DOWN TO EARTH
GARDENING

Also by Lawrence D. Hills

Down to Earth Fruit and Vegetable Growing
Grow Your Own Fruit and Vegetables
The Propagation of Alpines
Alpine Gardening

DOWN TO EARTH GARDENING

Lawrence D. Hills

FABER & FABER
3 Queen Square London

First published in 1967
This edition published 1975
by Faber and Faber Limited
3 Queen Square London WC1
Printed in Great Britain by
Whitstable Litho Ltd., Whitstable, Kent
All rights reserved

ISBN 0 571 10868 7

To

My Wife

who also loves gardening

Contents

Illustrations

PLANS AND PLANTING TABLES

PLATES

(*between pages* 96–7)

11. The polythene leanto 'annex' saves frame space in spring

12. *Lilium hollandicum*, formerly *L. umbellatum*, is the easiest of all for every garden

13. The climbing *Hydrangea petiolaris* is a splendid self-clinging climber with white flowers in summer

14. The Russian Vine, *Polygonum baldschuanicum* grows and flowers with fury

15. A well-pruned *Wisteria sinensis*, see page 87 for summer pruning and feeding this lovely climber

16. The fruit of *Chaenomeles cathayensis*, large as pears, is best of all for jelly and cheese

Preface

I have written this book for all the hundreds of beginner gardeners who wrote to me during my seven years in the *Observer* and demanded a small and simple book about 'ordinary flowers'. There are so many more 'flowers' than it is possible to imagine when you begin gardening and so much more to know when you have everything to learn, that this book cannot be small, but it is as detailed as I can make it.

For brevity is not simplicity and I have tried to tell very much more about how to grow the hardiest, easiest and most striking species of alpines, perennials, annuals, trees and shrubs, rather than far less about a wider range of subjects. Then when new gardeners know more about what they really like they can buy more specialized books about the subjects of individual chapters.

Most new garden trees are planted by those who will know enough in ten years' time to wish they had planted them somewhere else, and the beginner needs his knowledge all at once in sufficient detail to help miss most of the more expensive mistakes. So I have expanded this book from the articles in which I struggled to get a quart into a half-pint glass, and I would like to thank the editor of the *Observer* for his permission to reproduce those portions which appeared in his pages on Sundays.

This book is essentially a companion to my *Down to Earth Fruit and Vegetable Growing* and the two together make a large, complete gardening book of the kind that all beginners need when gardening dictionaries are useless because you cannot look up what you cannot spell. I have therefore included a large chapter on Pests and Diseases, which covers fruit and vegetables as well as the rest of the garden where blackfly attacks the dahlias and nasturtiums as well as the broad beans, and dieback disease and leafcurl can curse flowering prunus as well as peaches and plums.

This has been enlarged from the pamphlet 'Pest Control Without

Poisons' which I wrote for The Henry Doubleday Research Association, and I would also like to thank the President of this association of amateur gardener experimenters, Mr. Robert S. W. Pollard, for his permission to use so much of this first booklet written to help British gardeners to use fewer toxic and persistent chemicals. In small gardens it is so easy to spend more than the value of a crop on a tin of something deadly to defend it, that will have rusted through the tin and eaten a hole in the potting shed shelf before it is even quarter used, that even the most chemical-minded will appreciate the advantages of evasive action, wherever this is possible. There is no need for those who feed the birds in winter to poison them through the summer, when there are safe alternatives.

Because I have spent my space on practical details that beginners need when they start their gardening in new houses, I have had less room for more fashionable fields. Those who feel that I have neglected rhododendrons, camellias, grey foliaged plants, hostas, hellebores and hemerocallis, and enlarged on the ordinary, obvious and rather hackneyed good qualities of plants in every garden, will perhaps understand that I am writing for very ordinary gardens. They will in most cases find their favourites among the shrubs in the many lists under colours, soils and situations in the last chapter.

In conclusion I would like to express my appreciation of the labours of Mrs. Helen Gainsford who read the proofs and wrestled with the plant names. These are standardized by the Royal Horticultural Society's *Dictionary of Gardening*, because most catalogues have now caught up with this massive work, and I have chosen to avoid confusion among gardeners rather than the latest schools of thought among botanists.

Then I wish to acknowledge my debt to Mr. Malcolm Hickling, who drew the illustrations, and the photographers who supplemented my own rather amateur efforts, Mr. J. E. Downward, Mr. D. Woodland and Mr. H. Smith, who is responsible also for the coloured frontispiece of helianthemums.

Bocking,   LAWRENCE D. HILLS
November 1965–December 1966

1

The Picture and the Frame

Every garden is a picture that changes through the seasons, and through the years as trees grow tall. Every beginner gardener with his first garden knows nothing about art but knows what he likes and, as in painting, his liking depends on certain broad principles that make the picture 'look right'.

A painting is a window view of what the artist saw, but we 'walk through the window' when we go round our gardens, seeing other pictures beyond the trellis, round the corner or even over the hill, with each one separate and 'framed' by something that shuts off the view of the rest. Large gardens have room for whole galleries; small ones for a single picture, because the eye takes in everything at a glance.

Small front gardens are nearer heraldry than landscape painting, for each is a personal picture, limited by the road and the neighbours' fences as knights were by the size and shape of their shields, but blazoning the choice and skill of the Englishman whose castle lies behind his garden gate. His lawn is the green background to his flowers, and the straight paths to garage and front door the 'quarterings' or divisions of his shield. This garden has three viewing points: one from the road, one from the front windows and a side view from the garage path which is always to one side. The straightness of these paths and of the house itself make it very difficult to copy wild Nature successfully.

A miniature wood with daffodils in rough grass can be part of a garden with about 100 ft. of frontage, and the house at least this far back, but it will look fussy and untidy in a 28-ft.-each-way square, because the house will dwarf it, and when the trees grow they will block the view from the windows. The first principle for owners of a small new garden is never to plant a tree nearer than 25 ft. from the house, for the ten years before the the poplars start to tower fly faster than you think.

Straight lines should answer straight lines in what is called 'formal gardening', which uses grass as a background for colour, not to save labour. The idea that lawns are labour-saving comes from envisaging large gardens where one man with a 36-in. motor mower can keep pace with the wide sweep of turf falling away to a clump of silver birches. Their white stems in winter set against blue distance are one of the most rewarding tricks of landscape gardening, and with *that* kind of view even small gardens can use it. The Canoe Birch, *Betula papyrifera*, with bark that once made Red Indian canoes, is the whitest, but the Swedish *B. pendula laciniata*, is nearly as good and easier bought.

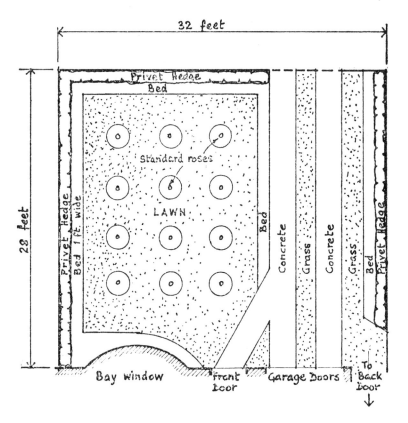

Fig. 1. Lawns waste labour. Small front garden with 490 square feet of fortnightly mowing and 165 feet of edging.

If your lawn is 18 ft. wide and 23 long, and if you fill the front garden with a 1-ft. wide bed round the edges and space out a dozen standard roses in 2-ft.-square beds on it, then you have 96 ft. of work with edging shears once a month round these alone, apart from 82 ft. round the outside. With hand mowing between once a fortnight taking longer than mowing the whole area, because of awkward corners, lawns are more work than beds that exploit the several ways of growing flowers with minimum weeding.

Keep the lawn for the middle, with its centre clear, as the green backcloth for beds beside it, so the mower goes on and comes off with least trouble, leaving no awkward small pieces to clip or finish afterwards. If you have a slope it is very much easier to level this off to a gradient of about one in six, so that you can mow it easily instead of leaving it steep enough to demand shears.

Just as trees of one kind, in small gardens that they can monopolize, grow as fast as they do where they fit a landscape, cars are roughly the same size for everyone. There is no need for a large garden to have a main path wider than the 7–8 ft. which takes one straight into the garage. There was a time when wide gravel paths swept in a circle round a central bed on the Victorian (and earlier) one-way system that saved backing the carriage and pair, and gave plunging room for frisky horses. Even at speed they were too slow to throw gravel at the windows as tyres do; but today concrete, or one of the various cold-laid bitumen and stone preparations, makes the best main paths.

The weight of a car driven in and out day after day is too much for amateur crazy paving, and while you are having the drive-in done you may as well have the front door path laid while the men and the mixer are there. Concrete is, however, a good servant but a bad master, and all small front gardens suffer from too much path in relation to their area. Therefore have only the really indispensable paths. To have one running all round the front of the house to walk on when you clean the windows is the most wasteful of all, because this route is taken too rarely to wear the grass. Have a narrow bed, even a foot wide, instead and plant wall shrubs, or even fruit; for a Morello cherry will thrive on a north-facing wall, while a south one will take pears and peaches with white blossom against red brick. Ceanothus, forsythia and 'japonica' go with white walls, and with well-trained wall shrubs one can reach across for window cleaning.

Another space-saving device is not to have a solid garage path but two strips of concrete 18–24 in. wide, which will be rather cheaper, and instead of the usual awkwardly mown strip of turf up the middle, have aubrietia. In its way the 'aubrietia drive-in' is as rewarding for gardens with only a view of the houses opposite as silver birches are for those who see blue distance from their windows. A wide strip of solid purple or crimson through April and May, in return for a single cut-back and weeding after flowering every year (although splitting and replanting should be carried out about every fifth autumn), is a real gain for far less work than regular mowing. Everything in this chapter is discussed in detail later, and a full account of how to make and look after one such drive-in will be found under 'Alpines'.

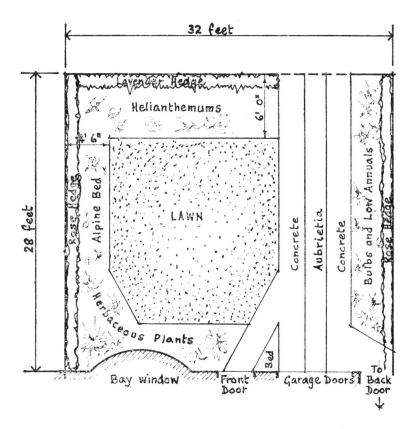

Fig. 2. The same garden with wide, labour-saving beds and 265 square feet of grass with 45 feet of edging

Narrow beds are to be avoided because they limit our gardening to perhaps one row of scarlet salvias and an edging of alyssum after perhaps a double row of tulips. Only beginners feel their gardens are vast spaces to fill, and they soon learn that there is never room for all the plants that one can grow.

The bed on the garage side must as a rule be narrow, but the one that meets the neighbour's, if your house is semi-detached, gives space for the herbaceous border. This is for perennials, which are plants that stay in and come up every year, unlike hardy annuals which are sown to flower the same summer and finish. They need at least 5 ft. of border width because they should be planted with the tall ones at the back and short in front, on a slope towards the view-point, in this case from the side and diagonally from the road and windows.

Because they must go at least a foot apart, and some need 18 in., 6–7 ft. is a better width for a front garden; but not more, or the lawn will look too small, and the herbaceous border looks best in proportionate width to the inescapable garage path. The heights vary, but the narrowest bed for success with 4-ft.-high subjects at the back is 5 ft., coming down quite steeply in 'steps'.

These are always called herbaceous *borders* because they need something behind them to take the wind, for even with staking the tallest plant can break. They also face the viewpoint, and their back view reveals mostly stems. In large gardens there can be double-sided borders, also sloped upwards from each end, and there are some very fine collections of perennials in big beds of this type at Wisley.

The Royal Horticultural Society's gardens at Wisley (near Ripley, Surrey) or those of the Northern Horticultural Society at Harlow Car, Harrogate, Yorkshire, both admit non-members for a small entrance fee, and are far better value for amateur gardeners in search of ideas and knowledge than Kew, or any local park.

At both of these there are examples of the traditional herbaceous border for large gardens. This sets off the bank of flowers sweeping up to tall delphiniums at the back against a high evergreen hedge, ideally clipped yew, thuya or other conifers, as a kind of 'vertical lawn' to contrast bright colour with darker greens than grass. This is rarely possible in small gardens, for it demands rather more than 3 ft. at the back for the width of a tall hedge, and room to clip it behind the lofty spires in summer.

Those who love delphiniums, or hollyhocks, can use a triangle bed with its high apex in the angle between house and neighbour's fence, sloping down as it widens into a corner cut off the lawn. This can go up into any corner with protection from wind from two sides, and it is quite effective to start the border narrow at the road end and swing out in a curve; but not an in-and-out wobbly edge, just one good curve for a bed large enough to follow the herbaceous border principle.

This shows the major difference between gardening and painting: for you do not have to wait to see the Van Gogh till the sunflowers are out, but you must go to Kew in bluebell or rhododendron time to enjoy these flowers. A large garden can afford not to have all the pictures in its gallery on show, with a rhododendron walk and an iris garden only for June. Small ones, that blaze with Russell lupins in every bed, are an untidy blank for the rest of the year.

Well-chosen perennials can flower from April to the last Michaelmas daisies in the autumn, and planning for a range of colours through every month is a skill that grows as we find what we like and what does well. Though herbaceous borders can stay without replanting for more than five years, buying or raising new plants to replace failures, or any disliked, is the means by which gardens grow as their owners find how much more there is to learn.

The 'tall at the back, short at the front' principle applies also to shrubs; but though these are labour-saving, because they stay there growing larger without replanting, unless the bed is planted so widely that it looks almost empty for its first five years they crowd and need autumn removals. Plant philadelphus, weigela, ribes, buddleia, forsythia, and all the ordinary shrubs that make up cheap collections, a foot apart each way to 'fill the bed' and they will be a crowded thicket before they have a chance to show what they can do uncrammed.

The small garden problem is not so much labour- as room-saving, and so many shrubs have such short flowering seasons in relation to their size that small gardens need very few. Of these the lovely potentilla, 'Katherine Dykes', with golden flowers the size of florins from June to October, is one for every garden and rare only because it is new; for it is tough and hardy on any soil. Remember always that trees grow tall but shrubs grow wide, so choose for the longest colour in the least space—never with the object of filling the space cheaply.

It is their length of flowering season that has made roses our national flower, apart altogether from their vivid beauty. Rose beds need not be wide because the principle of slope does not apply, though some bush varieties are shorter than others. Those who love roses will want a large bed of them, and a good one, with standards, right in the middle of the lawn. This gives a view from all three points, but they can also fill any triangle bed awkwardly left between garage and front door path.

Floribunda roses, the cluster-flowered bush type that began with the Poulsen family, and hybrid teas (illustrated on so many chocolate boxes), are formal. As bushes and standards they are utterly out of place in herbaceous borders or shrubberies, for their blaze 'kills' everything else. They are always 'formal' and traditionally rose gardens are paved, with steps and statues, both of which are hard to fit well into a small front garden, though it can be done by concentrating on a single picture and sticking to roses only.

Rambler roses, especially the class called 'Perpetuals' make the finest of the flowering hedges which can frame our gardens—at higher planting costs but with far less work later than the constantly clipped Lonicera and privet whose roots can transform the soil near them to dusty deserts. They will fit a foot-wide strip, for their roots can spread under concrete, but wider beds are better, and 4 ft. allows ample room in front for bulbs before the roses, as a 'Stay-Put Bulb Bed' with *blue* annuals sown to hide the dying foliage of the daffodils and the tulip varieties that will stay in the ground without replanting, or in the traditional bedding system.

A hedge is a straight line, therefore the bed should be straight and formal, and here a regiment of tulips above forget-me-nots, or these and wallflowers can be replaced by lobelia, which is a glorious long-flowering blue annual in its own right, used as a carpet not an edging, and dwarf French marigolds, brown, yellow or orange.

Rose hedges are the flattest of all for they are not clipped but tied in to cattle wire; this is wide-mesh wire net made to hold a bull, supported on iron or concrete posts which roses soon hide. There are several modern shrub roses which grow good hedges without support but they spread about 2 ft. across, not the 8 in. of well-trained ramblers. This is done with the little pruning they need after the bed below is cleared for winter, and the two good thornless kinds, 'Zephyrine Drouhin' (deep pink) and 'Kathleen Harrop' (pale pink) are a pleasure to tie.

Flowering hedges, of which roses are only one, need the contrast of grass, for they are not a dark green background, but more like upright flower beds that make the frame part of the picture. This does not matter so much for those with short flowering seasons, but a rose hedge is a blaze best set off with turf below.

So have the hedge beds narrow if you want more roses and at least 3 ft. of grass, not a thin path before the central bed, or one wide enough to take a collection of lower-growing bush varieties, in other colours, beside the garage path. Here also is a better place for a quieter feature like an alpine border.

This is a rockless rock garden, where alpines grow as a miniature double-sided herbaceous border rising to about a foot in the middle, and flowering long and well. They are small but brilliant and these beds are by far the best way of enjoying them on a flat site where a natural rock garden will look out of place.

One of the best developments of this idea is the helianthemum bed or bank, planted with only the more compact and weed-holding varieties of this lovely race. Because they offer reds, pinks, yellows, oranges and even browns, and these when roses are at their best, they can back on to a spring-flowering hedge such as one of white Spiraea, which their 8-in. height will not hide, but they are best against grey lavender.

This is a good small hedge, though it will reach 3 ft. with time and care, and grows well against a low brick front garden wall, with a 3–5 ft. (allow 1 ft. for the hedge width) bed ideally slightly banked up at the back, so it is in full view from the front windows. This is also an excellent site for an alpine bed and with this there is always something in flower from February to November if it is planted well.

The rock garden, like the miniature wood, is hampered by the small frame of garage path and neighbours' fences, but its best site is where the front garden slopes up to the road, so your window view is away from the straight lines of the house. A slope the other way reserves the best picture for passers-by.

Making the whole one large rock garden is rarely successful because few people can afford enough good stone. The larger the rock garden the bigger the rocks must be or it will look like a load of rubble shot down a hillside. A lump of Westmorland, Cheddar or Cumberland limestone as big as a biscuit tin weighs close on half a hundredweight, and a large rock garden needs many even twenty times this size.

If you can spend the cost of a new car on a good rock garden which will last far longer, go to Chelsea Flower Show, or any one where the firms who still build big rock gardens show their skill, and choose one with a style you like. Handling heavy rock on steep slopes is no job for amateurs, who do far better with biscuit tin sizes, and Chapter 8 shows how to make the result as natural as possible. With stones of this more manageable size you could make a small outcrop, to go with turf, a heather (Erica) bed for almost year-round colour, silver birches and shrubs to make a picture recalling the quiet corner of the mountains where alpines grow. Its problem is mowing the turf on steep slopes which in Nature are usually grazed by sheep or rabbits.

Rough grass cut perhaps twice a year with shears or a sickle or bagging-hook (whatever its local name), and with naturalized bulbs, is probably the best answer for the top of a slope steep enough to be a burden. Silver birches are not only graceful, but cast least shade, and both lavender and helianthemums are among the shrubs that are evergreen to prevent rainwashing and also have a good ground-holding roots, as well as tenacity for suppressing the weeds that can triumph where one goes least often. The summit of a back garden sloping steeply up from the house is the place for a miniature wood of flowering trees, or even an orchard, but have a seat at the top of the path, both for the view and because you will need a rest after every barrow load wheeled up the garden.

Terracing is the best answer for small, steep spaces because it uses straight lines to fit those of house and fence. Dry walls need roughly oblong square-shaped stones which are far cheaper than those for a natural rock garden which usually have to be fetched from further off. Like rock gardens they need larger stone for greater length and height for they must slope back and transfer the thrust of the soil behind to push downwards. Planted with strong-growing alpines, and using soil instead of cement, they can be a long-flowering main feature for the steep garden sloping up or down. If possible avoid having one that looks towards a house facing north, for it will have so little sun that the plants it can grow will be limited to ferns and the mossy saxifrages. The best face away from the house, and the window view of terraces going up and up makes your garden look far smaller than it is. Looking down from the terrace to the level beds between has the reverse effect.

You cannot use the other landscape trick (invented by the famous 'Capability' Brown) of narrowing paving, long lawns and avenues towards the far end, to fake the perspective and make them look much longer than they are. It only begins to work after about 100 ft. of length, so will not fit small gardens.

Dry walling on a small scale is easy, provided that you remember

that the backward slope should be 2 in. in the foot up to 2 ft., 3 for
a yard high, and 4 at the 4-ft. maximum, which means that it comes
back 16 in. in all; this ensures not only that the plants will get some
rain caught on the ledges of the stone layers but also that there is
strength to take the thrust. Over 4 ft. high, or steeper than this, they
are best cemented, which means drainpipes at intervals to let the
water through; ideally, a job for a builder. This is especially wise
where a garage drive-in must be cut down to the road, and it pays to
get the outer wall run up high so that soil dumped behind it can
bring the garden up nearer window level.

Builders will leave holes through for plants, but these are often dry
and unsatisfactory. It is better to plant in the bed above with strong
trailing species that hang down. For high walls one of the most
effective is clematis, even the ordinary jackmanii and its relations,
but there are many alpines that grow too fast and far for ordinary
rock gardens and these walls alone give them a chance to do their
best.

The problem of the front garden that we inherit is usually its trees.
New gardeners are always in a hurry and often plant the cheapest,
which are also the quickest grown, and these were cheaper still in the
1930's. Thus laburnum, cherry, prunus (ornamental plum), almond,
double red may, or mountain ash may well dominate the garden.

Very few long-flowering and brilliant garden flowers will grow in
the dry shade of trees, and a walk in any wood will show that the few
flowers like violets or bluebells are all over before the leaves close in.
It is possible to buy special grasses that will endure shade, but this
can only grow a range of plants if it is damp. The London garden
that grows ivy, periwinkle (Vinca) and the yellow *Hypericum calycinum*, but little else, does not suffer so much from smoke and soot
as from too many trees.

With a large garden one can walk round and see one's trees whole
from a distance, but in a small one they rob light and shade so much
that the choice is between growing trees, or flowers and vegetables.
Wait for a year if you take over your garden in autumn, to watch
your trees through their full cycle to see if they are worth making the
main feature of your garden, and if not take off branches, but never
cut them down. This leaves a stump in the ground that is far more
trouble to remove than cutting through the roots and using the
stripped trunk to lever the whole out completely.

A tree that flowers gloriously every year, a copper beech that has
delightful shapeliness in its foliage, or a tall cedar with boughs that

sweep out over the lawn, is worth gardening round, with shade grass, bulbs below including the autumn-flowering cyclamen, seats beneath it, and paving; but not a pool, for this will block with leaves.

Another compromise garden is the courtyard, used where houses crowd in cities, and likely to be forced on many more people as rising building-land prices lower garden standards towards the 'courts' of Victorian slums, with houses round a shared central space for drying of washing and children's games. Everyone's garden is nobody's garden and at the worst this development sinks to a small and inferior park, or such neglected gardens as can be seen behind tall London houses converted into flats.

The courtyard with one owner can be successful on an entirely different principle from that governing ordinary gardening. It must look inwards towards a central feature, with paving and plants in tubs and boxes round the sides and a pool with a fountain in the middle. Modern electric pumps to stand on the pool bottom, sucking and squirting high, are a delight for goldfish and beautifully cool in city summers, even for those who do not make their pool large enough for swimming or at least private soaking and sunbathing. Grass is unsuitable for pool sides because bare wet feet and dripping bathing costumes wear the 2-3 ft. of immediate surround far more mercilessly than lawns are worn by dry walking.

Make no attempt to be natural, for the idea is Moorish, and the courtyard was made for a hot, dry climate to serve as a personal 'oasis' of family peace, shutting out the dust, the glare and the flies of the crowded Arab town, with a fountain to sit by, as we would sit by a roaring fire with the rain and snow outside. We can shut out the noise, exhaust smoke and clamour of a London just as crowded, but it is important to make sure that there is a way out for the accumulated rainfall of a British winter (or summer) falling on a solid paved area in the middle of a house.

Arab gardens look inwards, but those of England are made to look out over broad and peaceful acres, with birches against blue distance, and rows and rows of little houses; with room to dig off a bad temper in privacy, and every small front garden bright as the shields knights wore when they died 'a-babbling o' green fields'. A garden of one's own is a privilege that we have freedom to enjoy and use as we will, with the widest range of personal choice in its design and planting that is left to most of us today; and, like all freedoms, it must be defended.

2

Lawns, Paths and Layout

Most homes have two lawns, and one is the background to the picture in the front garden, which has very little wear. The other begins as a place for prams and has a clothes line across it, even in spin-drier families; then it grows to a toddling ground, and graduates to a tent site for Red Indians and the pitch for ten-year-olds' Test Matches.

The first needs a good fine 'without ryegrass' mixture, which should be mainly fescues and bents, costing from 70p to 90p a pound (1974 price, like all in this book) and from any firm good enough to sell to beginners, it should have what is in it marked on the packets. If a lawn is shady it should be a 'Shade Mixture', based on *Poa nemoralis*, the species of grass that will do best with least sun.

Ryegrass is the one with long wiry stems that miss the mower and carry seed heads with flat seed blocks arranged like a Sergeant's stripes up a straight stem. A wavy stem means *Italian* ryegrass which is only found in cheap bad bargain mixtures, which grows very fast, strangles the finer grasses and dies after about eighteen months, leaving bare patches. It is grown by farmers for brief grazing, and the rejects have been included in lawn mixtures, which is why gardeners should always buy from good firms who blend the best grasses as blenders do tea.

Perennial ryegrass is the one in a 'with ryegrass' mixture, and it adds wearing power to a lawn as nylon does to sock wool. The best way round the seed head problem is to pay about 60p a pound for the top grade of this cheaper type which can cost as little as 45p, and have 'S.23'. This is a pedigree grass bred for most leaf and fewest seeds, which makes it more expensive but good value for both lasting lawns and pastures.

The normal sowing rate is 2 oz. a square yard, but with more care to distribute the seeds evenly 1½ oz. is better and comes cheaper when you have multiplied length by width in feet and divided by nine to find how many square yards you have. If possible buy seed treated with a bird repellent which will keep them off it long enough for the plants to get away, but the old trick of swirling the seed in a basin with paraffin and spreading on newspapers to dry before sowing is also quite effective.

Fig. 3. Lawn grasses can be told apart by their seed heads. *Left to right,* Brown Bent (fine), Chewing's Fescue (fine), Perennial Ryegrass (hard wearing, coarse), Italian Ryegrass (coarse, non-lasting).

The difficulty with turf, especially bought locally from a man who offers it cheap, is Couch Grass (*Agropyrum repens*), also called 'Twitch' and by other names, which is a weed grass that makes a tussock or high tuft; and when you mow the lawn it shows a bare brown middle and rather pale green coarse shoots spreading like a flat hand. It spreads by long white roots that can even pierce potatoes, and no turf with these in should be bought.

Other weed grasses are Creeping Soft Grass (*Holcus mollis*) and Yorkshire Fog (*H. lanatus*) which look much the same in mown turf, but are without the creeping white roots. These can be chopped out of existing lawns to a depth of 3 in. and replaced with fresh turf fragments whacked firmly in place, ideally in September or October. Grasses of course defeat selective weedkillers, and digging is the only answer for Couch Grass.

So dig with care before you sow, removing the long wicked roots of which every fragment will grow, taking out the stones and builders' rubbish, especially the large lump of flat cement from where they may have mixed mortar or plaster. Builders and jobbing 'landscape gardeners' often lay turf over these mixing places, which means yellowing and bare patches in the lawn in every drought. Smash up these lumps and save them, with all builders' rubbish like brickends, not for a 'rockery' but for path foundations and drainage.

New houses are usually handicapped by raw subsoil from levelling of sites with bulldozers, and dumping from the bottoms of trenches. Only about the top foot of any soil is alive, and this lifeless subsoil is usually lighter coloured; but digging among the weeds in the uncleared part will give a sample for comparison.

If your front garden has been scraped down to bare subsoil, buy a bale of peat, chop it down with the spade, water it to swell and spread it 2 in. thick over 300 square feet of the dug soil: which is lasting value for about £1.50. On this scatter $\frac{1}{2}$ lb. a square yard of equal parts of fine bonemeal and fishmeal and dig it in shallow, not more than 3–4 in. deep before raking and rolling ready for sowing.

A cheaper way to make raw subsoil grow good grass is 2 lb. a square yard of dried sludge (£2 cwt. delivered in the London area, but made and sold by many wise corporations) without the peat, forked in the same way, and 1 lb. is worth using even if the soil is merely poor and sandy. It is a non-smelly, dry grey or black powder, sold extensively for sports ground turf dressings, and excellent for garden lawns, especially on soils where lawn sand is 'coals to Newcastle'.

If yours is the lucky garden that had the top soil scraped on to it, or the original surface is intact, there is no need to add plant foods or humus from sludge or peat to stop clays baking or sands drying. Extract as many couch grass roots as you can, and use a garden line to mark out the shape of the beds, which can share the lawn dressing to start them on subsoil, even if they are not to be planted immediately.

The best lawn sowing times are from March to May, and in September, but no later, because the grass must have time to grow strong before winter, but spring is the favourite, while later than May risks a summer drought.

Regular sowing is important, so stretch the garden line 3 ft. back from the edge of the rolled potential lawn, and rake the surface to roughen it. The best way to be sure of sowing evenly is by punching holes *downwards* into a shallow tin with a large nail or the point of an old-fashioned tin-opener. Weigh out $1\frac{1}{2}$ oz. of grass seed and tip it in a glass, marking how far it comes up with stamp paper, and this is a measure for refilling the tin after you have sifted contents evenly over the first square yard. Garden measuring 'glasses' are made in plastic, and marked in fractions of an ounce of nearly everything.

By the time the first row of yards is done the job goes faster as you learn how thinly to sift the seed. Before moving the line sift fine soil roughly $\frac{1}{4}$ in. thick with an ordinary cinder type sieve for an even covering, and roll firm when sowing is finished. Those who are doubtful about paraffin or bird repellents can tie folded paper on strings stretched across, both as extra bird discouragement and as a reminder that the lawn is sown and there can be no more short cuts across it.

Roll again when the grass is 2 in. high and when it is standing up again, clip any tall places or tall weeds with the shears. Then mow with the knives set as high as they will go, and if the machine is an old one have the knives sharpened first. Leave the grass box off and leave the mowings as they fall, to add humus as worms take them down.

A spring-sown lawn that is up well and early will take three mowings in its first summer, firstly to stop the stronger grasses that are up first pushing out the finer ones, and secondly to get rid of the annual weeds which can crowd from the top inch of soil. It is not safe to use a selective weed-killer until the second spring.

These are to be avoided unless the weeds are very bad, for lawn mowings are a very useful humus supply for small gardens, and they are poisonous even on the compost heap for six weeks after use of selective killers. An older clover, daisy, dandelion and plantain killer without this disadvantage is 7 oz. sulphate of ammonia, 3 oz. sulphate of iron, mixed with 10 oz. of dry sand, either sprinkled directly on top of the worst weeds, or broadcast at the rate of 3–4 oz. a square yard if they are very bad.

Older lawns have other problems, and one of the commonest is moss. This is easily killed with Mortegg, which is a winter tar oil wash for fruit trees, at the rate of a $\frac{1}{4}$ pint (the makers supply a measure with the tin) stirred in a 2-gallon watering can and watered with the rose over 8 square yards after an April mowing. Moss may well grow again, for lawns can have deeper problems. Most moss is a protest against mowing without feeding, so spread 4 oz. of poultry guano or $\frac{1}{2}$ lb. of dried sludge per square yard about a week later. Brush it in by dragging a piece of inch-mesh wire netting weighted and stiffened with stout wood, which also spreads wormcasts as top dressing instead of as mud on the mower.

This treatment should be used for new lawns with a large number of wormcasts, for the top dressing of fine soil from these helps to keep grass growing happily. Those who insist on killing worms for 'tidiness' should use one of the Derris preparations sold for this purpose, not Chlordane, which has a 'House-that-Jack-built' chain reaction. Worms half poisoned as the effect wears off add up to a danger dose that means infertile eggs among all the birds that hop on the lawn and keep the worm population balanced.

Lawns can be mossy from holding rain after too hard rolling, but a rake or piercing gadget to let in air, even a fork thrust in often enough, is the remedy worms give free. Rushes or mares tail (*Equisetum*) among the moss show bad upbringing—the lawn was not properly laid or drained. If you have this trouble, start drastic treatment by filing the spade edge sharp, then cut a line a foot inside the edge of the lawn. Chop the strip into foot squares and thrust the spade under till they lift like tiles to stack moss-side down and rot for potting soil.

With creeping buttercup and cocksfoot (the grass that leaves rooty patches after mowing, worth digging from any lawn) among moss rather than rushes, easy drainage is possible by spreading a cubic yard of builder's sand over 15 square yards. Dig it in or hire a man with a rotary hoe to mix it into the top 6 in. before levelling and rolling for turf, or sowing shade lawn mixture under trees.

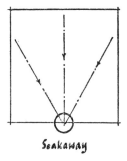

Soakaway

Fig. 4. 'Broad arrow' drains
fit small, square lawns.

Wet lawns need soakaways 4 ft. deep and 3 ft. square dug at the worst corner. Then dig three narrow trenches, one to the far diagonal corner and one to the middle of each side, 1 ft. deep at the far ends and 2 ft. where they join the soakaway. Their fall can be guessed, but it is easily tested with a spirit-level on a plank edge, and a scratch on the brass to show where the bubble rests at the right slope. Then 4 in. thickening to 8 in. at the soakaway ends, of cinders or broken clinkers go on the bottoms, with small coke a substitute for farm drainpipes in towns. Add a layer of dead leaves, or even folded newspaper, on top of the coke to stop replaced soil filling trickle spaces. Mix one part of sand to six of soil so that it treads firm enough not to sink but lets water through.

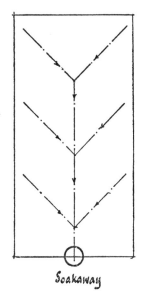

Fig. 5. 'Herring-bone' drains are needed for long, large lawns, 10 ft. between the side drains.

Soakaway

Fill the soakaway above drain coke level with hard rubbish such as bricks or bottles and finish with top soil for planting the border above. Then sand and dig or rotary hoe the lawn before levelling and rolling to take the turf fitted together with soil brushed on to fill cracks and hard whacking with spade or turf beater. Use the sprinkler generously in drought and mow with the knives set high the first summer, with selective weed-killer (for any weeds imported in the turf) before a feed next spring.

The rotary hoe or Rotavator is the answer for couch grass in new gardens, for those who can afford to wait through a summer before September lawn sowing. In most local papers there will be contractors who advertise this service, and three or four complete rotavations between May and August will leave a garden in beautifully easily dug condition, but one rotavation merely means more weeds.

Ideally, hire before the house is finished, in dry weather, first burning off surface grass that would wind in the machine, and if there are perennial nettles or blackberries, the same contractor can usually clear with a motor scythe, and burn. No small garden needs machines of this type, so it pays to hire a strong, skilled man with a big 6–7 horsepower Rotavator which will break up even heavy clay that has been pasture for years.

Motor-mowers pay to buy for they are used once every 2–3 weeks, but even small rotary hoes are three times as expensive and are used only for spring or autumn digging. A large one hired to start a garden well can alter an almost undiggable clay by churning in sand as recommended for lawns into the top 8 in. of the whole area. This lightens far better than digging in for the sand is evenly spread, and so is dried sludge for those unfortunate enough to have their whole garden of bared subsoil.

After the first two complete rotavations, one shallow and one going deeper, wait till the couch grass (growing with green spears) and other small weeds appear. These will be germinating from buried seeds, and they can be thick as cress. Then hire again for a single rotavation, and a third after another wait, each one going as deep as the machine will. Sand or sludge rotavated in is best on the second visit, when the ground is already well broken.

Unlike lawn sowing, this operation needs summer warmth, and drought, for the knives leave the soil full of air that dries out and kills the weed roots, apart from destroying three crops of young weeds before they can set more seed. It can cost as much as £30 for the three goes, which is a great deal cheaper than employing a man to dig the garden carefully and pick out all the couch grass. Even if it is possible to get one who will dig solid clay, he will 'turn the weeds under to rot' without knowing which have roots that grow from every fragment. Beginner gardeners should turn to Chapter 12 for a 'Rogues' Gallery' including convolvulus, couch grass, creeping buttercup, celandine, ground elder, mares tail, oxalis and winter heliotrope.

There is a quicker way to clear a garden that starts infested with any of the above. This is by using ammonium sulphamate, the weed-killer that the Forestry Commission use for killing wild rhododendrons, and where selective and other modern chemicals fail. Roughly speaking it is sulphate of ammonia made crooked, so plants that take it in choke, but after about a month it straightens to the ordinary artificial fertilizer, unlike sodium chlorate which stays poison till it washes out. It can only be applied between March and the end of July, because when weeds and grasses slow for winter they are not taking nitrogen, and this chemical kills as a bad diet rather than a poison.

Dissolve 2 lb. of the white crystals in a 2-gallon can of water and spread it over 200 square feet with the rose. Tall foliage is best cut down before the watering, and blackberries or the perennial nettle, which has yellow roots as strong as wire ropes, can need a second dose after a month if they are still growing.

At first nothing happens, then foliage greys and dies as the chemical goes right down to the tips of the roots that you would never find in a single digging. No precautions are needed, it is not inflammable like sodium chlorate (for its most usual use is flame-proofing curtains) and it is harmless to the animal kingdom, which includes soil bacteria and earthworms as well as pets, birds and ourselves.

The second effect is a thick crop of chickweed, groundsel and other annual weeds from seed hidden under the powerful perennials, all growing fast and sappy, safe to dig or rotavate under. There will be an increase of earthworms as more move in, and rapid multiplication of soil bacteria as both turn the slaughtered weed roots to humus.

The drawback is the cost, for ammonium sulphamate was 44p a pound in 1974 though cheaper in larger quantities, and value for all really frightful weeds. It is safe right up to the trunks of large trees which will have only big roots with no small ones feeding at the 6 in. depth. Ammonium sulphamate penetrates, unless it falls on leaves. Bush fruit are surface rooting, so are rhododendrons and it cannot be used to clear these or other shrubs of couch grass.

Garage drive-ins must take car weight and wear and the one to the back door takes the deliveries, the carrying of dustbins in and out, the prams and all the traffic of a home. They are therefore strong concrete and like the front ones usually laid by the builder.

Garden paths have wheelbarrow wear, and however small barrows are they must fit an adult between their handles, which will be 21–22 in. apart. The legs will be 18–20 in. apart, and so the path must be 2 ft. wide or the barrow will tip over unless it stands dead central for those who make theirs narrower. There is no point in wasting room on wider paths in small gardens with one barrow and no passing problem.

If a garden is made only for adults to walk round, with lawns, large shrub beds, herbaceous borders and roses, it does not need paths at all, for the wear is spread over the lawn area. If it narrows in to steps down and another picture at a lower level beyond, you can use flat paving pieces set 1 ft. apart as stepping-stones in the turf, needing no edging and taking the wear which occurs only where treading shoes are concentrated by going through a narrow opening.

This kind of layout needs a strong wooden 'ramp' made of inch-thick timber that fits on the steps to get the motor mower up and down, and the barrow that carries the grass. The steps must be cemented and strong because even small motor mowers are heavy.

It is a basic landscape garden principle that every path must have an objective in view, and a wide grass one 4–6 ft. across, made to mow in four double trips, with a seat, a sundial, a statue with a fountain or pool, or a gate to the orchard, is a fine contrast to broad beds beside. Grass paths are best made wide enough for two adults to walk abreast, and this allows a rubber-tyred barrow to choose a different track each time. Their edging is the hard work, until a satisfactory motor edger can be invented, but even this is less trouble than edging a network of small beds.

Leaving turf strips undug for grass paths in new gardens can mean reserves of couch grass spreading into beds, but if they are turfed and sown like lawns and not less than 3 ft wide, they can serve even vegetable gardens. The wide surface of fat rubber tyres cuts them far less even in winter than narrow iron wheels.

The smaller the garden the harder its paths must work, and veget-ables feeding a family, plus prams, toy motor-cars and tricycles (which all fit 2-ft. barrow width) ridden with increasing vigour mean far heavier wear than an 'admiration garden' four times its size is likely to suffer.

The best paths for hard wear without trouble are concrete, and for efficiency they should go straight down the middle of the garden. This gives easy dumping on both sides for loads of manure wheeled in from the front gate, and takes vegetables up and materials down to bonfires, leafmould and compost heaps at the bottom.

The alternative for narrow gardens is a path to one side, and this also suits one where a neighbour's privet hedge makes a root-robbery area that will grow little, and there 2 ft. can best be spared. The path can go 8 in. from privet main stems without harm.

Gardens that run east and west can have a good south-facing wall or fence for trained fruit, or outdoor tomatoes moving up and down a sunny border alternating with early lettuce. This is best narrow, 2–3 ft.; and a path beside it, with another on the other side, leaves one large bed in the middle. This gives a fine long orbit for space tricycles, with the corners curved off as they should always be for easy barrow turning, but wastes twice the room on paths, apart from cost, and makes the garden look smaller. The straight central path carries the eye down and gives length on 'Capability' Brown's principle, applied in almost every suburban garden today.

Dig the top 3 in. of soil from the 2-ft.-wide strip of your path and wheel it away to stack for filling in fruit or other tree planting holes. Then fill in with rammed hard rubbish and stones, including the siftings from lawn covering and everything the builders leave. Even clinker from central heating furnaces is worth hoarding for a future path foundation.

Buy 2 in. × 1 in. timber for the sides that hold the concrete in place, because though it is best bought ready planed, to ensure as little as possible sticking to it, enough will cling to spoil it for carpentry and this size makes good supports for raspberry training wires. If available choose 2 in. × 1½ in., for this does tree stakes also, with both sizes sawn up, pointed and creosoted afterwards.

Set the wood on edge at the path sides to leave 2 ft. clear between, and drive pegs on the outside to hold them. A piece for across the end is needed, and one 3 ft. long to have two loop type shed-door handles screwed to one narrow edge, but not enough for both sides all the way down a long path. The concrete will have set enough overnight to move the wood and do the other half even if the whole job is done in a single week-end.

A good mixture is three parts fine gravel and one part each of sand and cement, with water to mix it thick as porridge with the spade. This spade should be washed afterwards before it dries, or it can be so clotted with set hard concrete as to be useless for digging. The barrow needs just as careful washing. Wheel the mixed concrete on to the foundation rubble down to the start at the far end of the path. Level each load nearly flat with the spade, but use the 3-ft. length of 2 in. × 1 in. held by the handles to pack the concrete with the lower edge. This will leave a ribbed, non-skid surface like a concrete road or aircraft runway, because smoothing with a bricklayer's trowel (not worth buying for one job) can mean a slippery surface on a wet path. This is most important where a garden slopes, and where the path must go down as steep as a 1 in 4 to save steps.

Though motor mowers will go up or down slopes this steep (they will not mow them across, but will cut one way only) barrows are pushed and the weight comes on the handles. Cutting down before the dip and dry walling the sides, or building up dry walling for a ramp, with 1-ft.-wide beds between the tops of the walls and the path, are both good ways of making 1-in-6 or 1-in-8 slopes easier for wheeling. The best way of casting curves is to buy 3-in-wide strips of flat sheet iron and bend it round, nailing to the pegs. This is cheap and will do curves down to any size.

A barrow carries most of its load on the wheel and this is why crazy paving, unless it is set as a 'decoration' on top of concrete, tilts and digs in or breaks the cement in the cracks as the small part of the wheel with the weight pushing down moves from fragment to fragment. In crazy paving, very often these small pieces are mainly triangles pointing in all directions and do not have the broadening and lengthening effect of large paving squares. If you use real York stone, these pieces are costly both in mason's time for squaring them and in transport from the quarry; firmly laid in sand they make a splendid terrace, but an expensive path.

Precast concrete is cheaper, and slabs 2 ft. wide and 3 ft. long cost about £7 for 35 ft. of path. Dig out as before, add some hard rubble foundation, but fill in with rolled and trodden sand to bed them level on. Though curves cannot be made without specially cast slabs, they have the advantages that the path can be moved and its slabs can be levered up to dig out determined weeds that thrust up through the joints.

The growing of plants between paving is attractive in theory, but extracting weeds from the cracks is a worse job than digging them from a gravel path; and weed-killers wash along and kill the carpeting alpines. It is for this reason that planted paths are only for those prepared to spend time on their knees.

Gravel paths are rarely made today, and those who have one that is wide and weedy can save endless work by digging out the sides and replacing with soil, leaving the middle as the foundation for a 2-ft. concrete one. Where a path is a feature to treasure, for example one between lofty yew hedges, weed it with sodium chlorate (not ammonium sulphamate, for this will bring up the annual weeds from seeds in the gravel) 1 lb. in 2 gallons of water spread over 200 square feet. Gravel paths are usually made below bed level, so that weed-killers shall not run and poison where they are not wanted, while concrete ones go higher because they are permanent and weed free.

Whether the garage is separate or detached it will be to one side of the house, so the place for the garden shed should be behind it and against the fence on that side, so it is as near as possible to the kitchen door. A very great deal of gardening is done in intervals of cooking, so a short journey to take out tools, put them away, change gardening shoes and above all fetch vegetables, is essential.

It is possible to store dahlia tubers, gladioli bulbs and anything that needs to stay dry and unfrozen on 1-in.-mesh wire netting stapled to a framework of 2 in. × 1 in. timber, hoisted to the garage roof and lowered for inspection or when finally needed. This is not so easy for stored potatoes, carrots, onions and fruit that are wanted often and quickly.

All these freeze, and the sweet taint of potatoes kept cold for too long, even if they are not frozen black, does away with the advantage of growing your own for better flavour than you can buy. Tools, mowers, barrows and bicycles do not freeze, but need to keep dry, so two sheds (or one with two divisions) will be ideal, with the second lined for heat insulation.

Shed making is so fiercely competitive that there is little saving on making your own badly when you can buy design and craftsmanship for so little more than the cost of the timber. The cheapest are asbestos, about a third less; but sheds are tenant's fixtures and can go on the van when you move, and even the rather more solid asbestos roofing will arrive smashed. The other disadvantage is that a knocked-over bicycle or carelessly put-away mower can smash thin asbestos like glass, while thick asbestos costs little less than timber.

Red cedar and Meranti (a new Malayan hardwood) are the best, for they need no painting, but both go grey with age and a coat of raw linseed oil or transparent Solignum every four years will keep their original warm brown. Soft wood sheds are cheaper, and ordinary green Solignum allowed to dry thoroughly, or creosote, will act as a rot-excluding undercoat for a good outdoor paint. Brunswick Green is the most lasting pigment and also less glaring in a garden than modern pastel colours made for those who enjoy frequent house decorating rather than gardening.

Dryness depends on gutters, which are an extra often neglected, but it is the unseen drip from gutterless eaves between shed back and neighbours' fence that brings damp soaking up to rot and rust. Lean-to sheds are slightly cheaper than span roof, more easily lined, and need only a single gutter, which cuts out another across the end to lead two gutters to the water-butt, so the cost is about £3 instead of £6 for the popular 6 ft. × 8 ft. size.

A good shed firm will quote for variations on their standard sizes and the ideal for most gardens would be two 6 ft. × 6 ft. lean-to (or span roof) sheds joined together with a partition in the middle. The tool, mower and bicycle section needs the door in the end, for easy wheeling in and out. It does not need extra length, for 5 ft. of length takes bicycles comfortably and they will have to come out if you want to get at anything beyond them. Width counts, and 22 in. for one, 30 in. for two bicycles leaning against the side leaves room for mower and barrow, in a shed 6 ft. across, but 5 ft. wide can bring the tools plunging off their pegs as you struggle to extract a bicycle or put one away in the dark.

This shed can have a concrete floor (laid like a path but an inch higher than the paths outside) for the shed to stand on, not bolt to, for bolted it ceases to be a 'tenant's' fixture, which you can move if you sell your house. Cold strikes up through concrete and the storage one needs a wooden floor, which is best for both if the two are combined. Set the joists on breezeblocks, or bricks set flatways, so no wood rests on the ground. These can go on concrete but sheds need an air space below to prevent dry rot, which is why houses have air-bricks to let air in under their floors.

The storage one can have the door in the side so there is no need to go right round to the far end for vegetable fetchings, and this allows room for another small window in the end, as well as at the side by the door. It needs to be light, for one of its uses is sprouting seed potatoes in those Dutch tomato trays with raised wooden corners, stacking on top of each other, that are also splendid for storing apples.

The cheapest lining is roofing felt stretched tight on the rafters and side beams with large-headed nails, and painted afterwards with a white bitumen paint which takes on tar. Asbestos or hardboard will do but cost nearly half as much as the shed. If it is a span roof, nail short lengths of 2 in. × 1 in. timber across so that the lining does not go right up into the apex of the roof where it is awkward to fit.

If tools must be stored in this shed, nail a plank along to take the backs of forks and spades (that would rub through the felt), and a piece of 2 in. × 1 in., 6 in. away from the high side of the lean-to will take a row of hooks for hanging bunched onions. Further short lengths between beams will keep fat potato sacks away from the lining. A small lean-to well lined is far better than anything large and draughty, and will store seeds, bast, small tools and the few pesticides small gardens really need, on shelves above the cartons full of sand that store carrots safely.

Apples need to be stored at between 33°–45° F., pears 40°–45° F., and the roof space of a modern house is far too warm for them, yet most garden sheds are too cold and damp. If it is possible to connect electricity to both sheds, have an adapter above the bulb in the roof to take a plug for a second bulb mounted on a board and covered with an inverted biscuit tin with holes pierced in the bottom to let hot air out, and propped on wood fragments to let cold under. With a 100-watt bulb inside, this emergency convector heater will keep a small, lined shed frost free in even hard weather. The tin goes over the bulb because stored fruit prefers winter darkness, and curtains of old blanket over the windows will exclude light and increase warmth. The bulb is cheap heating, far better than paraffin which can taint fruit, but is too weak for a greenhouse, which loses far more heat through glass than is lost through the wood and the lining of a dry and frost-proof shed.

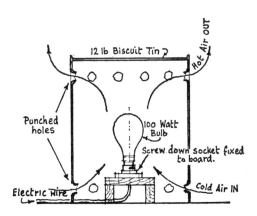

Fig. 6. Home-made electric heater to keep frost from fruit store sheds.

Beyond the shed is the best place for a cold frame, near the water-butt for dipping cans, and set so that its sloping glass side faces south for sun. This is essential and so is nearness to the house for trips to water and open and shut the wooden 'lights' that hold the glass. If the shed has electricity, a socket high on the outside can take a 75-watt soil-warming cable for the frame, which can also be used inside to keep fruit from freezing.

A small cold frame is more useful to beginner gardeners than a full-sized greenhouse, which will usually spend most of its time growing more tomatoes than the family can eat. One with lights that are about 3 ft. square or less, so that they can be easily lifted, is the best, while 'Dutch-lights' with single large panes of glass are to be avoided, for one careless handling or blow from a cricket ball smashes them completely. The smaller pieces in the older type are easily replaced.

Dig out 4 in. of soil below the frame and fill in with hard rubble as if for a path, topped off with cinders and ashes. Stand bricks on it to take the sides and ends, then fill in finally with more ashes to about 2 in. up inside it, treading and levelling these firmly. Coal dust or 'slack' is best for this final filling for it is tarry and grows no moss. This will take pots, seedpans or boxes standing level for even watering, and let the water away afterwards. Soil-warming cable can coil $\frac{1}{2}$ in. deep in this layer or hang on hooks round the sides in spring if tender things are raised. The normal early brassicas (cabbage tribe) lettuces, and easy annuals, followed by herbaceous and rock plant seeds and these potted to grow on through winter till planting time, need no heat.

This row of utility features along one side of the garden needs a wider path beside it than the 2 ft. minimum, because the barrow will have to stand outside them and be walked past; so have it 3–4 ft. across which leaves plenty of room for the lean-to shed side door, if you have one, to swing open.

The lawn beside it can therefore be extra wide, but the path will not be in the middle. If, however, it is taken across diagonally to the centre vegetable garden path this leaves space for a good-sized herbaceous border. The path can curve, but a curve joining two straight paths looks odd, though not if the far path also curves.

A flowering hedge before the vegetables start makes a frame for the first picture and the path goes through a 30–36 in. gap, which is even more necessary if you are planning grandly with a red brick wall and pedestals at the end. Make it just a mere 2 ft. and knuckles of other gardeners can be barked for a hundred years.

This plan gives a long lawn narrowing at the end, with room for toddling, cricket and teas, shut off from the vegetables beyond, but the essential is to draw a plan before you start, and gardens which look as if they had 'just grown naturally' were usually planned the most carefully.

Beyond the hedge have your bush fruits because you pick them over a long period, while tree fruit such as apples, you just harvest once for storing. Picking a few raspberries every day for tea, from kinds chosen to fruit in succession, entails planting them near the house, not at the end of the garden, especially with a steep slope up or down. Another advantage is nearness to the lawns, for bush fruit can be kept weed free with a surface coat of mowings, and only the surplus has to be wheeled down to the compost heap.

This area also fits the strawberries and rhubarb, while herbs are handy for quick picking beyond the first hedge. A second hedge can be *thornless* blackberries and loganberries, before the main vegetables, for easy training, and because you can pick both sides and do not share half the crop with your neighbour, with his the larger share if his side faces sun.

There can be another cross hedge after the vegetables if you are concerned with hiding the compost and leafmould heaps that lie beyond it, for convenient wheeling out to the vegetable area. This could be of blackberries and loganberries, but a hazel hedge is excellent and those who have only eaten long-dried bought nuts have no idea how good these are from your own bushes. Walnuts are slow to bear, roughly fourteen years from planting to the first real crop, though they are splendid large 'climbing trees' with non-slip bark for your grand-children; but hazels are the best small garden nut.

Compost and leafmould heaps can be shaded without harm, and go well under the standard fruit trees. Vegetables can grow under new planted trees, but rough grass with daffodils is the most labour-saving ground cover afterwards. Those who keep chickens should put them here, using a semi-intensive house, for manure from the dropping boards is excellent in the compost heap which destroys the 'fierceness' of its nitrogen that grows potatoes all top and no tubers. Allow the birds three times the recommended run area, so they are 'free range' under the trees, and act as efficient pest controllers.

Those who have a garden with a view beyond, either flat or sloping, should buy extra-tall standards with 7–8 ft. stems to plant in mown grass, for ducking and dodging the branches as you mow between becomes a burden after five years, when the trees begin to grow. Commercial orchards are grassed down once the trees are established, after the fifth year, and those who are tired of edging small beds round fruit trees can save labour by turfing them in for less awkward mowing. A 'Shade Mixture' is best for sowing in small gardens, especially under bush trees, for they are at minimum spacing and shade quickly. This grass needs to have fallen leaves swept off it, for trees are designed to kill grass under them.

Concentrating trees at the far end of a garden is particularly rewarding in gardens that slope up, for orchards have least material wheeled to them and only the crop will have to be carried down. Varieties chosen for beauty of blossom, spread over a long season, are flowering trees in their own right, and they do not hide each other even from the bedroom windows. Peaches as bushes or standards can crop better half-way up a hill than on walls, for frost flows downhill. This is why, if your garden slopes the other way, it is best 'open ended' without a high wall or hedge. One before the trees begin to block off unsightliness is better, with a gap in the middle to let the cold air through.

Evesham was once called 'the village where they opened the gate to let the frost out of the field', because its famous fruit growers were the first to learn how spring frosts behave. Plant standard trees if you have a hazel hedge, so that you see them from the house over the hedge-top, for it is hard to believe in the splendour of blossom when you plant your first trees small.

With this kind of garden it is worth paying extra for an outdoor water supply, and worth having a standpipe as far up the garden as possible, with full 2-gallon cans weighing 20 lb. each. Have the compost heap behind the first hedge if possible, for least weight wheeled, and it pays to alter the layout if you find your garden steep to climb.

Have the vegetables nearer the house, and behind a hedge have a separate garden for sitting and walking. You will not enjoy it from the house, but a separate picture between the vegetables and the orchard means fewer journeys up and down, though this matters less when you are young. Soils are usually poorest at the top of a slope, and plums and cherries thrive with even only a foot or less over solid chalk.

Where a road has cut across an old drainage system, the bottom of a down-sloping garden can have a boggy place where trees will not thrive because their roots lack the air drawn down as water sinks in the soil. This is more common in flat gardens on clay, where rushes, mares tail, moss and general sogginess show lack of drainage. Land drains can make all the difference to a wet garden, even one that is merely clay that stays too wet for early digging. Lightening the soil with sand or humus will usually cure this, but rushes are the sign that land drains are needed.

These are the same as lawn drains but must go deeper and carry more water, so farmers' drain pipes 3 in. thick and 1 ft. long costing about £8 a 100 are best, bought from builders' merchants. They can go under the path, but are usually better to one side of it, the wettest one, and a single row straight down will drain both sides for 15 ft. of bed.

A drain that starts 15 in. down near the house, with the minimum fall of 1 in 96 for a good flow, will be 30 in. deep after 120 ft.; and the soakaway wants to be at least 1 ft. deeper, so the further you drain the harder the work. Begin by digging your trench 1 ft. wide and deep, heaping the top soil to one side, then take it down roughly to the slope you need, putting the subsoil on the other side for putting back in the same order.

Greater care is needed with levels than for lawn drains, so put a 4 ft. straight length of the ever-useful 2 in. × 1 in. wood inch side up on a level surface and prop one end up $\frac{1}{2}$ in. Put a spirit-level on it and the bubble will move from under the 'bridge' in the middle that shows level. Scratch the brass on each side opposite its middle in its new position. Then use the piece of wood to test the levels along the trench, with the spirit-level bubble in the new position. Scrape away soil, or add more, so that you have a constant fall and your drain will trickle happily away for years.

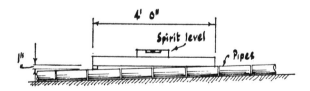

Fig. 7. Measure the slope of the drains with a spirit level on a plank on edge, blocked at one end to give a constant fall.

Set the pipes in the middle of the trench, just touching each other; and without cement, for the water goes in through the small gaps where they meet. Cover with 3–4 in. of cinders, and newspaper on top as with the lawn drains, before replacing the soil. The soakaway is the same, but in a flat garden it saves digging to put it in the middle and lead the drains to it, because it is so much easier to dig a wider hole than one deeper than 4 ft. Never have it under a lawn, because it may well sink considerably in course of years, but in a dug bed with about 18 in. of soil over the drainage material it is an asset.

Fig. 8. Lay the tile drains end to end with cinders above
to stop the soil filling the joints

Either at the end of a border, or where they can be part of a rock garden, soakaways provide an ideal home for the glorious damp-loving primulas. A garden with a boggy place at the bottom can be drained towards a soakaway left open, with the sides sloped off the 1-in-4 and filled with primula soil over the drainage material; then surrounded by rockwork as a kind of 'pool', but growing tall, damp-loving plants in shelter. This is a garden feature made from a disadvantage.

These primula bogs can be made artificially in dry gardens, and a water supply can be arranged for them in sloping gardens by planning ahead when you make the path. Mark the middle in the 3 ft. length of 2 in. × 1 in. and plane away from this the edge without the handles, taking it down to ½ in. at each end. This will shape the path as you ram so that it is slightly lower in the middle and the water trickles down the centre. At the lower end lead it into a drain to your bog, a full account of which will be found in Chapter 11.

The layout of back and front gardens follows the same broad principles, but with more scope for several pictures; however, it is still important not to attempt too much in a small space, and to avoid mixing formal and informal. The place for primula bogs and rock gardens is away from the straight lines of the house and vegetable garden. A slope sweeping down to the back windows can have bold outcrops of grey stone and a waterfall tumbling down, but this needs space for success.

However poor a soil, however small and awkward a garden, it will grow something really well, and by devoting enough time and trouble you can grow even the 'impossible', with the courage to try and to learn from failures entirely your own.

3

Evergreen and Flowering Hedges

A hedge is more than the frame of our picture. It must provide privacy as well as excluding dogs and children and adults hoping to take short cuts across our gardens. Chainlink fence, or the far cheaper sheep or cattle wire, will provide the last quickly, but neither of these offers any privacy at all.

Walls and wooden fences are up at once compared with hedges that take years to grow, and they provide an opportunity of growing trained fruit, especially if facing south for sunshine and with bird-proof curtains hanging as effective and temporary protection. If you choose an oak fence, however, get one with concrete posts, for even creosoted wooden ones can rot at ground level, to crash in a high wind and destroy the espalier pears (with branches trained horizontally) when these have just achieved their finest crop.

Wind must be considered, and also concealment of the hideous, which is an increasing problem for modern gardeners. Any wall or fence high enough to hide must be strong and expensive if it is to withstand wind, and when it is up and paid for it may look worse still. It is far better to endure, and wait for a living screen to grow.

Damsons grow the finest tall hedge which will hide a ruined view or temper the wind for draughty gardens. They provide a foam of white blossom in spring and fruit for jam, cheese and tarts through August and September. Two are especially commendable: 'Merryweather' is best as single trees planted 12–14 ft. apart in an orchard with others, for it has the largest fruit and crops the second year after planting; but 'Farleigh' is the fruit farmer's favourite windbreak. It grows taller and faster and has a thicker web of upright twigs.

Half-standard 'Farleighs', branching about 3 ft. from the ground and planted 4–6 ft. apart, can crowd themselves like trees in a wood, reaching 15 ft. more quickly than costly conifers. Insist on modern non-suckering stocks, for the old 'Mussell' types can sucker in the middle of a lawn from wandering roots, and fill the bed beneath, leaving no room for early daffodils.

Dig their holes 2 ft. square to allow room for compost or manure at the bottom and between every 4 in. of replaced soil. (Or a pound of coarse bonemeal for each layer.)

Damsons need no pruning, but from early May to mid-June is the safe time for shortening branches or clipping twigs to keep the tree hedge flat.

The 'Farleigh' damson blossoms late and so misses frost, and a screen of standards or half-standards lets spring frost flow through if it must go at the bottom of a down-sloping garden, which is why commercial growers use it, especially in the north. It does not produce the sudden hush experienced behind the eighty-year-old tall yew hedge of a stately home that costs hundreds of half-crown entrance fees to keep clipped every season. The twigs reduce the force of the wind and bend without breaking, hiding to some extent in winter but leafing solid for privacy in summer. If tall screening is not required, an 8-ft-high hedge will grow from the cheaper bush specimens planted at the same spacing, but both should go with stems 3 ft. from the boundary, and have this much to spread in on the garden side, for tall hedges grow wide.

Red Cherry plums planted this way also make good tall hedges, from half-standards or from the ground up with bushes. Their white flowers are nearly 1 in. across in March, and the penny-sized plums are delicious cooked or used for jam in August, though crops come usually every other year. Prune them like ordinary plums for the first two years, snipping off any dead shoot ends in May, but afterwards they have so little die-back or silver leaf risk that Somerset hedgers used to chop large branches to weave into high barriers around their orchards.

Weaving alone is easiest in gardens, with stakes between bushes for a solid 'basketwork' of bendy shoots, tying down the sideways ones with the uprights left for tall hedges of up to 20 ft. Bushes of the species (*Prunus cerasifera*) are far cheaper than grafted specimens, but have plentiful suckers and far less fruit.

For later blossom and the largest crab-apples for jelly, add 'Wisley Crab' for crimson flowers in April and a plentiful purple fruit. Prune these in winter, shortening the side shoots by two-thirds to an upward pointing bud, not an outward one, as in the case of apples.

The ordinary garden needs a hedge that is quick growing, evergreen, flowering if possible all the summer, suiting all soils and not needing clipping very often. Unfortunately it does not exist, and those who see one advertised should beware of fraud. The first lesson that gardens teach their owners is that one cannot have everything at once, and we can only make the best of what God gave us.

If we insist on cheapness as well, our hedges are limited to privet and *Lonicera nitida*. These are fast and evergreen, while those who are more patient can have their Lonicera for only time and garden space, if they wait till a neighbour clips his hedge in October or November.

Sort out pieces 8–12 in. long, then make a spade cut along the garden line, pushing the handle each way to widen to a narrow 'V' 6 in. deep. Sprinkle sand down it and insert your cuttings untrimmed in a close row, then tread back the soil firmly against them. By about May a great many will be rooted and growing, but though hedges have been made by just putting a row down like this, it is better to dig up the rooted ones and transplant 4 in. apart and 8 between rows to grow larger ready for planting permanently the following spring.

Green privet can be raised in exactly the same way, but as it is stronger you can cut the main shoots down to 4 in. from the ground when the cuttings are growing again after transplanting. Golden is less easy and is best from 2–3 in.-long soft shoots from July clippings inserted in boxes of sandy soil in a cold frame (see Chapter 11) and left there till the following spring before transplanting to grow large enough for hedge planting.

Both green privet and Lonicera are cheaply bought grown large to give the flying start new gardeners need. Buy 2–2½ ft. size to plant 1 ft. apart along the line of the hedge, in October and November or February, March or April, the two tree- and shrub-planting seasons.

If you have privet cut it back to 4 in. above ground so that it will make more shoots low and not go bare at the base later, as it will if left unshortened. Lonicera needs no cutback, but always clip it narrower at the top, so a 4-ft.-high hedge 2 ft. across at the bottom narrows to 1 ft. This keeps it solid all the way down by letting the light to the shoots below. Both can have thick branches cut out with secateurs if they grow too large in October, when it does no harm and provides plenty of cuttings.

The privet problem is robbing of roots, which makes it impossible to grow anything in the bed below. Gardeners who are cursed with a neighbour's hedge can dig out a trench 18 in. deep 1 ft. from the main stems and set sheets of corrugated iron, bolted together and coated with bitumen paint to stop rust, on edge against the privet side, then tread back the soil behind them firmly.

Another way is to build a rough wall like the one round a primula bog, using the same cement mixture and following the three principles of wall building. These are: (1) Wet the bricks, stones, clinkers or even empty bottles so that the cement sticks to them. (2) Never have two joints above each other, but always overlapping. (3) Wash the garden trowel and mixing spade so that no cement sticks to them.

The idea of the wall or corrugated iron is to prevent water, and the fact that you have manured the bed, from baiting the roots to your side, for they follow the trickle of plant foods through the soil and either barrier blocks the message. Golden Privet and Lonicera are far less greedy and need no walls.

These three hedges are common because they are cheap, but their advantage of growing fast for quick privacy means constant clipping. Anyone who pays a gardener to clip his hedges very quickly spends more on wages than the first cost of far better evergreens, even though the price of a dozen may buy a hundred privet.

Two new Cupressus will make evergreen hedges that suit all soils, including chalk, and that will clip to 3–4 ft. high or grow as 10 ft. windproof barriers. The faster grower is *C. Leylandii*, costing about £1.25 each when bought in tens. This is a cross between the old *C. macrocarpa*, which so often dies, in patches or completely, when gales break its brittle taproots, and the tough Canadian *C. nootkatensis*. The cross has the speedy growth and foliage (but grey instead of pale green) of one parent and the hardiness and spreading, safe roots of the other.

The best *C. Lawsoniana* variety is the new 'Green Hedger'. It clips as well as *C. Leylandii* but grows more slowly, sparing small gardens these powerful roots in the bed below. The cost is near £1.50 each, £1.40 each if bought in hundreds.

Like all evergreens, both are best planted in March, April or even May, which gives time for delivery if ordered in autumn.

In readiness, dig a 3-ft.-wide strip, manured, if possible, or with 2 lb. coarse bonemeal to a yard as a lasting feed for the first five

years. Plant firmly 2 ft. apart. Leave unclipped the first summer but
in the next August clip the sides and top straight and level so that
the upward shoots are shortened. Both are best with only August
clipping, though the faster Leylandii may need a spring one, too.

The cat-, dog-, rabbit- and cattle-proof evergreen hedge is *Berberis
stenophylla*, strong, spiny and staying 4–5 ft. high. Plants cost about
£1.30 each, go in 18 in. apart, and need clipping in April or May,
when the bright yellow flowers on young branches are over.

A slow-growing hedge for beauty is *Osmarea Burkwoodii*, with dark
green glossy leaves like non-prickly holly; they cost around £1.80
each, planting is 18 in. apart. Clip after April when the large clusters
of scented white tube flowers, each $\frac{1}{2}$ in. across, have finished. If you
take little off the top it will reach 6 ft. in time.

There is no green hedge that the gardeners buy one half so splendid
as the one they sow. For plant breeders' skill has now made flowering
broom (Cytisus) easy from seed, and hedges that are impossibly
costly at £1.25 each for grafted specimens, need only a 17p packet
for every 20 ft.

Hurst hybrids of broom are a mixture of crimson, purple, pink,
white, cream, yellow and brown with two colour combinations also
among their 1-in.-long giant gorse flowers. Unlike gorse blooms,
these are not spread thinly through the kissing season, but blaze
from late April and on through May.

Older races, even the *Cytisus Andreanus* hybrids in reds and yellows only, grew too tall and woody, but the new one will make a
solid evergreen hedge, growing faster from packets than anything
planted small for cheapness. Its roots are pea-tribe fertility gatherers,
thriving on poor, dry soils without making these poorer and drier,
as privet will.

Soak the seeds in cold water overnight to swell, and sow at 1 in.
intervals along a $\frac{1}{2}$-in.-deep furrow in May. Water to start them away
and weed through the summer.

Seed can germinate patchily in the open with a poor summer, and
those who have a cold frame can sow the seeds individually 1 in.
apart each way in boxes of sandy soil, in March or April. This brings
them ready to transplant 3 in. apart and 8 between rows in July instead of September from sowing outdoors. Take care to break as few
of their tender roots as possible, and because they are fully hardy
they can spend the winter growing ready to plant in April in a single
row along the hedge centre line which should be 1 ft. from the
boundary.

Small seedlings make better hedges than if you waited to plant the larger later. Water well if the spring is dry and keep them un-swamped by weeds that summer. By the next April they will begin flowering as a narrow, 2-ft.-high hedge, and after this preview, clip the top level and the sides straight, ready for a real show the next summer. It will then be about 4 ft. high and 3 across, needing colour photography if your descriptions are to be believed.

When this display is over clip it hard (shears will cut the just finished flowering shoots easily). Make the hedge roughly 1 ft. lower and 6 or 8 in. narrower. This removes most developing seedpods before ripening: these waste strength. Next year's flower shoots can then grow with a level start from the flat top and sides, and the hedge will keep its shape on one clipping a year.

If it grows too tall or wide with age, shorten the best strong branches with secateurs to grow young shoots again, but always after flowering, never in autumn or spring, when brooms hate pruning. Clipping again in September for tidiness will lessen the flower display and late-grown shoots may die in winter. A spring clip can restore neatness but not lost strength and brilliance.

Hurst hybrids came through the winter of 1962–63 without harm, but *Cytisus monspessulanus*, with plain yellow flowers and leafy in-stead of whippy branches, was killed by the severe frost. This can be raised in exactly the same way and stands more clipping for those who insist on neat hedges. Both will seed themselves, especially on sandy soil, and you could watch for seedlings to transplant like the others and so get plenty for replacements and extensions.

Broom hedges do well beside vegetable gardens, for though 2 ft. of width is lost in each hedge, Cytisus belong to the pea family (Legumi-nosae) and the lumps on their roots hold bacteria that gather nitrogen from the air which is drawn down to them as water sinks in the soil. So, unlike privet, they do not rob the soil (if anything they enrich it), and potato rows can go right up to the hedge, leaving you room to get behind for the summer clip.

Because their blaze is a garden feature they are best with low crops in front of them, and potatoes, carrots and onions set the show off as a lawn might. They will hide a fence but need tying back to it for they lean forward unless they can spread both sides. They can divide two front gardens, if nothing tall is grown in front of them, but as a front hedge they shut out the view from the road. A better low background hedge for a front garden is lavender.

The Old English lavender lives long as an 'evergrey' hedge, but not for ever, and if branches die suddenly in summer, or if the hedge grows bare at the base with past neglect, it is time to think of replacing it. Choose young shoots as cuttings—3 to 4 in. long without flower buds, and springing from the sides of older branches. Pull them off gently downwards so that some old wood comes away with each cutting. They root well in boxes of sandy soil in frames or greenhouses, but with modern rooting hormones replacements are easily grown in the open. Dig a trench in a shaded bed 4 in. deep and 8 in. wide and half fill it with equal parts of sand and garden soil.

Dip the old wood 'heels' of the cuttings in Seradix 'B' (Strength 2) and insert firmly about half their length deep and 2 in. apart. Water well and cover with clear polythene weighted with stakes against wind—an old dress bag will cover hundreds of cuttings. Remove this about twice a week for watering in the evening with the rosed can; leave the cover off at night as the cuttings grow, and entirely in about six weeks.

In October plant those that have rooted 4 in. apart and 8 in. between rows to grow plump and ready for 15 in. hedge spacing in autumn next year. Dig in compost or manure generously on heavy clay—4 oz. coarse bonemeal and 4 oz. lime a yard of hedge row on poor sand, and bonemeal alone on the thin soils over chalk, where lavender thrives.

To keep an established hedge in good shape clip the dead flower spikes along with 1–3 in. of stem growth to make the top level and the sides even. Remove dead branches whole, cutting down to clean wood (as when pruning plums). As a tonic for ageing lavender scatter 8 oz. a square yard of dried sludge or Gunos to a square yard of hedge, and hose it in.

Strong but neglected hedges can be cut to shape in October, using a saw on thick branches, or in the spring when they can also be clipped—but not later than March, or flowering suffers. The previous summer's tonic will bring new shoots to bared branches then and new life to well-loved hedges.

If you are buying lavender plants, for planting in October or March, 'Munstead' is dwarf for edging; there are near-pink and deeper purple kinds for hedges up to 18 in.; only Old English *Lavendula spicata* will grow 3–4 ft. high. At 40p each, they are bargains, giving a hedge that may last thirty years and will need clipping only once a year.

Mid-August is the time to replenish or replace lavender bags. For these, cut flower spikes of full stem length when they are full out and lay them no more than three deep in shallow cardboard boxes stacked alternate ways for the air to circulate. Drying will take a fortnight in shade. Drying them in sun or airing-cupboard heat wastes the scent.

The finest and narrowest hedge is one of roses, but unfortunately there are only two thornless varieties to give the great advantage of easy tying. They are long-flowering, long-lived and sweetly scented, at their best when trained tall and flat as hedges round small gardens.

'Zephyrine Drouhin' began about 100 years ago (1868) as the first thornless rose, with deep pink semi-double clusters. It can begin flowering in May and continue until Christmas, for it is one of the old, almost evergreen, 'perpetual roses'. Its main show, however, is in July. In 1919 it produced a variation, the shell pink 'Kathleen Harrop', which is just as good-tempered, fragrant and thornless. Each costs about 78p, and November is the best time for planting them, 4 ft. apart; but order in summer, for their hedging value has been discovered after years of neglect and they usually sell out before spring. The thorned rose to add prickles for a 'keep-off' hedge is 'Souvenir de Claudius Denoyel', with dark red double clusters that flower as fragrantly and as well with the same minimum pruning.

Rambler roses need support to make a hedge, and sheep fence of thick galvanized wire is stronger and more lasting than wire netting, but half the cost of chain-link, which will be wasted if hidden under roses. It is only made 36 in. high, so those who need slightly more height can buy 45-in. cattle fence, while those who suffer from small dogs can buy 'Universal Fencing' with wires 2 in. apart at the bottom and widening to 6 in. square, that train roses well. This type is made up to 4 ft. high, and if it is necessary to keep out rabbits, buy a roll of 2-ft.-width 2-in. mesh wire netting, and halve it down the middle. Twist the cut ends frequently to the bottom of the Universal fence and bend it into an 'L' with the lower arm 6 in. long. Dig a trench along the line of the fence about this wide and deep, and bury your 'L' with the arm pointing away from the garden, filling in the soil when the fence is strained tight. Rabbits trying to dig under will find the buried wire, think they have come to metal subsoil, and give up. A mole is more intelligent and will turn back and dig under, though 2 ft. buried straight down will stop one who is not very determined, and so will a privet wall.

Metal posts for ends, corners and intermediate support at 15 ft. intervals, with strainers, can be bought made up to fit all three types.

A coat of bitumen paint dried hard all over before they go in makes them last the life of the hedge, and this also makes the wire netting last longer.

Dig a 2-ft.-wide strip beside the fence, tucking compost or manure deep in the trenches with 8 oz. of coarse bonemeal a yard to give a lasting feed on poor soils. Getting the roses off to a good start can mean a solid hedge in two years, which is quicker than small privet or 'Macrocarpa'.

Plant only as deep as the soil mark shows they grew in the nursery. Train the smallest of the shoots in fan formation, but tie the two strongest level along the fence and about 6 in. above ground. One in each direction makes sure that shoots from it will grow up and keep the hedge from going bare at the base.

Each summer, tie in any stray shoots that straggle out, and every November tie them all in flat to make a tidy hedge. This is pruning time, and after some years any elderly branches that are dying back, weak, or making bushy heads that sway out awkwardly should be shortened to the lowest strong, young shoot, which is then trained in as a replacement.

Until thornless yellows and dark reds are bred, those who want to add more colours must use ordinary thorned ramblers and train with care for hands and nylons. They need to be chosen carefully for they must grow with minimum pruning, flower long and well, and so far as possible avoid mildew, which is the curse of 'Crimson Rambler'.

'Climbing Golden Showers' is about the best clear yellow, and 'William Allan Richardson' is more apricot, while 'Danse de Feu' is a really scarlet red, and 'Guinée' a very dark maroon crimson, all with the same qualities as 'Zephyrine Drouhin' and 'Kathleen Harrop', the two essentials. A rose is not *necessarily* better for being old, so beware of 'Mermaid', the large yellow single, once often recommended, as it is faddy about soils and often fails to thrive.

The wire to support ramblers acts as a fence while they are growing, but there are a number of bush roses that make good hedges without support. The 'Hedge Roses' of 1961 were only reject budding briars sold cheaply by misleading advertising, and exposed by the National Rose Society and the late V. Sackville-West in the *Observer* as the mean-flowered sprawling frauds they were. Any really cheap offer of roses for hedges should be viewed with suspicion—demand a picture of an established hedge and the size of the bushes before sending any money. There are always briars that do not grow stems thick enough for nurserymen to bud roses on, and these bought cheap by cut-price firms are the basis of bad bargains for beginners.

Real roses cost about 95p each, cheaper in dozens or hundreds for planting 2 ft. apart for a thickening hedge by the third summer. This is nearly as fast as privet, but with a show as they grow, for roses make a hedge to enjoy—hardy on any soil, dog-proof, cat-proof, and even rabbit-excluding.

Take out a spade-deep trench 1 ft. wide along the line of the hedge and fork compost or manure into the bottom. Then scatter ½ lb. of coarse bonemeal to each yard of trench, with extra manure, compost, leafmould or peat on sandy or poor town garden soils before replacing and firming the topsoil ready for planting.

Two modern shrub roses make the best hedges, 4ft. to 6 ft. high, and separately or together, for they grow at the same pace, making a level barrier without gaps. 'Bonn' has semi-double orange scarlet flowers 3 in. across, and 'Nevada' even larger single white ones. Both flower from June to October, but the second is almost thornless for easy training.

Rabbit exclusion demands thorns, and the Scotch roses 'Frühlingsgold', with large, bright yellow single flowers, and 'Frühlingsmorgen', just as large but pink, have plenty to keep the young shoots unnibbled while they grow. The Rugosas, with small double flowers in clusters like ramblers, 'Pink Grootendorst', 'Parfum de l' Hay', crimson and one of the most fragrant of all roses, and the double white 'Schneezwerg', also make thorny hedges, 3 ft. to 5 ft. high.

Small gardens need narrow hedges, and the best value in colour for space are two floribundas, 'Frensham', with deep crimson, fadeless clusters right through the June-October rose hedge season, and 'The Queen Elizabeth', clear pink with long-stemmed clusters that last well cut, and fewest thorns. The lovely and vigorous yellow 'Peace' also makes a good 3 ft. to 4 ft. hedge, with 'Ulrich Brunner' or 'Hugh Dickson', dark reds with matching growth speeds.

The first year they need no pruning but in the second spring drive two 2-ft. sticks or canes in each between bush gap. Then shorten their long shoots by a third and weave them in, basket fashion, between the sticks as hedgers once wove briars. Tie them, too, and aim to have the strongest near ground level, pegging them down with stout wire hooks. From these grow upright shoots that fill the gaps.

The next year shorten, weave and tie again, taking off any that thrust outwards completely, and then with its main branches stout and low the hedge grows on through the years, needing only removal of dead wood or weak branches. Tidy it by training and cutting back only between March and April, for a hedge of roses is not for clipping, but enjoyment through years of splendour.

There are other flowering shrubs suitable for hedges, but they grow more slowly than roses. They provide a background when out of flower, but if you make the frame part of the picture you want to be able to see it. Flowering hedges fit best round the vegetable garden, and conifers at the back of the herbaceous border.

The longest-flowering is a form of our native Potentilla, *P. fruticosa* 'Jackman's Variety', bred to be clipped and grow a thick and bushy hedge up to 4 ft. high. It suits all soils except solid peat, and glows from late June to September with flat, buttercup-like flowers over 1 in. across. It takes about four years from planting to make a solid hedge, but it is one well worth having, with the longest show of anything but roses.

Dig a 2-ft. strip for it, taking out all perennial weeds, especially couch grass roots, for these strangle and stunt young hedges. Use manure if possible, if not, 4 oz. of coarse bonemeal to each foot, and as much dried sludge on subsoil or poor sand. Plant 1 ft. apart between October and April, as deep as the bushes were on the nursery, and tread firmly round them.

Let the bushes grow the first two summers, then in the following March clip the back and front straight and the top level. Do this every year, leaving most on top till the hedge reaches its full 4 ft. in about six seasons. Never clip after the first week in April, for this leaves no time for new shoots to grow and flower.

Potentilla has small leaves which clip neatly instead of halving to unsightliness like those of laurel, but they fall in autumn, leaving bare twigs. Those of the hedge Spiraea (*S. Thunbergii*) turn orange and near scarlet, hanging till December like a brighter beech hedge, and a new light green crop starts in February. This is a shrub for a 4–5-ft. hedge. The shrubs are planted 18 in. apart, so a dozen at about the price of Potentilla go further. Treat it the same way as Potentilla but wait until April before clipping—then the small white flowers that cluster thickly on the young branches in March will be over. Cut short back and front but on top leave about 3 in. of shoots that have flowered, until the hedge is high enough. Clipping later leaves little time for next year's foot-long flowering shoots to grow.

Another hedge Spiraea (5–6 ft.) is *S. arguta multiflora*. It does not have the long-lasting autumn leaves, and the scented white flower clusters (which give it its other name of 'Bridal Wreath') appear in April and May. It suits chalk soils which *S. Thunbergii* dislikes, and as it clips a month later they cannot be mixed. Cost and planting distances are the same.

Both are hardy, better as a hedge than separate shrubs, and glorious with naturalized daffodils in the bed below, chosen for early or late flowering to contrast with the Spiraea.

Nut trees and hazel nut hedges come together, for the hedge is the best way to grow them in a small garden, either across it as a division, or as a boundary. It was the pollination problems, first discovered when the men of Kent began developing varieties of the wild hazel, that gave us our nursery rhyme:

> I had a little nut tree, and nothing would it bear:
> But a silver nutmeg, and a golden pear.
> The King of Spain's daughter came to visit me,
> All for the sake of my little nut tree.

The little nut tree for gardeners is 'Merveille de Bolwyller', because it suits the widest range of soils and climates; its nuts are broader and rather bigger than bought cob or filberts and it bears about the third season after planting instead of waiting till the sixth or seventh as larger-growing varieties do. It is self-fertile which means that it sets a crop with its own pollen, so you need have only one tree.

Two-year-old bush trees, pruned to cup shape, cost about £1.75 each for planting 12 ft. apart each way to grow like small apple trees or as in the nut orchards of Kent. Those for hedges are cheaper, especially by the dozen, because they do not have to be carefully trained with clear stems, and they go 3 ft. apart along the hedge line.

A very attractive hedge can be made with Purple Filbert, which has purple-brown leaves, planted with a 'Merveille de Bolwyller' or a 'Pearson's Prolific' (also self-fertile, but waits longer before cropping) to every four, not only because their green (especially in late spring), is a fine contrast, but as pollinators; for without them, purple hazels have few nuts. The side facing the sun always has most, so if it is a boundary hedge have this on your side if possible.

Nuts will stand up to a north aspect, shade from a house and poor soil, but they like shelter from the east wind. Plant them 6 in. deep, spreading the roots well and treading the soil firm. Dig the hole deeper if you have chicken feathers or the inside of an old feather mattress to bury below as lasting feed. November is the best time for planting but even March is not too late so long as you water if spring brings drought.

Shorten any upward pointing shoots to 18 in. long at planting time so that they branch instead of running up too high for hedges. Then leave the bushes to grow till the following March, when it will be time to put in two short, stout stakes between each, and weave the young and bendy branches like those of Cherry Plum. Tie some down to ground level so that their new shoots start low for a solid hedge. It can be clipped in May or June if it is untidy, but the best time is August, levelling top and sides as the summer pruning; this puts the strength into forming tassel catkins which must cast their pollen on the insignificant female flowers with the help of the winds of February. This is why pruning and training should wait till March when long straight-up shoots should be shortened and young sideways ones woven in as a regular routine. A spring 'weave' and an August clip will keep the hazel hedge tidy and fruiting, with nuts the third year on a 'Merveille' and the sixth for the other two.

These garden varieties are less powerful than wild hazels and they produce fewer 'suckers'. These are young shoots coming straight up from the roots, often in the border below, where they are not wanted. Unlike those of other fruit trees, these will grow new bushes, for hazelnuts are not grafted or budded on something else. Wait till they are about 1 ft. long, scrape away the soil from round them to where they join the main root, and cut them off carefully to avoid breaking the roots they will have round them. These will not be enough to support the leaves on the shoot, so shorten it to about 6 in. and re-plant in rows as you would Lonicera or privet, ideally in March. Transplant again to 1 ft. apart each way, shorten the shoots the following March, and they will be ready for hedge extensions in October.

If you do not want more hazels, or if the suckers are a problem, do not cut them off, for this encourages more to grow from the same place. Take hold of them firmly and *twist* as though you were unscrewing them. This will leave a wound, but this closes quickly and means no more suckers. This is the treatment for these shoots round all fruit trees, and for roses, especially those in hedges which will have different leaves from the rest, but these need gloves for gripping.

Another way of increasing hedge hazels is by 'layering'. Choose young side shoots near the ground and twist a piece of wire round about 1 ft. from the tip, so that it is tight on the smooth, lightish-brown bark. Put a handful of sand on top of the soil and bend the branch down so that this comes under the wire. Then peg it down either with a gipsy type clothes peg or a long 'hairpin' bent from

14–18-gauge galvanized iron wire about 6 in. long. Leave it alone, and when it is growing well cut it away from the parent plant and replant it with plenty of roots to grow on, like the suckers.

Nut trees grow more fruit per bush, and they need shortening of *all* their new shoots to 15 or 18 in., whichever measurement comes above a joint. The next March, shorten all side shoots to three joints (or the lowest spent catkin, whichever is the shorter) and the main end shoot of each branch to six. Choose strong shoots round the outside to shorten to 15–18 in. shoots that will come on and replace old ones that cease to bear on established trees; but screw off any that thrust up in the middle as though they were suckers.

Nuts for Christmas should be allowed to stay on till they are dropped from all-brown sheaths, but eat some young and green-sheathed in the autumn for the delicious flavour of their fresh, milky kernels. Perhaps the Kentish countryman warned the King of Spain's daughter against pruning the rooted sucker she took home with her at apple-tree time, for cutting away the shoots before they grow the catkins is the main reason for all tree and no crop.

Adjoining houses have one hedge or fence owned by a neighbour and one their own, so hedging both sides of a garden always means agreement on one side. Anyone will agree to a half share of your flowering or nut hedge, but a neighbour's corrugated iron or other fences, or blank walls, may need something to cover them quickly.

The climber that most quickly hides the hideous is *Polygonum baldschuanicum*, the 'Russian Vine', which can grow 15 ft. in a season. So long as you support it properly, its creamy plumes will give you a foaming cascade from July to October in sun or shade. It grows on any soil and in even the coldest gardens. Polygonum climbs without tying and can cover a high chainlink fence in three years, for though its leaves fall in winter, its matted stems still act as a screen and a windbreak.

On blank walls or corrugated iron fences, use horizontal wires 8 in. apart. Thread these through 3 in. vine eyes, fixed with large Rawl-plugs for brick or concrete, or screwed into the posts. Twist the 14-gauge wire (38p per $\frac{1}{2}$ kilo—about 52 ft.) round each giant screw-eye, so that the weight does not all bear on the ends.

The bed below need be only 1 ft. wide to take holes this square and deep—8 ft. apart for Polygonum, 6 ft. for other climbers. Put manure or compost on the bottoms and 1 oz. of coarse bonemeal to every 2 in. of top soil replaced.

Buy pot grown Polygonums to plant between October and April

without disturbing the roots as they come out of the pots. They need no pruning at planting time, only tying, well spread to the wires so that the new shoots advance on a broad front. When they grow too large, snip out whole branches about half-way up in mid-February. The stronger honeysuckles will also cover a screen of this type, and they will be discussed in Chapter 6 with the other climbers.

Gardeners who have something to hide now have a faster answer than any climber or hedge—*Miscanthus sacchariflorus*, a giant grass from China. As well as blotting out ruined views with a 10-ft.-high barrier of foliage, it has the added advantage of dulling summer traffic noise. Because it grows fast and high each year on all soils (except thin ones over chalk or rock) start by digging in compost or manure generously with 1 lb. a square yard of coarse bonemeal as lasting food. Then plant the clumps firmly in March or April, 4 ft. apart and 4 ft. from the boundary they have to screen.

During the first summer the clumps will grow 2 ft. to 3 ft. high with wide, grass-like leaves which spring from the joints of stout stems and arch downwards. In the second season, when the thicker shoots reach 6 ft., the effect is of a green fountain, and in the third and later seasons these fountains reach a height of 10 ft. or 12 ft. meeting in a curtain with the noise-deadening qualities of a yew hedge.

The leaves die in autumn, but the light brown foliage should stay on as both winter protection and screen until March, when the clumps should be cut down, with shears or secateurs, to a height of 6 in. The pithy stems should be chopped up for compost material. Then spread a 2-in.-thick coat of manure or leafmould, with sludge or Gunos under it, on the surrounding bed. This feeding starts the shoots racing away in spring so they may reach their full height by July.

Established clumps may flower in August with wide and lofty plumes which can be dried as room decorations for tall vases. They cannot set seed in our climate and as their roots go down instead of spreading and shooting in all directions, as hardy bamboos can in mild gardens, there is no risk of this giant becoming a science-fiction-size couch grass.

Leaving leaves on through the winter is also the best policy for Pampas Grass—*Cortaderia argentea*—which can be clipped down to 1-ft.-high domes in March (take care that the razor-sharp leaf edges don't cut your hands). Alternatively, the accumulated dead foliage can be burnt out with a blowlamp or flamegun on a dry day when it will burn too fast to harm the waiting shoots. The grass also appreciates a surface-manure mulch round its clumps after spring cleaning about every fourth year.

Miscanthus make striking lawn plants grown as single specimens, since they have no wandering roots or savage leaf sides. For this purpose the small species, *M. sinensis zebrinus* with golden cross stripes on smaller leaves, and *M. sinensis folius striatus* with cream ones down the leaf middles, are excellent, serving also for 4–6-ft.-high screens.

Both flower in July and August with red-tinted plumes and can be raised from imported seeds sown in April, 6 in. apart and 1 ft. between ½-in.-deep furrows. Hoe to keep them free from weeds.

4

Trees for Small Gardens

Many unfortunate small gardens suffer from too many trees, not only on account of shade but also because of the robbing roots that suck the moisture away, often under the fence to the next-door garden. Here the privet wall as recommended for a hedge can be used to keep neighbours' roots within bounds.

Trees differ from shrubs, for once their tap roots are down they cannot be moved to allow more room between, so they must be chosen with care and planted no nearer than 15 ft. from each other, which is the minimum. It is essential to choose fairly slow-growing varieties, and nothing that is evergreen, for though conifers will make a hedge, and the tall flame shapes of cypresses make avenues that carry the eye across the park to the imitation Greek temple, this is not for small gardens.

Large hollies, pines and cedars need room to show off their shape, and if they are beautiful and inherited, garden round them and put up with their disadvantages. Anything evergreen dries the soil under it and makes it impossible to grow bulbs in the bed below. The more overshadowed and dried by trees a garden is, the fewer crops it will grow well. Those who buy old houses may follow an owner who has been content with laurels, periwinkle, ivy and sun-starved irises under crowding trees. Either they must limit their gardening to dry-shade-tolerant plants, which excludes fruit and vegetables and almost everything that flowers long and well, or they can take out a tree or two to let in light and air.

Wait a full year round before you begin felling trees in a garden new to you, especially if you move in in winter, for something gnarled and old that seems merely a space-waster may fruit deliciously, or flower with a perfection that makes endurable the burden the tree may be for the rest of the year. It is so easy to fell a tree that has taken perhaps eighty years to grow that it is as well to make sure that you want it down.

The easiest way to fell a tree is the traditional gardener's method that removes it completely, like taking out a tooth. Saw off the branches first to leave a tall stump at least 10 ft. high, using ropes to lower the large ones and help to pull them down. Buy new clothes line for this job or, better still, stouter rope from an ironmonger, getting enough to allow for standing well clear. Then dig a trench about 1 ft. wide and 2–3 ft. deep round the tree and 3 ft. from the trunk, cutting through each root as you come to it with a sharpened axe. Tie the rope firmly near the top of the tall stump and pull and release, repeating this and digging and cutting more roots, till the levering action breaks the tap root and brings the tree down with a crash.

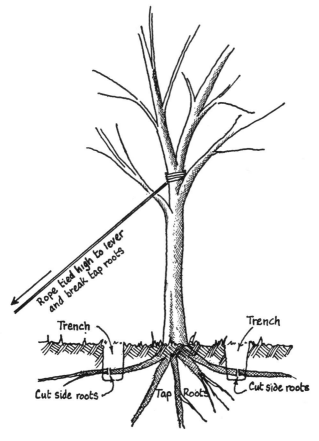

Fig. 9. How to fell a tree in a small garden.

Two adults should be able to fell a tree under 1 ft. in diameter with safety, provided that they take their time and keep together, for one pulling on the rope and the other chopping can mean a broken back when the trunk comes down. Large trees should be felled by tree surgeons, especially if they are likely to fall against buildings or other people's property.

If anyone is employed to fell a tree, insist that it comes down this way, because cutting of the stump near ground level with a power saw makes it impossible to use the trunk to lever out the roots by the traditional gardener's method. The timber merchant or woodman is merely concerned to get it down cheaply and on the lorry with the largest possible quantity of usable wood. The gardener wants it extracted like a tooth so that he can grow something else in the room.

Where a stump has been left in it can only be rotted or burnt out. Drill four holes about 6 in. apart in a 1 ft. wide stump (more for larger), using a brace with a $\frac{1}{2}$-in. bit to go down about 4 in. Clear out the sawdust and fill the holes with sodium chlorate weed-killer, corking up the openings. Uncork after about a fortnight and refill, for the weed-killer will have vanished into the sap channels of the tree.

Three fillings will usually kill any stump, even an elm or poplar, but if it shoots again the next spring, repeat the dose. The sodium chlorate will stay inside the roots and not cause trouble, and the stump will slowly rot. As the chemical is inflammable it is possible in summer to light a bonfire on top of the stump, and once it has been got well alight it will smoulder away, reducing the buried wood to charcoal which can be dug out.

Sawing off branches from the neighbour's trees needs his permission, but it can make a real difference to the light and air in a crowded garden. Always saw *upwards* under the branch, then down about a foot away from the trunk, in case the branch gives suddenly and tears the bark down the trunk, which can kill a tree. Then saw off the final stump to leave a clean cut level with the trunk so it will heal over, and paint the cut surface to keep out the wet, ideally with a plastic emulsion paint.

In sawing ornamental trees, remember the principles of fruit pruning, 'stone fruit in summer, pip-fruit in winter' and flowering plums, peaches, cherries and even almonds are in the summer-pruning class. Saw them before 15th July to remove dead wood and crowding branches, because from May to mid-July is the safe season when the spores of silverleaf and die-back diseases are least likely to be blowing about. These can attack laburnums, too, so laburnum branches should also be sawn then.

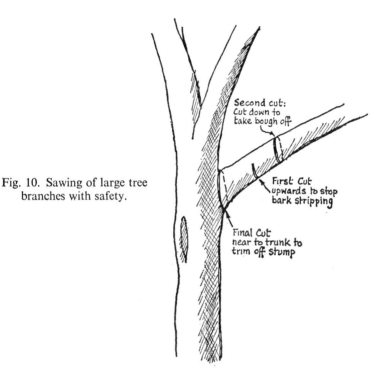

Fig. 10. Sawing of large tree branches with safety.

Second cut:
Cut down to
take bough off

First Cut
upwards to stop
bark stripping

Final Cut
near to trunk to
trim off stump

During this safe season look over ornamental trees in the plum family, especially if newly planted or within up to four years ago, to see if any shoots have died at the tips. Snip these off with the secateurs and if there is a brown stain in the middle, snip again and again till the wood shows white and clean. If none have died back there is no pruning to do, exactly as with plums or cherries in the fruit garden.

Most gardeners expect to grow some fruit and often cram a garden with an assorted dozen, but one of the ways to save space is to plant the finest-blossom varieties as flowering trees and enjoy the fruit too, choosing the kinds for succession so that the whole show is not over in only a week or so. By choosing some of the less usual ornamental trees it is also possible to enjoy fruit, if only for cooking, from the same trees that are a feature of every spring.

Perhaps the finest tree for small new gardens is *Prunus persica* 'Aurora', which grows fruit, and is a beauty too. It is strong and easy, reaching 25 ft. in about five years, with large, clear, rose-pink double flowers in March and early April, and a crop of small peaches for eating, stewing and making jam, in years when frost misses the blossoms.

Next best is 'Clara Meyer', with smaller flowers but more chance of peaches. Neither variety needs pruning, but, as with ordinary peaches, both share leafcurl risk—so spray them in February with a proprietary lime-sulphur wash. Spraying with Alginure or Maxicrop seaweed foliar feeds is also effective, and has the advantage that you can wait for the leafcurl to appear before applying either feed.

Full standards of both varieties cost about £4 (bushes cost about £2.50; plant them like fruit trees). Dig holes 2 ft. square and deep and drive a stout, well-creosoted stake into the centre of each one. Fit the tree roots around the stake and fill in firmly with all the top soil mixed with 3–5 lb. of coarse bonemeal, which will act as a lasting feed.

Secure the stem in at least two places to the stake with either of the plastic tree ties that 'give' as stems become trunks; or use an old nylon stocking. These are the perfect tree tie, knotted firmly round the stake twice so that the tree stem is cushioned against the knot, then tied again to hold the tree firm with plenty of 'give', yet rotproof strength. They last at least a season and, unfortunately for budgets, there are plenty of replacements available in most families.

Flowering almonds can fruit in lucky frost years, but most of them have nuts that are bitter and poisonous with hydrocyanic acid. Choose *Prunus amygdalus macrocarpa* for an upright habit that shades the bed below least. It has large pink flowers that are as lovely as any almond, and 'sweet' nuts that store for cracking and eating with raisins.

The flowering crab that provides most jelly from least space is 'Wisley Crab'; it has deep crimson blossom and the largest purple fruits. 'Dartmouth' flowers white with rather smaller crimson fruit, and the new American variety, 'Katherine', bears plenty of scarlet crabs after really beautiful double pink blossom—each bloom measuring 2 in. across.

Mountain ash or rowanberry jelly is sharply pleasant, with roast meats, and *Sorbus aucuparia* 'Jackman's Crimson', with white flower clusters in May, has the largest bunches. Birds often strip these in smoky towns where rowans thrive. The answer is to plant *S. aucu-*

paria xanthocarpa, which has vivid orange autumn tints; the birds rarely attack the yellow berries.

Laburnums have the disadvantage of untidy black pods that hold seeds poisonous to children, but with room for an extra tree, choose *L. Vossii* for the longest 'golden chains' and the best show in late May and June. Whenever they go in during the October to March tree planting season, they can fail to leaf in spring, not because they are diseased or damaged, but from a fit of the sulks which has produced many complaints for long-suffering nurseries. If they fail to leaf by September, then something is wrong, but usually they recover their normal temper during July.

The flowering thorns are also on the fast side for the smallest gardens, but the double varieties make a striking show in May. The best are *Crataegus oxyacantha masekii*, a very good double pink, and *C. oxyacantha plena coccinea*, which was once called 'Paul's Double Scarlet Thorn', not because it is scarlet but from its bright rose red that is near the colour of 'Paul's Scarlet', the lovely climbing rose.

Almost every other flowering tree (with some exaggeration) is now a *Prunus*, for the cherries, almonds and plums are all lumped together. 'Kanzan', which was formerly called 'Hisakura', is the most popular, with strong, upright branches and large double rose blossom; 'Shirotae', or 'Mount Fuji' is a dazzling double white, while 'Fugenzo' has a flat and spreading habit with pale pink double flowers that start later and last longer than all the others.

There are many flowering plums, and of these the American hybrid of two Japanese species, *Prunus* 'Trailblazer', has early white blossom, dark purple foliage all the summer and small fruit rather like large, oval cherries, excellent for jam, pies and stewing. This is new to British gardens and there are now towering specimens, but stock plants on nurseries have produced plum crops that will make it impossible to plant as a street tree.

It is merely the risk of theft, and damage by those who steal fruit, that prevents us from planting fruiting trees in front gardens, and, generally speaking, the unusual kinds described here are safe, because they will be thought poisonous. Apples, however, are obvious and should stay in the back garden.

For planting apples between November and before February ends, means not only fruit for the future but at least fifty springs of blossom. Loveliest of trees is 'Upton Pyne', with rose-pink flowers so large that it is worth growing for beauty alone, though its large yellow cookers sweeten for eating, too, stored from January to March.

'Sunset' provides a contrast of paler pink blossoms and near-'Cox' flavour for eating in November and December, matching pollen for a crop on both.

Together they fit 'Ribston Pippin', which awkwardly needs two pollinators to produce its delicious, long-keeping eaters, russet-skinned, crisp, yellow and spicy, and flowers like scented snow in spring.

For early beauty, plant 'Arthur Turner', with rose-pink blossom and cooking apples to pick small for pies from July onwards, so thinning the crop for larger bakers in October and November. Add 'Laxton's Epicure' for plentiful, paler flowers, and soft, sweet, juicy apples in September and October, eaten straight off the tree to get the full flavour that quickly fades. Another for picking and eating in July and August, is 'Laxton's Early Crimson', far nicer than 'Beauty of Bath', and also fruiting alone for one-tree gardens.

Where frost blackens early blossom too often, or if you want to extend the glory of apples in bloom, plant 'Edward VII', a better-than-Bramley cooker that keeps from November to March. This also fruits on its own. With room for three, have 'American Mother', with a show of later flowers and soft, sweet apples for October and November, and 'Heusgen's Golden Reinette' for an eater of taste lasting until April.

'Orleans Reinette' is famous as the most delicious of all for eating till February, and is just as lovely with late blossom, but is not as strong a tree. It deserves a place in small gardens, where most failures come from choosing the wrong pollen partner. Heusgen's stronger but less tasty variation fits perfectly.

For June blossom, plant 'Crawley Beauty', the fruit of which keeps for cooking and eating from October to April. If it fails to fruit well alone, add 'Royal Jubilee', an excellent cooker till Christmas.

All these uncommon apples are easier in Scottish and northern gardens than 'Cox', and thrive also in the south. Here 'Cox' can go near 'Arthur Turner', or the spicy-flavoured 'Red Ellison', which is a better 'Cox' pollinator than 'Worcester Pearmain'—or it can crop alone.

Buy full standards, for half standards are too low to motor-mow under without ducking at every tree, and are just as awkward with a hand mower. It is worth ordering early from a good nursery and asking for extra-tall standards not only of apples but of all flowering trees, because having the branches high and clear leaves room for leafmould and compost heaps under them at the bottom of the garden, and allows some light and a view below them where they are near the house.

Dig the holes for apples 15 ft. apart each way, which is the minimum spacing for any tree. Unlike shrubs, they cannot be moved once they are in, and lopping can spoil their shapes as they grow into each other. Keep the bulge where the graft was made 2 in. above the surface, and plant with the essential care to leave no airspaces among the roots. Plant without haste, for time is well spent planting trees for fruit and beauty too.

Standard apples should be grafted on M. XIV or M. XXV, and any good nursery should know these new, faster-fruiting, semi-dwarfing stocks for small gardens. There is no real difference between pruning apples for blossom and for fruit, but it is possible to get more fruit from a flowering crab by giving it the normal apple treatment. This means shortening the longest and strongest of this year's shoots on every branch to a third of its length in winter, and its lesser contemporaries to the third or fourth bud, whichever points away from the centre of the tree. The exceptions are the varieties which fruit at the shoot tips ('Worcester Pearmain', 'Lord Lambourne' and 'Blenheim Orange') and these merely need to have dead or crowding branches sawn out to keep the middle of the tree open.

Just as the crab is a tiny apple grown for blossom, there is an ornamental pear, *Pyrus communis* 'Beech Hill', which grows straight up in a tower of blossom in spring, casting little shade. It makes a lovely tree in a small garden, going up and up like a Lombardy poplar, but without those fiercely thrusting roots that go under house foundations which should keep all poplars out of small gardens. Its pears, however, are small and scarce, for this new variety is bred for blossom and needs no pruning.

Ordinary pears are value not only for the foam of white blossom in spring that they all share, but for the beauty of their autumn foliage, apart altogether from their fruit. This is rarely appreciated because most gardens allow room for only one pear tree, and this must be one of the two self-fertile varieties. 'Conference' is long, thin, juicy and sweet, while 'Fertility' is pear-shaped, but as tasteless as most imported fruit, and neither gives really striking autumn colour varieties.

It takes two pears and their paired pollen to make a crop that is worth while for both beauty and flavour. In the narrow beds of little houses today, on walls that face south for sunshine, we can grow the forgotten tastes of a kind that the great gardens once grew.

White walls contrast with the crimson autumn leaves of 'Triomphe de Vienne', whose rich pears, picked in August, ripen a red-flushed yellow for September eating. This kind can fruit happily single, but is better paired with 'Thompson's'; the fruit has a finer flavour, keeping for October and November, and leaves are as rich a red. A third, with matching pollen, is 'Glou Morceau', with plain brown leaves but sweet yellow pears for December and January.

'Glou Morceau' should also nowadays partner 'Doyenne du Comice', the finest-tasting of all—picked the first week in October to eat later that month and in November. ('Laxton's Superb', once its popular pollen companion, cannot be planted for it takes Fire Blight, the new, incurable disease.)

Against red brick walls pair 'Beurre Superfin' (yellow-leaved, and pears picked in mid-September for October eating), with 'Durandeau' (yellow leaves flaming slowly to orange, and fruit to pick a fortnight later, ripening for November). Add 'Joséphine de Malines' to either for the longest-keeping flavour, lasting through December to February.

Horizontally-trained trees with two 'storeys' cost about £6.50 each, or with three 'storeys' £8. Plant with the middle stem below the window centre and branches tied to wall nails till they grow strong. The tip shoots—never pruned—are trained back round bays and finally upwards. Cordons (about £1.95 each) with single stems are planted 30 in. apart and trained straight up the house. Both should be grafted on dwarfing quince, and the bulge where the pear wood begins is planted above ground. Existing wall-pears with buried bulges should have soil scraped away so that any roots from them can be cut, for these can 'un-dwarf' a pear to grow more wood and less fruit.

Pears planted between October and March are not pruned till next winter, cutting back side-shoots to the third or fourth bud then and every December. Each August shorten the growing side-shoots to six leaves, but do not cut away the short, chubby ones that bunch as 'fruiting spurs' along the branches.

A glory of white blossoms in the spring may mean too many pears to ripen, so thin the fruit in June to 6 in. apart. Run a hose in the border to stop thinned fruit from dropping in drought years.

When picked, store apart from apples, with care for tender skins. They need 40°–45° F., and modern attics with fibreglass insulation in the rafters bring that same perfect ripeness of pears that were once stored in stable lofts and eaten by candlelight.

5

Shrubs for Small Gardens

Shrubs are space fillers for large gardens, but the relatively short flowering season of most varieties means that a blaze is followed by a long gap. There is no problem where a large garden has space to fill, and lawns and shrubs are the least-labour answer. Small gardens need to use room to the best advantage, and the longest display from the least space.

The *Potentilla fruticosa* varieties are a bargain in providing the longest life and taking the least room, with blooms nearly 1 in. across, like flat single roses. They flower from early June until the end of October, and suit all soils however poor, any garden, however cold, and tolerate some shade, though they are best in full sun.

'Kathleen Dykes' is lemon yellow, 'Jackman's Variety' deep yellow, 'Mount Everest' white, and 'Primrose Beauty' nearer a rich cream. Normal pruning time is March—the second after planting: cut out a quarter of the main branches to leave 2 in., so that there are always some of the new shoots to flower full length each summer. All these kinds grow 3–4 ft. high, and as much across, pruned this way.

In narrow beds or in tubs or large pots, where they do well, cut *all* the old branches back to 2 in., so that they flower like fury on only the young shoots and keep far smaller—usually about 18 in. high and wide.

Plant them between October and March 2 ft. apart in narrow and crowded beds. Dig in 8 oz. of coarse bonemeal to a square yard, for this lasts longer than the fine stuff, with manure or compost tucked in the trench bottoms. They will last for ten years without re-planting.

They drop their small, strawberry-like leaves in winter, so there is space to plant small bulbs and daffodils between them for colour. As the Potentillas grow after pruning, they hide the dying bulb foliage, which is best covered with a 2-in. coat of leafmould or peat, with a scatter of fine bonemeal below it, to prevent weeds, and give food and humus for both bulbs and shrubs.

For contrast, plant *Spiraea japonica* 'Anthony Waterer' at the back of the bed. They have large, level-topped flower heads from late June to August. *Ceratostigma Willmottiana* will give clear blue flower clusters from late July till the end of October. Both take the March cutback that gives bulbs room to grow, with 'Anthony Waterer' shortened to leave 2 in. of every smooth-barked young shoot, and Ceratostigma cut right down, for it looks dead every winter, but grows from underground each April.

For the dry, shaded places under trees, dig as for a sunny bed, with ample manure, and plant the evergreen *Skimmia japonica frag-rans*, which needs no pruning, at the back of the bed. Short spikes of cream flowers will appear in May and June. At the front have *Symphoricarpos Chenaultii* with small scented bell-flowers and purple berries that linger on for Christmas decorations. For yellow cups in July and August plant *Hypericum calycinum* 1 ft. apart each way, shortening them to 8 in. when they go in. Cut both back every March to keep them flowering cheerfully.

Follow the same principle with Ceanothus, snipping back the shoots that flowered from July to October to 1 in. length in March. These have tassel flowers. 'Gloire de Versailles' (pale blue), 'Topaz' (dark blue) and 'Perle Rose' (deep pink) are splendid sunny border shrubs best planted from pots in April or May. The evergreen species for walls with blue ball flowers in May need only removal of crowded shoots and tying tidily after flowering.

The graceful *Tamarix tetrandra* should have its slender shoots shortened to 2–3 in. long when its broad pink plumes wither as May ends, while *T. pentandra*, with taller plumes from July to September, needs the same pruning in March.

November is the time to 'blue' the pale pink hydrangeas that thrive in sheltered corners of town gardens. 'Madame Riverain', as the hardiest of the pot-plant kinds, is most frequently found, and blues beautifully. The usual crimson, 'Parsival', turns muddy purple.

Blueing compounds are expensive for large bushes, but aluminium sulphate or alum (which is aluminium sulphate and sulphate of potash) are cheaper; they can be got from chemists. Buy 4 oz. for each square foot the plant covers and scatter the crystals among the stems and round under the spread of the branches, then water the crystals, to start them soaking to the roots where they can last two summers.

Limy soils mean only patchy, dull mauves, but the soil can be un-limed by watering 2 oz. of Epsom salts dissolved in 2 gallons of water on each 4 square feet in March and again a fortnight later. This produces better blues, except on chalk.

Hardy hydrangeas can be planted in the autumn, though spring is better in the north. The best outdoors are 'Vicomtesse de Vibraye', pale pink or Cambridge blue, 'Ami Pasquier', deep pink or royal blue, and 'Hatfield Rose' which is crimson and changes to purple. 'Westfalen' is the brightest crimson of all, and blues to blue-black ink colour.

These flower from July to September and the Lacecap varieties with wide flat plate flower heads, not the familiar domes, finish in August. The best varieties of these are 'Blue Wave', whose large outer florets stay white while the smaller ones in the middle go pale pink or sky-blue, and the deep pink 'Lilacina', which blues with a purple centre.

Forced pot plants are soft so should not be planted before May when their shoots need shortening to two joints to ripen buds for next summer's flowers. Prune outdoor bushes in March, cutting back their smooth-barked shoots to the first pair of fat buds, or their lowest joint with none. Overgrown specimens can have old branches shortened by half then, but not all at once for they miss flowering till new shoots ripen.

Hydrangea species will not blue. *H. paniculata grandiflora*, hardy in the coldest gardens and in shade, has tall white domes in July and August. Shorten its flowered shoots to half length each March and spread a 2-in. coat of peat over the roots, with some manure under it. This helps all kinds on poor, dry soils.

When forsythia fails to flower it is usually because of lack of ripening time for the smooth-barked young shoots that bear their splendid stars. 'Tidying' them to a dome shape in summer, leaves only shortened flowering shoots, but April pruning lets these grow full length, with time to ripen buds for next year's blaze.

Some flower only on the smooth, brown-barked shoots that grew last summer. Of these the deepest usual yellow is *F. intermedia vitellina*, the palest *F. intermedia primulina* (near primrose) and the latest is the golden *F. viridissima*. Others flower also on older branches: *F. intermedia spectabilis*, with clustered, crocus-yellow stars: and its large-flowered new variety 'Lynwood' is perhaps the very best of these easy shrubs for any soil and every garden.

Observe where the remains of the flowers are, for different pruning is needed. With flowers only on smooth-barked shoots, cut back those that have flowered to 1 ft, or quarter-length, whichever is shorter.

Where these shoots have grown from old branches, shorten these to leave not more than three, but if the bush is meant to hide something keep the strongest, rough-barked boughs unshortened. Snip back the young shoots on them as well as the stronger ones nearer the roots, to make the 'fruiting spurs' that grow long new ones to bear the golden fountain that is the crop.

Elderly bushes, too large for small gardens, can now have boughs even as thick as hoe handles sawn off to leave only 1 ft.: half could be done this way and the rest pruned normally. This drastic sawing (unsafe in autumn) with dead wood cut right out, can restore the splendour of the bushes and economize on space.

With old wood also look first for strong, smooth-barked shoots that did *not* flower, or flowered only a little, and leave these unpruned. They failed to ripen last summer, but can spend this one growing side shoots to flower together next spring.

Then go over the bush shortening young shoots that have flowered: to a quarter of their length if they are of pencil thickness, while the thicker shoots should be cut back to 1 ft. long. Take back trailing branches to the second or third strong shoot, but from the middle of the bush remove only weak or crowded branches, for if the pruning is mostly round the outside, this can start the centre flowering unhidden.

The golden trailing kind thriving on north walls is *F. suspensa*, and the pale lemon one with purple-tinted bark, *F. suspensa atrocaulis*. Both need to have their flowering shoots shortened to 1 ft. length, old weak branches which are growing none cut out, and young ones that were flowerless tied in to the nails or wires.

The finest is *F. suspensa Fortunei*, so strong that it needs to be taken down from the wall completely; train back only unflowered shoots (if any) and cut the rest off 1 ft. from the ground. Those that grow new need tying in through summer.

Flowering currants or Ribes, including 'Pulborough Scarlet', the brightest red, and deep pink 'China Rose', need forsythia-type pruning. Shorten the shoots to 4 in. as soon as their flowers finish. Overgrown *Ribes* can be sawn down to 1-ft.-high stumps after flowering: this gives them a brilliant second childhood.

This drastic treatment improves giant Philadelphus and Weigela, but leave their back stumps 3–4 ft. high and slope down to 6 in., so that the new shoots start in 'steps' with sun to ripen them. Then you will get towers of blossom, instead of thickets flowering sparsely on top. Prune these shoots, like those of small specimens, by cutting them down to two joints after flowering.

Buddleias overgrow to trees rather than thickets and they must be sawn and shortened in March, for their new shoots start in spring to flower the same summer. Saw half their unwanted branches one year and half the next, but never in autumn because wet and cold can kill their hollow stumps. The orange-ball *Buddleia globosa* needs May pruning when the flowers are finished.

Buy 'Royal Red' for 1-ft.-long dangling cones of rich red purple; 'Charming', the best pink; and 'Fromow's Purple', deep violet, to flower from July to autumn. Shorten their long smooth shoots to 3 in. in March. But wait till June to cut two-thirds off those of the orange-ball kind (*B. globosa*) that flower in May, and July for *B. alternifolia* (with unpaired leaves). Leave their straightest shoots to grow, for this kind make a tree.

Weigela (correctly called Diervilla), including the new 'Bristol Ruby'—brighter red than 'Eva Rathke'—and the best double-white Mock Orange, *Philadelphus virginale*, grow into giants if unpruned, so cut out the branches that have flowered through June and July when they finish, leaving about 2 in. of young wood.

Philadelphus, Buddleia, Weigela and Tamarix all grow tall and strong for the border back or to fill in space. They start small, so resist the temptation to cram them together. Give them at least 4 ft. each way, and remember that eventually they will need 'step' pruning to show their flowers at their best, which means a border planted one shrub thick, or with one large shrub at the back and herbaceous plants, bedding plants or bulbs in front to flower at different seasons.

In this strong and easy class come Deutzias, and *D. scabra* 'Codsall Pink', with rose-purple double flowers in June and July, *D. rosea carminea*, with rose-pink double hanging bells in May and June, and *D. pulchra* the white one, all grow 6 ft. high easily.

Prune them like Weigela after flowering, and though they can be moved when they are fairly large—about 3 ft. across—they are easy to increase by the hardwood cutting method that serves for Buddleia, Forsythia, Philadelphus, Ribes, Tamarix and Weigela.

These shrubs have made most reputations for 'greenfingers' by growing easily from sections of the many long shoots that grow each summer, about 1 ft. long, removed in winter, between November and January. Cut them always with a knife because the stems are hollow tubes and secateurs crush them so that they rot instead of rooting.

Insert these cuttings the way up that they grew, 4 in. apart and 8 deep, along a slot cut with the spade beside the garden line. Then tread the soil firmly round them, and they will be well rooted and growing by the next autumn. Transplant them 1 ft. apart each way to grow planting size in another year, cutting back to two joints any long shoots that have raced ahead.

The pea tribe shrubs can be raised from seed, which is slower but cheaper by far than buying them full sized, for those who have room to grow their own.

Three easy ones for any soil are *Coronilla emerus*, with bright yellow pea flowers from May to September, growing up to 4 ft. high, *Ononis fruticosa*, rather shorter, with larger pink pea flowers from June to August: and *Caragana aborescens*, with yellow ones in clusters of up to four, which are a striking show in May, especially when it eventually reaches 15–20 ft.

Two other beauties are *Amorpha canescens*, with slender blue-purple spires, 6 in. long, from July to September, and *Indigofera Gerardiana* with red-purple ones for the same long season. Both are fairly rare but easily grown from home sown seed. Amorpha is smallest, about 3 ft. high, while Indigofera can grow to 8 ft. but in the north it needs cutting down each spring to grow a fresh crop of 4 ft. arching flower shoots each summer.

Soak the seeds overnight to swell, then sow 4–6 in. apart along $\frac{1}{2}$-in.-deep furrows with 15 in. hoeing room between them. April is the best sowing time in the open, and by the following spring they will be small but ready to transplant to their permanent homes. Like the hedge broom, which belongs to the same family, they move best when young, and grow well from strong and sturdy seedlings.

Lilacs, now correctly called Syringa, are either grafted on privet, or raised by layering, which is far the best. Though they are usually planted in full sun they will take shade for some part of the day, which makes their flowers last rather longer without fading. Ideally plant for an all-round view, for a good large lilac is a pillar of spires in May and early June.

There is no need to have ordinary lilac, for there are a great many new and splendid colours. 'Sensation' has red-purple flowers with white edges to the florets which cluster together like those of a hyacinth. In fact one could call lilac 'hyacinth bush', for the colour range is nearly the same, as well as the flower shape. 'Mrs. Edward Harding' is a real red, 'Bellicent' is clear deep rose. 'Primrose' the closest yet to yellow, and 'Blue Hyacinth' (single) or 'Ami Schott' (double) are nearly true blue. It should be said that all lilacs wait about three years after planting to show in their true colours—new planted specimens are always paler than they will be when established.

As soon as the flowers are fading and brown, break the trusses off to dump on the compost heap. We have bred lilacs to flower far larger and more freely than they do by nature and if they try and set seed on the massive trusses they will be so weakened that next year's display will suffer. This truss removal is essential every year, and then is the best time to shorten straggling shoots and thin overcrowded branches, but otherwise they need no pruning.

Most lilacs are starved, for though they will grow on any soil, doing particularly well on dry and chalky soils, they do better if well fed. Spread about a 1-in.-thick coat of rotted manure on the surface covering a 1-yd.-wide circle round the bush, every alternate year, and cover this with another inch of leafmould. All trees and shrubs feed from the surface, and this policy of mulching with humus materials other than compost (which can contain weed-seeds unless it is excellent) is worth using every other year at least for the lilacs, but anything that seems to be sulking can be made to snap out of it with a dressing of farmyard manure and a mulch to hold it down.

Lilacs are scented gloriously after rain, but the finest scented shrubs of all are the viburnums, relations of our native Guelder rose and the Wayfaring Tree, named from the fact that its long beady shoots which supplied parcel string up to a hundred years ago, came in handy for emergency repairs to packhorse harness.

The most famous is *Viburnum Carlesii* with dome shaped clusters of scented white flowers in April and May. It thrives in sun, but the flowers last longest in part shade which it will take, and this whole race is excellent for north-facing borders. Even better for scent and flower size is *V. Burkwoodii*, also April flowering, while *V. plicatum grandiflorum* carries on the display till June, with the same white snowball flowers, but unscented, and set in pairs along arching branches.

The winter-flowering viburnums have glorious scents, perhaps enjoyed at their best when cut and brought indoors through December, January and February. The first and most popular is *V. fragrans* which has the same domed clusters of white florets at the tips of the bare shoots starting in November and continuing till February ends. The lovely new one is *V. bodnantense* 'Dawn' with pink flower clusters in pairs along the leafless young shoots from December till April.

All these viburnums grow well on any soil, reaching 6 ft. high eventually, and they need no pruning. The winter-flowering kinds should not have more than half their flowering growth cut in any season, because of the check to growth from reducing the leaf area. If they are used for winter decoration, give them a mulch with manure under it in spring as the shrub equivalent to the cocoa with rum that the Navy appreciates on wintry nights.

Another good winter-flowering shrub for any soil and cutting to bring indoors is *Cornus Mas*, with small yellow starry flowers on bare branches in February, which will coax into bloom a month earlier in a vase, and forsythia is excellent for this forcing. Any forsythia will grow enough new shoots to stand slaughtering for cut bloom every winter, but though Hamamelis, the Chinese Witch Hazel, is glorious, with its cowslip-scented yellow flowers like slender incurved chrysanthemums with twisted petals, it grows so slowly that one good vaseful will cripple a specimen for years.

Hamamelis hates lime, belonging to a large and lovely class of plant that demands peaty and leafy soil with loam that contains little calcium. Up till now every shrub in this chapter is one that will thrive on any soil, including solid chalk, for hydrangeas grow easily on the limiest soils, but flower in muddy colours when they are blued. The same trick with the Epsom salts will save any lime-hater on an ordinary soil that has yellowing leaves despite ample peat and leafmould, but not on real chalk or limestone, where the gardener should stick to plants that will grow happily.

Lime-hating shrubs on normal soils should be planted in holes dug 2 ft. square and deep-filled with a mixture of two parts of loam, and one each of leafmould, peat and sand, enriched with 2 lb. of coarse bonemeal for enough to fill a hole this size. The peat should not be the neutral sedge peat used in potting soils, but rhododendron peat which is far more acid. The coarseness of the bonemeal is important, because it has a smaller working surface for the bacteria of decay than fine, so lasts longer.

If rhododendrons grow wild in local woods, there is no need to go to this trouble, but remember that bonemeal, leafmould and well-rotted manure are necessary plant food providers on the kind of hungry sand that grows pine trees well but dries out fast every summer. Compost is also neutral if made with one of the many other methods than the old Indore one (see Chapter 14).

With a good lime-hater's hole dug and filled, Hamamelis will grow slowly and steadily from spring planting, for it should always go in

after it has finished flowering, and needs no pruning or other attention. Another delightfully scented lime-hater that flowers before the
leaves appear is *Daphne mezereum* with stemless rosy-purple flowers
in February crowded along the upright branches. Once it has got
established it can be cut for winter bloom, but never more, and ideally
less, than half the bush a season, and always with some feeding afterwards. They need no pruning.

Magnolias are also lime-haters, but because they are shallow-root-
ing a surface mulch, as suggested for lilacs, is still more appreciated.
For small gardens choose *M. stellata*, the earliest to flower in March
and April, *M. soulangiana alba*, with white cup flowers in April and
May, and *M. soulangiana rubra*, the mauve or purple variety. The
latest to flower is *M. liliflora nigra*, darker than the last and longer
flowering, with purple cups that are kept on till June, but less hardy.
All magnolias need a sheltered place and no pruning, with a dose of
Epsom salts if they need it.

Though azaleas and rhododendrons are now lumped together as a
single race, gardeners and nurserymen are perfectly clear on the
distinction between them. Azaleas lose their leaves in winter, and
rhododendrons are evergreens. Both hate lime and need little pruning, preferring a sheltered place because their flowers are large and
easily damaged by biting winds. They also flower for a comparatively short time, but on such a scale that new gardeners on chalk
will try to grow them, when a good bush of *Potentilla* 'Kathleen
Dykes' would be far better value for money and space.

The hardiest azaleas are *A. coccinea speciosa*, with vivid orange
flower heads of tubular florets, and *A. ponticum* (also called *Rhododendron luteum*) which has orange-yellow single tube blooms. The
A. mollis hybrids have wider florets but need more warmth and
shelter, while the Japanese varieties, which are nearly evergreen, are
plants for the south, though very lovely in a range of soft colours.
They can suffer greatly from drought in summer, and it is worth re-
serving rainwater from the butt for them, as from the mains it can be
hard, which means limy.

There are a very great many hybrid rhododendrons and the best
way to choose for a bed if you have room for them, is to visit Kew,
Wisley or the Royal Horticultural Society's Hall for a show during
their season from April to June to pick the colours you like. They
need partial shade, a lime-free soil, and summer moisture, which is
why they grow best in the western side of Britain.

Though they need no pruning, break out the dead flower clusters as soon as these go over, for they are still more weakened by fruitless attempts to set seed than lilacs. A surface mulch of leafmould (see Chapter 14 for leafmould making) is also important to hold moisture. Where the wild *R. ponticum* with the mauve flowers is growing in the woods, rejoice in rhododendrons and the easier azaleas, but otherwise small gardens do well to leave them alone.

The lime-haters, or rather peat-lovers, that are really worthwhile are the heathers, and though a lime-free garden can have them in bloom all the year round, planting only the kinds that suit limy soils will still give a long show, plus weed-suppressing evergreen foliage, once the bed is established.

Chalky gardens can grow healthy heathers with tidy, evergreen foliage that suppresses weeds, but chalk suits only the kinds that flower from November to May. Clay, sands or even sooty town soils grow these, too, but also kinds that give a full year's flowering, if gardeners remember that heather loves peat.

Rhododendron peat is best, £1.50 per cwt. delivered in the London area, which is enough for a bed 6 ft. square, though heavy clays need more. Thin soils over chalk and poor sands can starve heathers, so mix equal parts of fibrous loam (about £2 cwt.) with their peat and dig it in for a bed to last over ten years without replanting.

November and April are the best planting months, and though heathers cost 40p to 50p each, nothing offers so much colour so long for so little trouble. Plant 1 ft. apart each way, deeply, with the foliage sitting firmly on the soil, and in staggered rows so that the round domes meet quickly and leave no room for weeds. Place the winter kinds in view from the windows, so that you see their brave flowering through snow and sleet.

There are *Erica carnea* varieties for any soil, including chalk, with one-sided spires of small bells on bushes 6–9 in. high. Every other year they need clipping down to where the lowest bells finished, in May; all heathers grown for minimum weeding need this treatment sometimes to keep their foliage thick.

'King George' is usually first to flower, with near-crimson spires, beginning in November and lasting till March, with 'Queen Mary's' pink ones starting in December with the paler 'Winter Beauty' and 'Cecilia M. Beale', the upright white one that holds its flowers clear of mud splashes.

March starters to follow them and flower on through April are 'Springwood White', 'Springwood Pink', 'Ruby Glow', brighter than the older crimson 'Vivellii' but with the same coppery leaves in winter, and the deep pink 'Prince of Wales'. At the back of the bed plant the 18-in. *E. darleyensis*, rose pink, *E. mediterranea* 'W. T. Rackliffe', white, and 'Brightness', the best red of these taller, any-soil kinds that flower from March to May.

Non-chalky gardens can fill June, July and August with *E. cinerea alba major*, the white bell heather, 'Cevennes', clear shell pink, 'C.E. Eason', a strong red, and 'Colligan Bridge', the best purple.

The Cornish Heath, *E. vagans*, overlaps these, and flowers on through October, with 'Mrs. D. F. Maxwell' the finest, with carmine full circle spires that can hide the dark green foliage. 'St. Keverne' is a good pale pink and 'Lyonesse' the finest white, but with them plant the old *E. vagans grandiflora* for purple spires that go on till carneas come round again.

6

Climbing Up and Climbing Down

Vertical space up and down house and garden walls can add extra room to small gardens with the additional advantage that walls need no weeding. The south-facing house walls should be treasured if they have beds rather than concrete below, for they provide the shelter and warmth for peaches and pears.

The others offer homes for a range of flowering wall shrubs and climbers, planted in beds narrow enough to reach across for window cleaning and kept weedfree with close, low-growing alpines. These should be dug out 2 ft. deep and 1 ft. wide because the higher and wider a climber spreads, the more plant foods it needs and the more water.

Beds beside houses are often full of builders' rubbish which should be removed with the hungry subsoil. There is no fear of disturbing foundations because modern houses are built on concrete, and no climber has roots strong enough to get under, as poplars will.

Fork up the bottom of the trench, and scatter $\frac{1}{2}$ lb. of a mixture of equal parts of coarse bonemeal and hoof and horn meal to every foot of trench. Then fill in 6 in. with turf, grass side downwards, or good topsoil, and spread 4 oz. a foot of slaked lime, followed by another batch of bonemeal and hoof and horn, continuing till the trench is filled, using manure or compost for the top layer.

Most climbers appreciate lime, while coarse bonemeal and hoof and horn last longer in the ground than any other feed, and this kind of treatment in the past tided today's giant wistarias over their first fifty years. If the soil is sandy have a 6-in.-deep layer of leafmould or peat on the bottom of the trench, trodden firm, as a kind of emergency water tank, for these can hold on to moisture like a sponge.

When making beds against the house look for the damp course (a continuous dark strip of lead or other material to prevent water soaking up the wall) and keep the soil surface at least 2 in. lower, so that not even surface mulches of compost or leafmould can go above it.

The bed should be lower than the path or lawn beside so that a hose can be left to play in it and soak the climbers thoroughly in time of drought. Peaches suffer especially from dry beds against walls and a real soak, not just a watering, will cure 'June Drop' which means most of the fruit falling at marble size; but it can make the drawing-room wallpaper come out in spots if the bed level is over the damp course.

Before planting beds round the house with expensive wall plants it is easy to foresee how they are going to look by growing climbing annuals, which are equally attractive, between new-planted climbers while these are mere small and hopeful beginners. There is no need to begin by hammering holes in the walls, or driving nails into the sides of sheds. Buy a tube of transparent Bostik, squeeze a dab like a thicker sixpence on the wall, and after about half an hour, press the end of your string into the dab and leave it to set overnight. It will hold for at least a season against wind and weather, provided that the wall was dry and unwhitewashed.

Morning Glories are in their glory every summer morning from June to September. Each day new flowers appear—saucers, 3 in. across, in blues, violets, reds and pinks, to fade at noon and die before dusk. Our grandmothers grew them from penny (now 6 new pence) packets as easy annuals sown in the open late in March or early April, and climbing 10 ft. up strings in children's gardens. Then they were called 'Annual Convolvulus', for they are distant relatives of this weed, sharing the same shape of flower but not its damnable, lasting roots.

Today we grow hybrids of tropical species. They have still larger flowers and more dazzling colours, but they need starting in a heated greenhouse and do best under glass. The vivid red 'Scarlett O'Hara' and the blue- and white-striped 'Flying Saucer' are as brilliant as the older 'Heavenly Blue', but they need large pots (using John Innes potting soil) and training up canes in sheltered courtyards full of sun.

The original hardy Morning Glory came from Virginia in 1629; it is *Pharbitis purpurea*, but catalogues list it as *Ipomoea purpurea*, among the tender kinds. This is still grandmother's mixture and although the old named varieties are lost, 'All Double Mixed' is another lovely survivor.

They should be grown on the sunniest and least windy side of a wall or fence. Do not plant them against a shed with no gutters, for the drip from the eaves can kill them with over-watering in wet summers. The bed need be only 5 in. wide, with compost or manure dug in 6 in. deep, or 1 oz. of dried sludge or poultry guano to each yard of this narrow strip.

Soak the large seeds 24 hours in cold water before sowing, edgeways, 1 ft. apart, with about ¼ in. of soil over their upper edges. Spring sunshine warms the soil to this depth, but deeper sowings can fail from cold soil. When they are 3 in. high, thrust in a metal skewer by the side of each as an anchor for the string, the other end being fixed in advance to dabs of Bostik, or wall nails, if annual climbers are to be a permanent feature of the garden. Add extra strings in fan formation as the plants branch and twine, flowering as they go.

Climbing nasturtiums flop because they have too little grip on string, and need stout sticks and rough bark for clinging, but their relation Canary Creeper (*Tropaeolum peregrinum*) shares neither their black fly nor striped caterpillar pests, and soars lightly and vividly even 12 ft. up the wall. Its flowers are bright yellow, 1 in. across, with two frilled upper petals and a lower lip split in four, rather like small orchids. They last in a generous show from July till October. Sow them like Morning Glory, but there is no need to soak the tough seeds. They are an easy annual for sun, shade, poor soil, and even summer winds.

The hardiest and fastest-growing self-clinging climber is the old Virginia creeper (now *Vitis quinquefolia*) harmless to concrete or modern mortar, but the new 'Ampelopsis', *V. Veitchii* 'Beverley Brook', is neater, brighter red in autumn, and better for small spaces.

One for southern gardens and a sheltered wall is the Climbing hydrangea, *H. petiolaris*, which needs no pruning and climbs with sucker-footed tendrils. Its large, heart-shaped leaves turn golden before they fall and its white flower clusters 6 in. or more across in June are a sight to remember in the shaded town gardens where it will thrive.

Both this rare and lovely climber and the tough and easy self-clinging creepers should be shortened to 1 ft. length when they are planted in spring with the cut ends leaning against the wall, for only the young shoots have grip enough to start climbing.

Among the loveliest of the wall shrubs that must be tied up the wall are the 'Japonicas' which can reach up 10 ft. in time and are splendid against white cement paint. There are two groups—one for walls, with crimson, pink, scarlet or even apricot flowers, like very large apple blossoms, appearing before the leaves or when these are just unfolding, between March and May, and a bush sort for shrub borders, with the same colour range and season, but followed by large fruit for jam and jelly. Both are easy to grow; the difficulty is in their names—a problem which began in Nagasaki, 170 years before the second atom bomb fell. In those times, Europeans were allowed only on a small island in the harbour, and Carl Thunberg, their Swedish doctor, was collecting the flowers of forbidden Japan by searching through the hay they were allowed to have for the cows, goats and sheep kept for milk and meat. He rescued our 'japonica' from the goats and called it 'Pyrus', because the withered twigs could have been a pear.

Seed was sneaked home by East Indiaman and in 1776 *Pyrus japonica* began to thrive on English garden walls. In 1874 a Mr. Maule, of Bristol, travelling in Madame Butterfly's Japan, found another kind that was so like a quince (*Cydonia oblongata*) that it was christened *Cydonia Maulei*. The two were so similar in flower and leaf that the wall one became *Cydonia japonica*.

Fifty years later it was found that only Mr. Maule's discovery was wild in Japan; the 1796 seed was gathered from a garden, and the Japanese had imported it from China centuries earlier. Still worse, neither was it a quince, but something between a quince and an apple, which was renamed 'Chaenomeles' (pronounced 'Kay-nom-ee-lees').

The wall japonica could not stay 'japonica' as it was not Japanese, so it became first *Chaenomeles lagenaria*, meaning 'with vase-shaped fruits', which it has when it does, and now finally *C. speciosa*, which means 'handsome' or 'good-looking', which it always was.

The real Japanese japonica that Dr. Thunberg discovered in the spring of 1776, like a dried hawthorn clipping in the hay, now gets its name back. It is *Chaenomeles japonica*, the bush with the big round fruits that Mr. Maule also found. This is the one which makes the jams and jelly. (See Appendix I for recipes.)

The best 'japonica' to flower and fruit in any soil and even on north-facing walls is *Chaenomeles speciosa* 'Boule de Feu'. It has scarlet flowers over 1 in. across in clusters of up to four that start in February, before the leaves, and finish as April ends. For four years in five they miss the frosts and produce a crop. The fruit is about 3 in. long and $1\frac{1}{2}$ in. in diameter, ripening yellow to make jam, jelly, 'cheese' or wine.

C. speciosa Moerloesii, with contrasting blossom pink outside and white within, has fruit red-cheeked like apples. Plants cost about £1.40 each.

Narrow beds against walls can be poor and, as already pointed out, full of builders' rubbish, so dig a trench 1 ft. wide and deep and 2 ft. long to hold compost, manure or 4 oz. of coarse bonemeal on the bottom, and fill with good topsoil. Allow 4 ft. between plants. Tie the branches to wall nails or wires on galvanized iron straining-eyes and train in all young shoots the first summer, when they need no pruning.

Chaenomeles age gloriously as they grow up a house wall (10 ft. perhaps). The old ones can be overhauled as soon as the leaves fall, starting with the suckers that can fill the bed from the grafting on quince. Dig down about 6 in. round these and twist them off as though unscrewing, for if they are cut they grow again. (Buy new plants only on their own, suckerless, roots.) Then take out any dead or weak branches completely, and tie the easy ones back to the wall. The branches and shoots that thrust untrainably outwards should be cut back to about 2 in. in length, finishing with a bud pointing *sideways*.

Young chaenomeles in their second summer need pruning in the same way after flowering, tying in the young shoots where there is wall space to fill. Strong shoots that are racing tall should be shortened by two-thirds in August.

The bush kinds that were *Cydonia Maulei* need this summer pruning only, with weak or crowding branches removed after flowering. The best bush fruiters are *C. japonica Simonii* (with crimson flowers until May) and the light red *C. japonica alpina* (rather more spreading but with as many golden fruit).

The pips from these fruits should be stored for sowing the following spring, exactly as with the pea tribe shrubs in the last chapter. Seed can be bought, but only species come true from seed—the hybrids will vary and have only a remote chance of being as good as their parents. On the other hand small 'japonicas' on their own roots, and about 6 in. high, move well, though they take at least three more years to get where good pot-grown specimens are from a first-class nursery.

Like many climbers they are grown in pots because if they are moved large their tender roots are broken, which is still more important with wistarias. These are slow but splendid, and more often inherited with a house than planted, so the first need is to know how to look after the one you have.

Summer pruning suits wistaria, both the ordinary *W. sinensis* and the magnificent Japanese *W. floribunda macrobotrys* with its 2–3-ft.-long tassels as shown on willow-pattern plates. To grow stronger flower buds, cut back their new, long, whippy shoots to quarter-length in July and August. Reduce this again to 4–6 in. long in winter if a specimen is overgrowing its wall or house. The best tonic for an elderly wistaria is a weekly watering through summer with a proprietary liquid tomato manure, a digestible high-potash feed. Failure to flower is usually caused by birds eating buds in spring, and the best answer is invisible black terylene thread laced across the strong branches.

Plant wistaria where it can go straight up the house, before you start training it across above the windows, for its tassels need room to hang. Start it with a tree-sized hole with lime at the bottom, as recommended for flowering trees, and give it a surface mulch with manure in its second summer. The best wistaria planting month is March, and during May it pays to syringe the bare branches with plain cold water until the leaves start, for they can sulk unless they are given a start. As wistaria cost about £4 each, very few people plant a number of them, and few small houses have room for more than one specimen when it starts to grow properly.

Wistaria needs and deserves the sunny south side of the house, but the toughest of all wall shrubs is *Pyracantha coccinea Lalandii* which can face north, north-east or east, however cold, bleak and windy the wall may be. It is evergreen, with clusters of flowers rather like hawthorn in June followed by bright red berries that last till January, for birds dislike them. Tie it back to the wall in August, the best time to tidy up any dead or awkward branches, but it needs no pruning. Neither does *Cotoneaster horizontalis*, which is equally easy, and it needs no tying either. If it is planted 6–9 in. away from the wall it will push up and outward in a fan thickly clustered with red berries in the late summer and autumn.

The escallonias have flowers rather like large single lilac florets in June and July, and need a south wall, for they are not hardy everywhere in the open, though they can be used as hedges in Devon and Cornwall. They will go about 10 ft. up a house in time, and the best are *E. edinensis* with clear pink flowers, *E. Ingramii*, rose red, and *E. Donard Brilliance*, which has crimson. They need little pruning, but they can be snipped back and tied in to the wall after flowering.

These wall shrubs have all relatively stiff branches, and can be kept tight against the wall with vine eyes screwed into holes made with a

Rawlplug tool filled with a Rawlplug or Rawlplastic, with stout galvanized wires between them. True climbers with slender stems need more to hold on to, and one of the plastic-covered, wire mesh support trellises, such as 'Netlon', or sheep fence, as recommended in Chapter 2, secured to vine eyes at 4-ft. intervals up and down, gives a grip all up the house. Use plastic-covered wire to secure it, for plain thin galvanized will rust away.

If the far cheaper sheep or cattle fence is used it should be painted with black or green bitumen paint to make it last, for climbers can keep so much moisture round it that it rusts. Ordinary chicken-wire netting will barely last five years against a wall. It is sold only in 25-yd. rolls, so it pays to buy and paint a roll to share with neighbours and to have a builder with a ladder to fix it to vine eyes so that it is about 1 in. away from the wall.

The powerful *Polygonum baldschuanicum* recommended for screening will reach the eaves of a two-storey house surprisingly quickly. Others for height and speed are the honeysuckles, *Lonicera americana*, with purple and apricot flowers in large clusters in May and June, *L. periclymen serotina* with gloriously scented red-brown and yellow flowers from July to September, and the plain yellow *L. tellmanniana* which flowers as long and is unscented but does well on north walls. All need nothing but removing of dead or crowding branches in spring, and climb by twining, so need no tying. The Evergreen honeysuckle, *L. japonica Halliana*, has scented, creamy flowers from June to October, and is also a twiner, but flowers best if the shoots that grew and flowered each summer are shortened to 1 in. length each spring. Once it is right up the house it is as well to let it alone.

For the earliest colour against a red-brick house choose *Forsythia suspensa* or the jasmines, which keep within reach of steps for pruning the shoots that have flowered back to 1 in. length, as soon as their display is over, and the tying in their new shoots need. The Winter jasmine, *Jasminium nudiflorum*, can flower in November and has usually finished by February, and the summer one is *J. officinale* with white, sweetly-scented florets from June to August, with a new hybrid *J. stephanense* that is just as sweet, but a light pink. These should never be pruned in autumn because they flower only on their pale green young shoots. These summer varieties need their cut-back in March, so they have time to grow new flowering shoots.

The most popular and lovely climbers for all levels are clematis which climb by hooking and twining their leaf stalks, so can go high up a house. Choose the varieties that need the least pruning for high climbing, especially the 'Montana' type, with clusters of small flowers in May, the kind that can be seen pouring over old sheds or summer-houses in neglected gardens. They only need removal of dead wood and crowding shoots in March.

The finest white one is *C. montana grandiflora*, and *C. montana* 'Elizabeth' has larger pink flowers and is scented. The Lanuginosa group (clematis should have the group against them in the catalogue and on the labels so that the buyer knows how to prune them) needs the same minimum pruning, and has ordinary large-flowered varieties available in a wide range of colours.

Some good ones are 'Beauty of Richmond', pale mauve, 'Beauty of Worcester', deep violet blue, and 'Belle Nantaise', lavender, all June- and July-flowering. 'Lady Northcliffe', deep lavender, flowers longest, from July to October, 'Lord Neville' is deep plum, 'Marie Bouisselot' is pure white, and 'Prince Hendrick' sky blue, all three in July and August.

The clematis everyone knows is *C. Jackmanii*, tough and easy, but flowering in summer on shoots that started the same spring. Cut them back in the spring after planting to 6–8 in. high, and just above a bud. Train them along a short stake to the wire mesh and spread the branches out so that they do not cross but climb with their leaf-stalks, pinching out the growing tips in May, July and August, so that they make planty of well-spaced branches going up the wall. Take out any buds that grow, because the first summer should be spent in growing the main branches.

The next summer they should grow shoots which will flower from the joints of these branches to tie in if necessary. The following February or March cut these shoots back to within 1 in. of where they join the branches, and do this every year through the long life of the clematis, even following it up the house on a long ladder, for the Jackmanii and Viticella varieties are some of the most striking. They will not go higher than about 10 ft.

The longest-flowering is 'Comtesse de Bouchaud', soft cyclamen pink, with flowers saucer-shaped rather than the familiar wide, fat crosses, and lasting from June to October. The original violet blue *C. Jackmanii* and the dark violet form *C. Jackmanii superba* are July- and August-flowering with a splendid show for two months rather than a succession, like dark purple 'Gipsy Queen', deep red 'Madame Edouard André', light blue 'Perle d'Azur', 'Star of India', violet with a red bar, and 'Victoria', soft heliotrope mauve.

The Viticella type have small, saucer-shaped flowers in great quantity from July to September. The original *C. viticella* is purple blue, 'Abundance' is deeper purple, 'Ernest Markham' is the best dark red, 'Huldine' a white, and 'Ville de Lyon' the nearest to carmine.

The Patens group of clematis, which includes the very popular 'Nellie Moser' which is pale pink with a deep red bar down the petals, flowers from June to September but on the old wood, like the rest of this type. Cut back the shoots that have flowered to the next strong bud below them, after flowering, and thin any overcrowded branches. Start them off like Jackmanii, keeping the branches well spaced.

The barred varieties are the most striking. 'Barbara Dibley' is violet, with a dark purple bar, 'Bee's Jubilee' is mauve barred carmine, and 'The President' is deep violet with a pale bar. There are many plain colours, and 'Elsie Spath', bright blue, and 'Miss Bateman', white, are both vigorous and free-flowering.

There are also a number of shorter species of clematis that need no more pruning than the Montana group which make good downward climbers. The *Clematis alpina* varieties have bell-shaped flowers in April and May, and trail down about 6 ft., or climb this high, with 'Pamela Jackman' a splendid sky blue, 'Columbine' pale lavender, and 'White Moth' a double, rather like a cup and saucer canterbury bell. The yellow *C. tangutica* has its bells closed into Chinese-lantern shapes from August to October, while *C. flammula* has small white star flowers, and *C. jouiniana* 1-in.-across lavender ones in clusters, from August to October. All do well upwards also, and the last two are excellent on cold north walls.

They are at their best, however, climbing down as cover for banks too steep to mow, but no sharper than 45°. Remove the turf, or if the covering is weeds, dig out as many roots as possible of perennial nettle, convolvulus and couch grass. Make a bed along the top of the bank as for upward climbers, with less elaboration if the soil is reasonably good, and peg black polythene firmly over the bank, with care to see that the wind cannot get under it and billow it into tatters.

Then plant the clematis and space the shoots out over the polythene, which will hold down the weeds till the clematis has grown thick enough to suppress the weeds, when the polythene can be pulled out from under. The drawback of polythene is slugs, and scattering slug bait between the clematis shoots is an answer if damage is discovered.

The evergreen honeysuckle, and the winter jasmine, are even better than clematis for banks because polythene is unnecessary, for they can be pegged down with 20-gauge galvanized iron wire bent into 'hairpins', so they root into the soil and help hold it. Their stems are far less brittle than clematis shoots, so weeding between them until they are thick enough for suppressing is easy without polythene.

The place for the straight-down climber is where a steep site means an awkward drive-in, and the only way to deal with the slope in the space is to employ a builder to make a brick or stone wall that curves with the path and has drainpipes let in to prevent water building up behind it. The safe limit for a 'dry' wall (built with soil instead of mortar, with plants between the stones) is 5 ft., and it needs space to slope it back (see Chapter 7); so the builder's cemented wall must be used where pathside and terrace walls have to go higher.

Though builders will leave 'pockets' for planting, these are usually too few and dry for a good show of wall plants, and the best way to treat these almost vertical walls is by growing climbers down from the top, because a bed at the bottom would complicate an already awkward entrance. Make up the planting trench in the same way as one by a house, and be ready to hose it if necessary during drought.

Wall shrubs cannot be grown, for they will strive to go upwards, but clematis, especially those that need minimum pruning, jasmine, honeysuckle and forsythia are all glorious scrambling down a blank and ugly wall. The problem is the thickness that builds up and can block the view at least up the drive-in, so be prepared to thin drastically, and not to plant *Polygonum baldschuanicum* unless you have cut a tennis court out of a hillside and want to hide a 20 ft. down slope. Clematis are by far the most attractive, and a range of varieties for all seasons, pruned by use of step ladder where necessary, replaces a problem with a striking garden feature.

A trial trip with annual climbers, as suggested at the beginning of this chapter for the up-the-wall planting, is just as easy downwards. The canary creeper will cascade down and is effective against grey concrete or red brick, but the ordinary climbing nasturtiums are superb even on the very worst soil, for their familiar flowers are least hidden by leaves when they are hanging down.

The two *Tropaeolum Lobbianum* varieties 'Lucifer', scarlet, and 'Spitfire', deeper red, with *T. majus luteum* the old bright yellow, or a sixpenny packet of mixed, will show what your wall will look like with a thick and splendid coat.

7

Walls, Paving, and their Planting

The dry wall is a method of supporting banks of soil, or bringing a slope down in terraces or steps, using squared stones with plants growing between them. Roughly speaking, it is a rock garden on edge, but a formal garden feature going with the straight lines of path, house and hedge, rather than attempting a copy of the quiet corner in the hills where alpines grow.

The only reason why old paving stones, flints and lumps of concrete are undesirable is that paving is too thin, and both flints and broken concrete are usually too rounded for firm building. If a garden contains too many brick ends (which are worth saving for shed foundations and air channels in the bottoms of compost heaps) or anything in the rough stone line, this is better built into dry walling than a 'rockery'.

The best source of supply is a local builder, ideally a small firm where a foreman will know when an old stone wall is being pulled down, and the nearest source of a square-faced limestone or sandstone which will not split and flake with the frost. Kentish rag, Bargate sandstone and Somerset cream are all types available in the south of England, but buy the nearest local stone. A full load, if possible, for transport is the major cost, so a little extra to finish may cost nearly as much as the main bulk. Allow roughly a ton of walling stone to 20 square feet of wall face, less if the stones are larger than about twice brick size, more if it is light material like overburnt bricks fused into clinkers.

A dry wall is best planted as it is built. Its cement is soil, and the plants are built into the vertical and horizontal joints as it goes up, with their roots going back into the soil behind. The best building time is October or November, for then Aubrietia and several other easy plants can be planted as bunches of unrooted branches. Hold four or five growing tips together, and lay them with about 1 ft. of mature stem running back into the soil behind the wall on the soil

'cement' of a stone layer, cover them with a little more soil, and set
the next rock firmly on top of them. The spring glory of the Aubrietia
is such a major part of the display from any dry wall that it is worth
waiting till the easy propagating time to build one.

Dry walls hold up steep banks, first by preventing small falls of
soil washed down becoming large ones (on the principle of bricking
a railway tunnel), and second, because they slope backwards, so most
of the thrust from behind is transferred to pushing the bottom stones
downwards. The standard lean-back is 2 in. in the foot up to 3 ft.,
3 in. in the foot for higher, up to 6 ft., which is about as high as it is
safe to go without cement. The backward slope also collects the rain
that drives against the face of the wall, for the benefit of the plants.

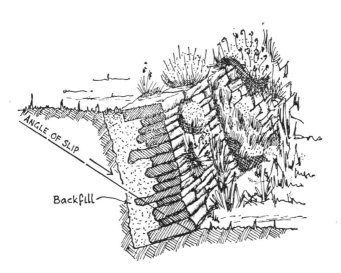

Fig. 11. Section of a dry wall showing backward slope and tie stones.

Start by putting down the garden line and digging a shallow trench
1 in. deep on the outer side against the line and 3 on the inner one.
Then set the first stones, which should be the largest and flattest
available, with their 'faces' (the straightest and longest sides) against
the garden line. They should sit firm and slightly slanting back because their job is to take the downward thrust of the soil behind, and
therefore scrape away soil and add it to take any lumps or hollows
under them so that they can be stood on without rocking.

Then ram the soil firm behind them, holding each in place with your foot so that they do not move outwards. Two rammers are useful, a short one made out of an old rake or hoe handle 1 ft. long for punching soil firmly into small spaces, and a stout post with the upper part rounded for easy gripping to ram the soil behind the wall.

Spread about 1 in. of soil over the firmed bottom course and then place the next layer of stones in place, taking care that the vertical joints do not come over each other, on the principle that the 'bonding' of any house wall will show. The stones may be all sizes, and one large lump may reach up several courses and compel locating of some joints above others, but these are to be avoided as the wall only holds together by friction between the stones and their weight.

The first foot of the wall is often left unplanted, but as the secondary object of a dry wall is to make a colourful show in a small space, clump-forming plants can go in along the second course. Aubrietia should have at least 1 ft. of trailing-down room, and nothing should go below it, but there is scope for thrifts, mossy saxifrages and sedums low on the wall, all of which break up and grow easily for divisions in the autumn. As a general rule the proportion of plants is one to an 18 in. each way square of wall surfaces, and the plants in the lists in Chapter 15 are divided into trailers, which can swamp them.

The best places for plants bought pot-grown, as alpines usually are, will be found in the vertical joints. Water them well or soak them by standing them, still wrapped, in water, then peel off the paper and squash them between the stones, with soil above and below, and plenty rammed firmly behind.

Some pot plants which happen to be autumn division subjects can be split into several before planting in the wall, especially aubrietia, which has incidentally the distinction of being the only alpine with two spellings. It is called after Claude Aubriet (1668–1743), a famous French botanical artist, and, by a unique and sensible compromise, both are correct. 'Aubrieta' is botanically accurate, because it was the spelling used in the first botanical description, but 'Aubrietia' is retained as the popular name of the garden varieties. It is therefore used throughout this book which is concerned with these varieties of *Aubrieta deltoidea*, the original species which is a washy pale mauve grown only in botanic gardens.

A dry wall usually goes up far more steeply than the bank behind it, which may be a raw face of subsoil. Filling in behind and between the stones will need a very large quantity of soil, and this will be all the alpines have to grow in. A standard mixture, assuming that the soil available is the upper 8 in. of a cultivated garden, is three parts soil, two parts peat or leafmould, and one part each of sand and loam. The last is only necessary on sandy soils to add the ability to pack firm behind the stones and some essential plant foods. On clay soils use two parts of sand and no loam.

As the wall rises in layer by layer of plants and stones, it is as well to include tie stones, especially if the height is greater than 2 ft. These are long pieces set so that their length goes back into the bank, and their short height and width are on the face, and they can go at 4–6 ft. intervals along every 2 ft. of height. They are more important on sands than clays, and most important of all when a wall has to be built of flints or other small and unsteady stones, for they add extra holding power.

The top of the wall is best finished with large flatter stones and should have room behind it for trailing plants to cascade over the edge from an alpine bed, even a narrow one, for nothing should go behind a dry wall that requires frequent digging.

A flight of straight steps can be built almost as easily as the dry wall itself but as it has got to take the weight of people walking up and down, it must be cemented in places and left until it has set hard. The bottom stones should go in flat, with a firm stone face 6 in. high but filled in behind with hard rubbish such as brickends. Water these well and mix up cement either permanent or temporary as advised for paths, work it into the cracks, and finish with $\frac{1}{2}$ in. of it ready to take the treading stones.

These must reach back 15 in. to the next 6-in.-high riser for comfort, wider if possible, and should be wetted on the underside so that the cement sticks tight before they are pressed in place and tapped level. Steps are laid like crazy paving, but always in cement because the wear and weight are concentrated on them, and an uncemented stone can so easily tilt and tip someone down the whole flight. The corners are made by saving up the longest stones and locking them between each other like a dovetailed box or brick wall corner.

Dry walls are frequently associated with paving, and many gardeners inherit large areas of this never very satisfactory path and terrace material. The best way to deal with paving that has dandelions, thistles, couch grass and docks thriving from blown seed in the crevices where plants once were, is to make a clean sweep of the lot with Amcide poured along the gaps between the stones and replant.

The slots and corners between the paving stones can be cleaned out with a kitchen knife or teaspoon if there is no room for a trowel, and fragments of suitable paving plants tucked down and covered with John Innes Sterilized Potting Soil. This has been steam-sterilized to destroy weed seeds so the paving plants have a long start on the weeds whose seeds blow on to the paving and wash down between the cracks. Perhaps the easiest carpeter for shade is *Claytonia australasica* with underground stems that spread along the cracks, pale green leaves in a mat, and almost stemless white daisy flowers the size of farthings from June to September. A slower and nicer species that appreciates leafmould, is *Hypsela longiflora* with the same low leaves from underground, and the same flowering season, but stemless five-petalled white and dark red flowers, *Linaria hepaticifolia*, with dark green kidney-shaped leaves and tiny stemless lavender snapdragons over the same period, and *Stachys corsica*, creamy white double flowers of the same shape, will flower from June to August. In southern gardens the miniature Mimulus, *M. cupreus* 'Whitcroft Scarlet', can be planted or sown direct in shade and can last as a perennial, while *Hutchinsia alpina* will also do well in shade, and its small white, candytuft-like flowers in May and June add earlier colour to a sunless corner.

There are plenty of paving plants for full sun and the best of those which will split and tuck between the stones are *Acaena microphylla*, with bronzy foliage and red chestnut burr seed-heads which will take unlimited treading on; *Campanula cochlearifolia* with blue bells and *C. pulla* with deep violet, both from June to September; *Frankenia thymaefolia*, with tiny gorse-like foliage and shell pink stemless flowers all the summer; *Sedum dasyphyllum*, with white flowers and grey foliage, *S. sexangulare*, yellow flowers and green, and *Thymus serpyllum major*, the strongest and darkest red of all the carpeting thymes.

Almost any low-growing alpine can be planted in between paving, but the true, tough carpeting kinds listed here will take the wear in the middle of the paths where people will be treading. Taller and less accommodating species can go towards the sides. A full set of lists under colours and flowering seasons will be found in Chapter 16.

This applies still more to the wall plants both trailing down and thrusting up, for nearly all the stronger alpines are better on walls than in the small rock gardens that are all most people have room for today. Several plants are hardiest in dry walls where they escape winter damp, particularly *Androsace lanuginosa*, a trailer with pink flowers in clusters, from June to October, *Onosma echioides*, with large yellow bell flowers in May and June and grey leaves, and *Zau-*

1. Lavender hedges are easy from October cuttings in the open ground.
Cut the flowers for drying when they are half open

2. The best cat-and dog-proof hedge is *Berberis stenophylla*; clip only in May after the bright yellow flowers are over

3. This giant Chinese Grass *Miscanthus saccriflorus*, grows ten feet high in a season and makes a hedge that dulls the noise of traffic

4. *Potentilla fruticosa* Kathleen Dykes, pale gold flowers from June to October, the longest flowering shrub of all

5. A well-planted dry wall. Note that the strongest trailing species go highest, and the dome-shaped ones nearer the ground

6. A sandstone rock and water garden; note the slight dip of the strata-line and the upright rock faces

7. 'No-Weeding' rock garden, planted with strong species that suppress weeds

8. A heather garden can be in flower almost all the year round

9. American Pillar is a strong and colourful rambler, ideal to train up
thick posts and stout arches

10. Mme. Grégoire Staechelin, a rose with semi-single flowers of glowing
pink, is a strong climber

11. The polythene frame 'annex' saves space in spring. The upper picture
shows it rolled for the day

12. *Lilium hollandicum*, formerly *L. umbellatum*, is the easiest lily of all for every garden. There are many varieties

13. The Climbing Hydrangea, *H. petiolaris*, with white flower heads in summer, is a splendid, self-clinging climber for a sheltered corner

14. The Russian Vine, *Polygonum baldschuanicum*, grows and flowers with fury, and hides anything hideous; fastest of any climber, but needs strong support

15. A well-pruned *Wisteria sinensis*. See page 87 for summer pruning and feeding this lovely climber

16. The pear-sized fruit of the white-flowered *Chaenomeles cathayensis* is best of all for jelly, cheese and wine making

schneria californica with grey foliage and scarlet tube flowers in September and October. Both the last are clump-formers.

The most important class is those which can be split for wall planting in the autumn, and if possible these should be bought in the spring and planted up to grow larger, unless they can be taken from existing clumps. Aubrietia are especially improved if they are cut back after flowering and left to grow on, for they make the main spring show from March to June. The others are Arabis, both the common white and the pink, *A. Sundermanni*, all forms of *Armeria maritima* (thrift) with 'Bloodstone' and 'Laucheana' the best reds of this excellent race of clump-formers; the 'Encrusted' saxifrages for sunny walls, and the 'Mossy' group for shaded or semi-shaded ones, the trailing sedums of all species with *S. spurium coccineum* one of the best, *Thymus serpyllum major*, the thyme that is strong enough to trail, and *Veronica rupestris* with clear blue flowers from May to July, capable of reaching 4 ft. down the wall.

Two others can be added to this class by working a mixture of equal parts of leafmould and sand into the clumps in June and July so that they root into it and by October can be taken apart for planting as split-off branches, like aubrietia. The alpine phloxes, both the *P. subulata* hybrids with gorsey leaves and the neater *P. Douglasii* varieties, can be increased this way, and reinforce the display from April to June, with pink, red and lilac flowers on evergreen trailing foliage. The other is *Polygonum vaccinifolium*, which has masses of willow-shaped leaves on red barked branches and a long succession of pale pink spires about 2 in. high from July till October. It is a powerful trailer capable of reaching 3 ft. down a bank in four years, and one of the longest- and latest-flowering of all wall plants.

There are roughly two hundred good wall plants and it is only possible to mention a few, but the majority will be found listed in Chapter 16, as trailers and clump-formers, under their colours and flowering months.

8

Rock Gardens and Alpine Borders

The traditional rock garden has two problems today: first, every increase in rail and road transport charges makes good limestone rock as used at Chelsea Flower Show more expensive; then there is the problem of weeding. There are many more attractive gardening jobs than pulling grass out of granite chippings to save small treasures from smothering in the scree.

Those who love alpines have a number of books written for them, but the ordinary gardener does better with the stronger and easier species grown on the 'no-weeding' system, which is a development of the 'no-digging' system of keeping the weed seeds under ground by disturbing the soil as little as possible.

'No-weeding' rock gardens depend on choosing plants that will themselves keep down weeds—for no selective chemical will kill the weeds and spare the alpines. But no plant can suppress weeds that grow from lasting perennial roots; these should be attacked now to ensure a weed-free future.

Roll back the rocks on existing gardens and dig out the wicked roots under them to their bitter ends. Two paintings, a fortnight apart, of Lornox on the leaves of convolvulus will kill roots that are out of reach, ready for safe planting in the autumn.

Dig well then, for no chemical is completely effective, though Amcide, as recommended earlier, is the best; and all chemicals are unsafe near trees or shrubs, or where spray can blow on lawns or beds. Here or in ordinary gardens two careful diggings, with time between for missed root fragments to grow and show, are a better answer.

Good Westmorland rock is frost-proof, kind to alpine roots, and grey to set off their vivid colours. In the London area it costs £2 a cwt., which is two pieces about as big as biscuit tins. It is cheaper if you collect the stone yourself, and then you also have a chance to choose long flat pieces for low gardens or tall ones with the most weathered face to hold up slopes.

These faces should have their strata lines sloping slightly sideways in the same direction, as though the garden were a solid rock formation showing through soil. Slant the stones back against the slope so that the rain will run back into the soil, instead of off them like a roof.

John Innes seed soil is best for alpines. It costs £1.70 a cwt. almost anywhere. This amount spreads 3 in. thick over 12 square yards between the rocks. It is steam-sterilized to kill weed seeds and none can germinate from below through the thick coat.

Weeds do grow through carpeting thymes, but compact helianthemums make a 6-in.-high evergreen forest that kills by light starvation like a pine wood, reducing weeding to the digging out of strays. Perhaps the best are 'Ben Dearg', salmon red; 'Ben Hope', rose pink; 'Ben More', orange; 'Fire Dragon', flame red with grey leaves; 'Old Gold', the deepest yellow; 'Supreme', crimson; and 'Wisley Primrose'. But there are many more good weed-holders, among their eighty-odd varieties. Cut them back every other year when the first blaze is over to keep them bushy and a barrier against weeds.

Among them plant *Linum narbonense* 'Heavenly Blue', whose flowers on 1-ft.-high wiry stems provide a glorious contrast to the fiery colours below. Another good contrast is *Hyssopus aristatus* which grows 8-in.-high bushes and violet blue spires in August and September; a hardy creature if it is cut back for tidiness and a neat weed-holding habit.

For quieter colours plant Teucriums, which are rather slower growing, evergreen, compact bushes about 6 in. high. They flower in July and August with pale pink spires for *T. Chamaedrys*, shorter, yellow ones against silver grey leaves for *T. Polium* and crimson spires for *T. lithospermifolium*. With these plant the neater Dianthus, for the aim is a close carpet of foliage. The hybrid varieties 'Bombardier', with double scarlet flowers, *D. Elizabeth*, a double pink, *D. Graze Mather*, a double salmon, and *D. Keith* a crimson double in the same race are all very long flowering and good weed-holders. Cut them back in the spring, or in October if they straggle.

Campanulas should be chosen from types that makes domes rather than trail, and the *C. garganica* varieties, 'Blue Diamond' with deep blue stars, 'W. H. Paine' with white-eyed stars, and *C. garganica fenestrellata* with pale blue ones, are the best weed-suppressers and, like Dianthus, fond of extra lime in their soil, thriving on chalk.

Prunellas make a carpet about 3 in. thick with heads of small antirrhinum-shaped flowers from June till October. 'Loveliness' is a clear mauve, *P. grandiflora* deep red purple, and *P. incisa rubra* crimson. They go well with the 2-in.-tall pale pink spires (August to October) of *Polygonum vaccinifolium*. This loses its willow-shaped leaves in winter, but the mat of its red-barked branches is thick enough for weed suppression. Trim it with shears in April if it spreads too far.

Aubrietia are excellent early in the year, cut back after flowering to keep tidy domes. Alpine phlox follow on to flower through June. Choose from the strongest *Phlox subulata* varieties—'Betty', pale pink; 'G. F. Wilson', lilac; 'Sampson', deep pink, and 'Temiscaming', the new, real red. Cut them back after flowering only if they grow thin in the middle. Hand-forking in fine bonemeal among the clumps in July (8 oz. to the square yard) is a good tonic for these or any other large elderly alpine.

Plant these strong kinds of alpines roughly 8 in. apart each way in drifts as pot-grown plants (all cheaper by the dozen). Slower kinds need 6 in. spacing.

Among other treasures are *Aethionema* 'Warley Rose', famed as the perfect alpine, with tiny pink hydrangea heads from May to August, and *Lithospermum intermedium*. This is not the lime-hating 'Heavenly Blue' but the easy, any-soil species which looks like a grey-green hedgehog with heads of pure blue tube flowers hanging from 6-in. stems. It could be in every garden. Heavenly blue is the colour that flashes in the foam of waves breaking out of clean, deep water, of summer seas, of cloudless skies and of the flowers of the rock plant with this perfect name. They are shaped like single lilac florets, about $\frac{1}{2}$ in. across, or rather larger for 'Grace Ward', the newer variety of *Lithospermum diffusum*. Their blue tide spreads over dark evergreen foliage, is highest in May and June, and ebbs slowly until October.

In August lift up the 4-in.-high carpet of black-barked trailing branches and under it spread about 1 oz. of fine bonemeal to each square foot, for healthy ten-year-old specimens can be the size of a hearth-rug. Then add a 1-in.-thick layer of sifted leafmould, which in small quantities costs no more than peat, and lithospermums like it better.

Though awkward branches can be shortened now, they need no annual cutback, unlike aubrietia. If the black stems show bare in places, mix 1 oz. of dried blood with the bonemeal for each square foot, and give another ounce in spring as a tonic.

Never fork under a 'Heavenly Blue', because breaking of the tender roots has brought more failures than limy soil. If leaves turn yellow on well-fed lithospermums, then lime is the trouble—and curable except in chalky gardens. Stir 1 oz. of Epsom salts in a 2-gallon can of warm water, let it cool, and water in a square yard of plant and bed. Give a second watering the next day to wash in unused salts further. Epsom salts are magnesium sulphate and this with time forms insoluble calcium sulphate (gypsum) and magnesium carbonate, which lime-haters like.

'Heavenly Blue' is not grown to keep weeds down under roses, but they can be planted round it, with smaller floribundas like 'Yellow Hammer' (orange yellow) or 'Meteor' (scarlet) to set off its glory. On a rock garden, or planted at the top of a dry wall, it needs room to cascade over grey stome.

When planting lithospermum dig a hole 1 ft. wide and deep and 2 ft. long, in full sun, and fill with two parts of John Innes potting soil to one of sifted leafmould, or with the traditional recipe of two parts leafmould to one each of peat, sand and good loam.

Tread it and water well before putting in three plants 6 in. apart along the middle, taking care not to break the pot-shaped soil round the roots. The ideal time is September, with time to take hold before winter, or in spring. Any garden will grow them with this care and every gardener who has seen a good one wants to, whatever his soil—not because they are labour saving or trouble free—but because they are such a Heavenly Blue.

No gardener can ever understand why climbers risk their necks gathering edelweiss, with flowers like small starfish cut out of dirty blankets, but gentians are another matter. There are over four hundred of them and the easiest for every garden, even with chalk or the soot-and-pebble soils of London, is the true *Gentiana lagodechiana*. It costs roughly 25p for about twenty years' flowering without missing a summer.

Its sky-blue trumpets, wide as florins, look up singly or in clusters from the tips of trailing branches set with broad leaves in pairs. Water well in dry springs, for drought can kill it on sunbaked chalk, though lime never will.

Plant in sun or semi-shade, but not under trees, on a border front or on the lower slopes of the rock garden, with peat or leafmould dug in to hold moisture.

Others of this broad-leaved, easy type are *G. Freyniana*, the same but a paler blue; *G. septemfida*, 8 in. tall and floppy; and *G. Hascom-*

bensis, with stiff, 1-ft.-high stems, which is best for the herbaceous border. All sleep underground from autumn till April, missing winter smoke in towns. They are safe to dig up then and move, even when very large.

The lime-loathing gentian is *G. sino-ornata*, with narrow leaves like short grass on slender, pale green stems which carry indigo trumpets from October on to Christmas. The lime-free soils it likes can be too dry, so dig in leafmould or peat, and water in time of drought—as with all the narrow-leaved kinds that also die down in winter, including two that start flowering in August, *G. Farreri*, pure Cambridge blue and *G. Macaulayi*, cobalt with white throats and wider trumpets.

These will stand most lime and grow in any garden but a chalky one. Dig a trench 1 ft. wide and deep and fill it with equal parts of John Innes potting soil and sifted leafmould, feed with 4 oz. a square yard of fine bonemeal each spring. If foliage yellows in the summer, water with 1 oz. Epsom salts to a 2-gallon canful of water to cancel the intruding lime.

The Swiss *G. acaulis* is easy on any soil, including chalk, but prefers clay. Plant with the pot soil 1 in. underground and tread the surrounding soil, for firmness helps flowering. So does a teaspoon of iron sulphate watered in round each stubbornly flowerless dome of close-packed, 1-in.-long, evergreen leaves.

Try the other evergreen species, *G. angustifolia*, *G. clusii* and *G. dinarica*, which can flower when *G. acaulis* fails. In lucky gardens any one of these can be splendid, with deep blue trumpets 2 in.–2½ in. wide on short stems, in March, April, May or autumn. Always try, for there is no flower more lovely that beginner's luck can win.

The garden that really needs a rock garden is the steep one on sand where sandstone rock can be bought cheaply and locally. This is best set with only a slight backward slope into the hillside, coming down in a series of steps, with wide areas for planting behind them. Just as with the Westmorland and Cheddar limestone, set the rock the way up it 'grew', with the lines of the strata running across the slope, not upright or edgeways.

It is best to build a rock garden from the top of the slope downwards, for the rocks are not bonded into each other like stones in a dry wall, and the important stage is always placing the main rocks that are going to determine the strata lines and getting them just right. Choose two good ones with plenty of weathered 'face' for the nose of your outcrop, dig out the soil where they are going to stand, and try them in place so they meet in an 'L' or 'V' with a joint for crevice planting.

When the first rocks are set, tilted slightly back with the dip of the strata lines that gives unity to your rock garden, fill in the soil behind and ram it firmly so that there are no air spaces. Then come forward with another 'step' formation of sandstone with only a gentle slope on the soil between, which will be covered with 3 in. of sterilized soil for a weedfree start after rock placing is finished.

The steps come down irregularly because today plants are cheaper than rock, and the larger your planting areas the better. On sandstone the ideal weed suppressors are the heathers described earlier, and even *Lithospermum* 'Heavenly Blue', though most other alpines will grow there. Always add some lime for Alpine phlox, campanulas, dianthus and aubrietia.

The best example of good sandstone rock placing is the rock garden at Kew, where there are several areas that are entirely no-weeding. Edinburgh has a fine example, and at Chelsea, at almost any of the Royal Horticultural Society's fortnightly shows at Vincent Square, S.W.1., and in the Flower Tent at most large agricultural shows, there are table rock gardens built by famous alpine firms that are both patterns for beginners and the best sources of good plants. It is easy though to fall in love with a glorious alpine that is not hardy enough for a slug-haunted garden on poor soil. Mention in this book is restricted to those that are hardy anywhere, and for everyone, even though some are rare but worth hunting from firm to firm.

The alpine border today is far more popular than the true rock garden, for it is a miniature version of the herbaceous border which can be formal or informal, so that it fits into any garden layout, but especially the small front garden. It is a rockless rock garden, easier to weed, and without the problems of making expensive rock 'look natural' on a flat site.

Though it is possible to make one for miniature appeal, using tiny roses and dwarf iris so that it becomes about a foot-to-the-inch scale model, this is not easy and is inclined to look fussy in the open. In troughs, pans and window-boxes, however, alpines make excellent permanent plantings.

The real advantage lies in treating alpines as low-growing perennials with long flowering seasons and small but brilliant flowers. A
well-planted rock garden should have colour the whole year round
except for the depths of winter, and the alpine border should follow
the same principle, though there are cases where it is worth concentrating on a blaze for one season and labour-saving tidiness for the
rest of the year.

The 'aubrietia drive-in' is an example of a one-species alpine bed
which replaces the awkwardly mown grass between two concrete
strips that leads to some garages. Exchanging fortnightly mowing and
edging for one cut-back and weeding a year, and replanting every five
or six seasons, is a bargain in labour saving, apart from the solid
blaze of colour every spring.

Dig with care to take out dandelion roots beheaded by turf stripping. Also remove builders' rubbish, for modern Portland cement is
not 'old mortar rubble' and is as useless as brickends or plaster for
lime-loving alpines. Spread 1 lb. of lime to each yard run of these
strips (usually 30 in. wide) before the final digging.

On heavy clay spread a 2-in. layer of builders' sand (a cubic yard
does 36 ft. of strip). On sandy soils dig in leafmould or peat, but the
final level of the bed should be below the level of the concrete, to trap
water, and not banked high and dry.

Leave the pot soil unbroken when planting 8 in. apart in three
staggered rows, the outermost 6 in. from the sides. For long drives
use 'Monarch Strain', the 'Russells' of seedling aubrietia, for a patch-
work of colour at about £10 for 100. But named varieties produce the
best effect and are also cheaper in quantity. 'Bressingham Red',
'Magnificent' and 'Mrs. Rodewald' are strong crimsons; 'Magician'
is a red-purple outshone only by the rare 'Henslow Purple'; 'Gloriosa', a real shell pink, and *rosea splendens* a deep one. 'Carnival',
'Godstone' and 'Gurgedyke' are good, deep violets, and 'Mrs. J. S.
Baker' an unusual one with a contrasting white centre; 'Blue King'
is nearest the pure blue aubrietia which would be far more worth
breeding than black roses.

After the flower display is over in late May or June, and before the
clumps can waste strength on seed-pods and trailing untidiness, all
aubrietia needs drastic treatment to keep it growing as healthy evergreen domes of foliage. This is just as important in the rock garden,
and still more necessary on the dry wall.

Turn back the long tangles and shorten them with shears to leave
only 2 in. of the stems above ground. This must be done each year, to

avoid the hardened arteries of old grey branches and to encourage the young flower shoots.

Take the chance to remove stray weeds struggling through the aubrietia carpet, and fork in 4 oz. of fine bonemeal a square yard. Then water the cut-back plants so that this slow feed starts the compact clumps growing to meet again and keep down the weeds.

October is replanting time for carpets of aubrietia that are threadbare with age, for exactly the same reason as it is the best dry-wall building month—aubrietia can be split then and even bunches of unrooted strands can be firmly planted and will thrive.

Aubrietias no more need a car over them than alpines need rock to thrive, and this planting fits a narrow bed at the base of a flowering hedge, because an orthodox tall herbaceous border is going to hide the background. A hedge of yew or any other solid evergreen sets off the long herbaceous border in a big garden as a plain or small-patterned wallpaper does good pictures inside the house. If you make your frame part of the picture by growing your roses as a hedge to add extra room to a tiny garden, you need low planting in the bed below them.

When the aubrietias are planted, ordinary rather than miniature daffodils can go in and stay naturalized with lifting and dividing and replanting and replacing or replanting, about as often as the plants need an overhaul. Their foliage can be tidied roughly when the aubrietias are cut back each year, and as the bed is narrow it is possible to reach across for tying in rose shoots through summer and for pruning in October. Aubrietia beds do well below potentilla hedges, which flower after they are over, or spiraea or broom hedges with a contrasting colour at the same time.

The all-helianthemum bed is perhaps the most successful of all, needing a trim-back every other year and the same treatment as on the no-weeding rock garden. Take great care digging out perennial weeds and start off with $\frac{1}{2}$ lb. of bonemeal a square yard, digging in compost or manure too if the soil is poor, planting 8–9 in. apart each way in staggered rows.

Their roots are stronger than those of aubrietia, and they can hold soil on a slope of about 1 in 4. The best background for their yellows, flames, reds and pinks in a blaze through June and (with a July cut-back), again in September, is a lavender hedge with grey evergreen foliage contrasting with the dark green of the helianthemum even in the depths of winter. A wide belt of lavender with a wider one below of helianthemum is a cheaper and more colourful solution to a dry bank problem than a terrace, especially if the decision is made far enough ahead to raise the plants from cuttings or seed.

Helianthemum seed can be sown in $\frac{1}{2}$-in.-deep furrows in the open ground in April and the seedlings transplanted at 1 in. height for 6 in. apart each way. By the following spring they will have grown enough to show which are going to be compact weed-holders for moving to the bed as replacements, and which are tall or straggly types to discard. Seedlings will always be mainly pinks and whites, so the best increase is from cuttings 2 in. long taken from the tips of shoots, without flower buds, in August, inserted in pans of sand as described in Chapter 13. Enough to plant in broad drifts of single kinds in a long large bed add up to a considerable sum, even bought by the hundred and leaving the selection to the specialist nurseryman.

A single species bed for shade that can even be fairly dry is one of mossy saxifrages, which are also evergreen, and make domes of foliage that meet to make a carpet of sufficient thickness to keep down annual weeds. They can also be split and planted as foliage bunches like aubrietias in October, and need the same limy soil.

Because they are easy they are also common, but the best are rarely seen. Plant 'Flowers of Sulphur', the only yellow one, 'Knapton Pink', 'Sir Douglas Haig', still the best crimson, and 'Hartswood White' for a full range of colour, 9 in. high in flower in April and May.

The real alpine border to provide colour and interest through the year need not be restricted to weed-holders, for some of the nicest alpines are too slow growing and too small to fight British weeds on their native heath and win. It is a question of choosing the plants, and one man's (or woman's) weed-holder is another's cherished treasure, depending very largely on the weeds they have to face.

Though Amcide is expensive for clearing whole gardens it is ideal for small areas, and because it is not a hormone or poison it can be used on a bank in dry weather without risk of its washing down and slaughtering the lawn below. It is a total killer and cannot be used between bush fruit, roses, etc.

The alpine bed for small species needs the same weedfree start with John Innes Sterilized Seed Soil as a no-weeding rock garden, though aubrietia beds, helianthemum banks and any bed planted with the stronger species can manage with the addition of bonemeal and leafmould.

Start by digging out the top 6 in. of soil and piling it to one side. Then dig out and remove 3-4 in. of subsoil before returning the top layer into the hole, upper side downwards if it is thick with chick-weed rejoicing in freedom from couch grass after Amcide. Finally, spread the John Innes in a 3-in. layer on top, leaving all the weed seeds buried too deep to grow. The alpines can then be planted with any soil extras they may need, such as more leafmould, and they should make the most of their start in far better soil than any ordinary garden can provide. The grittiness of the John Innes is particularly valuable on clay, even though roots go down into the soil below.

Alpine beds are not planted like herbaceous borders, which start with low-growing plants in front and sweep up to lofty delphiniums at the back, because the viewpoint is mainly downwards. You can imagine you are about 10 in. tall with *Zauschneria californica* towering its scarlet tube flowers above your head, but the slope would be so gradual (for most alpines are much wider than they are high) that it would be hard put to it to do well enough to show.

Though a long and narrow bed can be planted with the shortest species in front and the tall at the back, it is best filled with drifts of varieties of a single species, or with front-to-back belts of several. The best system is the double-sided or 'island' bed made for a view from all sides, because the tallest alpine will be little more than 1 ft. high and cannot block the view of the low ones behind it.

They slope down to carpeting plants, as used for paving, which can have bulbs below them—autumn-flowering crocus under spring flowering carpeters, as an example. All the plants recommended for small rock gardens can grow in alpine borders and many, like gentians, do far better where they can be easily weeded if necessary and away from the summer drought of so many amateur rock gardens. Alpines that trail and need dry conditions are best on the dry wall today, for the stone between them grows no weeds, while the place for the dome and mat formers is in the alpine bed, leaving the difficult kinds for the alpine house of the enthusiast.

The main planting principle is to use a wide range of species so that there is always something in flower throughout the summer, and so that the colours contrast well without 'killing' each other. No end should be a complete blank at any time, and at no time is there any need to sow annuals to 'make a show after the aubrietia', for this is still a confession of ignorance when there are so many good perennial alpines that are both hardy and colourful.

Good alpine beds begin with plans, drawn to scale on squared paper, and Plan 1 is an example of one, 4 ft. wide and 12 ft. long, designed to bring in the fullest range. The seventy-four varieties on this plan are assumed to be planted in threes, except for the large spaces left for carpeters which should take six and need splitting as they spread. It could be done with one each of the smaller kinds and threes of the carpeters, by those prepared to wait longer for the display.

There is no room to fit the names on to the planting areas, so the alpines have been given numbers and the bulbs letters which can be looked up in the table which gives heights, colours and flowering times. No. 1 is *Hypsela longiflora* which likes leafy soil and semishade, and this end is assumed to be pointing towards the house and shaded. Round it everything that likes these conditions has been collected, with *Fritillaria meleagris* and *Erythronium dens-canis* as the bulbs under the carpeters, and *Iris lacustris* from the shores of the Great Lakes of Canada, because it likes the leafmould. This is a perfect miniature iris 3 in. high, hardy and easy, provided it is given these conditions which are also enjoyed by its taller relation *I. cristata*.

At the other end the bed is assumed to come out into the sunshine and here extra lime has been added for the two carpeting campanulas and other species that need it, for it is better to keep lime lovers and humus appreciators at opposite ends, with the many 'don't mind' plants in the middle. Heights in the table mean heights in flower, and the *Campanula pusilla* (more correctly *C. cochlearifolia*) varieties are about ½ in. high without the extra 2 in. for their nodding bell flowers.

The divisions vary in size because the plants differ in growth speed, with the large campanulas needing over twice the room that fits No. 28, which is *Armeria caespitosa* 'Bevan's Variety', the miniature thrift from the dry mountains of Spain, in the best form which has the deepest pink stemless flowers. No. 12 is the yellow type of the miniature iris from Albania, and like its smoky red parent at No. 59, it needs ordinary soil and sun, entirely unlike *I. lacustris*, which is often killed by getting the same treatment.

The bed is 4 ft. wide because this is convenient for weeding at need, taking cuttings or trimming back the tall centre species like *Serratula Shawii*, No. 38, which is the last plant to stop flowering before winter. Its pale pink powderpuff flowers on sturdy 1-ft.-high stems need cutting back when they go over, leaving the bed tidy till spring when Serratula will send up red-brown ferny leaves from a mat of underground roots that are fine weed-excluders, and will need splitting where they encroach on neighbours. A nurseryman once said, 'That and "St. Joan" were the best things he ever did,' but it is named for another Shaw. The plants in Plan 2 are chosen for close canopy effect, and their planting areas are larger because they are faster growing and tougher than those in a normal alpine border.

The two strong carpeters are *Ajuga reptans minima variegata* which has insignificant flowers, entirely unlike the glorious blue spires of its relation *A. pyramidalis*, but makes thick mats of white-edged leaves, and *Acaena microphylla*. This has grey leaves and seed heads like tiny, very long-spined red chestnut burrs that are on show all the summer. These two can have small bulbs below them, especially spring and autumn crocus, but the others are too tall for any but the larger alpine daffodils, and the *Iris reticulata* varieties.

The aubrietia and dianthus are all the stronger for the new double varieties to give the longest flowering seasons, and all will need the same cutting back as they would in a one-species bed. The veronicas and alpine phlox will need trimming back if they encroach on their neighbours, but *Hyssopus aristatus* should only be tidied in the spring. Its branches are hollow and winter wet rots them as it does pentstemons, so leave the dead shoots on all the winter, and cut them down in March or April to the new growth at the base.

The best time to make an alpine border of this type is October when the aubrietia can be split, and so can many of the others. The strong-growing *Armeria maritima* 'Bloodstone', can be torn apart then, and bunches of even four single shoots planted 3 in. apart each way will meet in time to flower the next summer.

Prunellas also tear easily apart, like the sedums, both ajugas, acaena, arabis and the polygonum. The alpine phloxes, which do particularly well in chalky gardens, can have a mixture of equal parts of leafmould and fine soil worked into their gorse-like foliage when their flowers have vanished, and they will root into this so well that they can be torn up like aubrietia for alpine beds and dry walls. The helianthemums, veronicas and dianthus are all easy from cuttings in a cold frame.

Planting alpine borders needs planning ahead in time as well as on paper, for the more of the bread-and-butter plants are home-grown, the more money can be spared for new and lovely species from the mountains of all the world.

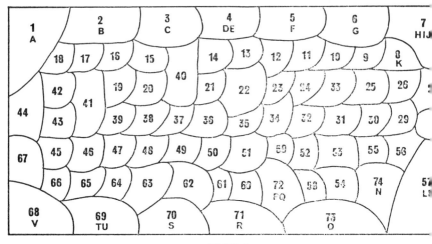

PLAN 1

Long-flowering Alpine Border

		COLOUR	HEIGHT	SEASON	BULB BELOW
1	*Hypsella longiflora*	White	1 in.	June–Oct.	A
2	*Gypsophila cerastoides*	White	1 in.	June–July	B
3	*Thymus* 'Bressingham'	Pink	1 in.	May–June	C
4	*Campanula pusilla* 'Miss Wilmot'	Medium blue	3 in.	June–Sept.	E D
5	*Antennaria dioica*	Grey–pink	1 in.	May–June	F
6	*Frankenia thymifolia*	Pink	1 in.	June–Aug.	G
7	*Campanula pusilla alba*	White	3 in.	June–Sept.	HIJ
8	*Sedum dasyphyllum*	Pink–purple	1 in.	Foliage	K
9	*Sedum cauticolum*	Rose-red	3 in.	June–Sept.	
10	*Saxifraga Elizabethae*	Yellow	2 in.	Feb–March	
11	*Veronica selleri*	Lavender blue	6 in.	Aug, and on	
12	*Iris melitta* (*Yellow form*)	Yellow	4 in.	April–May	
13	*Veronica corallii*	Salmon-pink (deep)	9 in.	July–Aug.	
14	*Dianthus* (*double*) 'Oakington hybrid'	Deep rose	6 in.	July–Sept.	
15	*Teucrium polyium*	Golden yellow	4 in.	July–Aug.	
16	*Teucrium lithospermifolia*	Rosy crimson	4–6 in.	June–Sept.	
17	*Potentilla ambigua*	Golden-yellow	2–3 in.	All summer	
18	*Polygalla Chaebuxus purpureus*	Purple	4–6 in.	May–July	
19	*Dianthus* (*double*) 'Pike's Pink'	Pale pink	6 in.	July–Sept.	
20	*Teucrium pyrenaicum*	Lilac cream	3–4 in.	June–Sept.	
21	*Scabiosa parnassifolia*	Rose mauve	4 in.	July–Aug.	
22	*Campanula carpatica* 'Isabella'	Violet blue	6–8 in.	July–Sept.	

		COLOUR	HEIGHT	SEASON	BULB BELOW
23	*Campanula carpatica* 'White Star'	White	6–8 in.	July–Sept.	
24	*Pentstemon Roezlii*	Red	6 in.	May–June	
25	*Achillea Lewisii* 'King Edward'	Yellow	6 in.	May–Sept.	
26	*Saxifraga Burseriana sulphurea*	Light yellow	2–3 in.	Mar.–Apil	
27	*Androsace semper-vivoides*	Pink	2 in.	April–May	
28	*Armeria caespitosa* 'Bevan's variety'	Pink	2 in.	May–June	
29	*Linum salsaloides nanum*	White	2 in.	May–Sept.	
30	*Teucrium chamaedrys*	Pink	6 in.	June–Sept.	
31	*Solidago brachystachys*	Deep yellow	9 in.	Sept–Oct.	
32	*Aethionema* 'Warley Rose'	Pink	4–6 in.	May–Aug.	
33	*Iberis gibraltarica*	White	6–9 in.	May–July	
34	*Sisyrinchium bermu-dianum*	Deep violet	9 in.	Nealy all year.	
35	*Zauschneria californica*	Orange scarlet	12 in.	Aug.–Oct.	
36	*Sisyrinchium brachypus*	Golden yellow	6–8 in.	June–Sept.	
37	*Rosa* 'Oakington Ruby'	Double crimson	8–9 in.	May–Oct.	
38	*Serratula Shawii*	Pink	9 in.	Oct.–Nov.	
39	*Rosa pumila*	Double pink	8–9 in.	All year	
40	*Campanula turbinata*	Purple-blue bells	6 in.	July–Sept.	
41	*Rosa* 'Baby Gold'	Gold and orange double	6–9 in.	June–Sept.	
42	*Iris cristata*	Mauve	6–in.	May	
43	*Gentiana lagodechiana*	Blue	4–6 in.	Aug.–Sept.	
44	*Saxifraga oppositifolia*	Large rosy crimson	1 in.	Feb.–Mar.	
45	*Iris lacustris*	Blue, gold crest	3 in.	April–May	
46	*Lithospermum inter-medium*	Blue	6 in.	May–June	
47	*Hypericum reptans*	Yellow	4 in.	May–June	
48	*Horminium pyrenaica*	Blue purple	6 in.	July–Sept.	
49	*Linum arboreum* 'Gemmell's hybrid	Yellow	6 in.	May–July	
50	*Chiastophyllum oppositifolium*	Yellow	4–6 in.	May–July	
51	*Lithospermum inter-medium* 'Heavenly Blue'	Blue	6 in.	May–Sept.	
52	*Dianthus (double)* 'Bombardier'	Crimson	6 in.	July–Sept	
53	*Campanula pulloides*	Violet	6 in.	July–Sept.	
54	*Achillea rupestris*	White	6 in.	May–June	
55	*Campanula glomerata acaulis*	Violet	2–3 in.	June–Aug.	
56	*Saxifraga Jenkinsae*	Pink	2 in.	Feb.–Mar.	
57	*Campanula pusilla* 'Miranda'	Pale blue	3 in.	June–Sept.	L H

		COLOUR	HEIGHT	SEASON	BULB BELOW
58	*Iberis* 'Little Gem'	White	3–4 in.	May–July	
59	*Iris melitta*	Smoky red	4 in.	April–May	
60	*Silene schafta*	Rosy purple	6 in.	Aug.–Sept.	
61	*Rosa* 'Pixie'	Pale pink and white Dwarf	6 in.	May–Oct.	
62	*Campanula carpatica* 'Blue Moonlight'	Pale blue	6–8 in.	July–Sept.	
63	*Prunella incisa rubra*	Crimson	6–9 in.	June–Sept.	
64	*Phlox Douglassii* 'Eva'	Mauve	2 in.	May–June	
65	*Dianthus* (*double*) 'Grace Mather'	Salmon	6 in.	July–Sept.	
66	*Potentilla verna pygmaa*	Dark green and golden yellow	Tiny	Succession	
67	*Saxifraga oppositifolia alba*	White	1 in.	Feb.–Mar.	
68	*Claytonia australasica*	White	1 in.	June–Sept.	U
69	*Mazus reptans*	Mauve	1 in.	May–Aug.	S T
70	*Nierembergia rivularis*	White	2 in.	May–June	S
71	*Thymus serpyllum major*	Bright crimson	2 in.	May–June	R
72	*Hutchinsia alpina*	White	1 in.	May–July	P Q
73	*Arenaria purpurescens*	Pink	1 in.	May–July	O
74	*Sedum lydium*	Green foliage turns scarlet	2 in.	Foliage only	N

Bulbs for Under The Carpeting Alpines

		COLOUR	HEIGHT	SEASON
A	*Fritillaria meleagris*	Mixed dark	8–10 in.	April
B	*Crocus Tommasinianus* 'Whitwell Purple'	Purple	2–3 in.	Feb.–Mar.
C	*Iris reticulata* 'Harmony'	Pale blue	9 in.	Feb.–Mar.
D	*Narcissus juncifolius*	Yellow	3–4 in.	April
E	*Crocus speciosus*	Blue	4 in.	Sept.–Oct.
F	*Iris reticulata* 'J. S. van Dijt'	Red-purple	9 in.	May–April
G	*Chionodoxa sardensis*	Blue	3–4 in.	March
H	*Crocus Sieberii*	Lavender blue	4 in.	Feb–Mar.
I	*Narcissus cyclamineus*	Yellow	6–8 in.	Mar.–April
J	*Crocus speciosus albus*	White	4 in.	Sept–Oct.
K	*Narcissus minimus*	Yellow	3 in.	Mar.–April
L	*Scilla praecox*	Blue	3–6 in.	March
M	*Crocus susianus*	Yellow	2–3 in.	Feb.–Mar.
N	*Iris reticulata*	Blue purple	9 in.	Feb–Mar.
O	*Eranthis hyemalis* (winter aconite)	Yellow	2 in.	Feb.–Mar.
P	*Crocus Zonatus*	Lilac	3 in.	Sept.–Oct.
Q	*Muscari* 'Heavenly Blue'	Blue	3–4 in.	Mar.–April
R	*Narcissus nanus*	Yellow	6 in.	Mar.–April
S	*Scilla* 'Spring Beauty'	Blue	3–6 in.	March
T	*Anemone blanda*	Blue	3–4 in.	Feb.–April
U	*Crocus chrysanthus* 'Snow Bunting'	White	3 in.	Feb.–Mar.
V	*Erythronium dens-canis*	Mixed	6 in.	Mar.–April

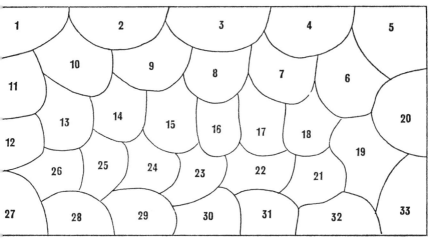

PLAN 2

Weed-suppressing Alpine Border

		COLOUR	HEIGHT	SEASON
1	*Sedum spurium coccineum*	Rosy crimson	3 in.	June–Sept.
2	*Phlox subulata temiscaming*	Red	4 in.	April–June
3	*Phlox Douglassii* 'G. F. Wilson'	Lilac	6 in.	April–June
4	*Phlox subulata* 'Betty'	Pink	6 in.	April–June
5	*Aubrietia* 'Thomas Hood'	Double purple	3 in.	April–June
6	*Prunella grandiflora alba*	White	6 in.	June–Sept.
7	*Veronica rupestris*	Brilliant blue	4 in.	May–July
8	*Helianthemum* 'Ben Hope'	Rose pink	6 in.	May-July
9	*Helianthemum* 'Fire Dragon'	Flame red	6 in.	Mar.–July
10	*Dianthus* 'Keith' (*double*)	Crimson	6 in.	July–Sept.
11	*Arabis albida*	White	6 in.	April–May
12	*Veronica pectinata rosea*	Pink	2 in.	May–June
13	*Ajuga pyramidalis*	Blue	6–8 in.	May–July
14	*Helianthemum* 'Wisley Primrose'	Pale yellow	6 in.	May–July
15	*Hyssopus aristatus*	Blue	6 in.	July–Aug.
16	*Helianthemum* 'Old Gold'	Deep Yellow	6 in.	May–July
17	*Helianthemum* 'Supreme'	Crimson	6 in.	May–July
18	*Alyssum saxatile*	Yellow	6 in.	May–June
19	*Polygonum vaccinifolium*	Pink	6 in.	July–Sept.
20	*Aguja reptans minima variata*	Foliage	1 in.	
21	*Helianthemum* 'Ben More'	Orange	6 in.	May–July
22	*Dianthus* 'Elizabeth' (*double*)	Pink	6 in.	July–Sept.
23	*Helianthemum* 'Ben Dearg'	Salmon red	6 in.	May–July
24	*Polygonum affine* 'Darjeeling Red'	Red	9 in.	July–Sept.
25	*Prunella* 'Loveliness'	Clear mauve	6–9 in.	June–Sept.
26	*Armeria maritima* 'Bloodstone'	Red	6 in.	May–July
27	*Acaena microphylla*	Bronze foliage red deep shade	1 in.	July–Aug.

		HEIGHT	COLOUR		SEASON
28	*Prunella grandiflora*	Purple violet		6–9 in.	June–Sept.
29	*Aubrietia* 'Greencourt Purple'	Blue purple (double)	3 in.		April–June
30	*Phlox Douglassii*, 'May Snow'	White	2 in.		May–June
31	*Aubrietia* 'Stock Flowered'	Pink	3 in.		April–June
32	*Aubrietia* 'Joan Allen'	Crimson	3 in.		April–June
33	*Veronica rupestris* 'Mauve Queen'	Mauve	4 in.		May–June

9

Bulb Gardening

The gardener divides bulbs into three classes—those that can stay in year after year and increase even if the flowers are cut, like crocus and naturalized daffodils; those that must be dug up, stored till autumn, and planted again with biennials between, like bedding tulips; and those that must also be dug up and stored right through the winter because they are not hardy, like gladioli and tigridias. Gladioli are of course 'corms', not bulbs, but our classification is for gardeners, not botanists.

One of the most satisfactory homes for the smallest bulbs is in the alpine border, and the names of the best will be found with their flowering seasons and colours in the plan in the last chapter. Planting is possible by turning back a carpeter in the autumn, but the neatest method is to use an apple corer to thrust down and take out a plug of soil and a disc of the plant, so the tiny bulb can be dropped down the hole and the 'core' replaced.

The low foliage of the carpeter prevents even the smallest and earliest flower from mud splashes and provides a foliage background or a flower contrast, but it is best to have the bulbs in bloom at different seasons. The relatively large flowers of bulbs can 'kill' the longer but more modest show of most low alpines.

Ordinary crocuses, like large daffodils, are best naturalized in grass because their spread by both offsets and seeding can swamp small alpines, and leave a mass of dead foliage to clear up. The species on the plan are all miniatures, and the only reason why very few people have a real show of the autumn crocus species from September to November is because these must be planted in July or August, though most gardeners expect to buy bulbs in autumn or spring. If they grow crowded and flower sparsely, dig up the carpeter, and take the bulbs up in July to catch them dormant, replanting the largest with an extra scattering of bonemeal. Small crocuses can be naturalized among shrubs.

The smallest daffodils fit the alpine border, with the 3-in.-high *Narcissus minimus*, like a tiny 'King Alfred', in March and April, following snowdrops and winter aconites in February. The 6-in.-high *N. nanus* lasts on till April, and so do the rush-leaved *N. juncifolius*, with trumpets that look upwards, and the 6–8-in. *N. cyclamineus* that has petals turned back like those of a cyclamen. Chionodoxas and scillas, especially 'Spring Beauty' and *S. praecox* (or *S. siberica*), and grape hyacinths add blue. But it is important not to have too many, because their foliage must have time to gather food for next year's bulbs before it is tidied up, and this can interfere with the carpeters.

The early *Iris reticulata* varieties, 'Harmony', pale blue, 'J. S. van Dijt', red purple, and the blue-purple original species are like 9-in.-high Spanish iris and are at their best under carpeters. So is *Anemone blanda*, the 3-in.-high miniature anemone flowering in March and April, with 'Royal Blue' the best variety, though it can also be bought as a mixture of blue, white and pink. Once these little anemones are going well, let them alone—the bulbs are so like small stones that they can rarely be found for splitting.

Another beauty that does best under carpeters is *Fritillaria meleagris* which should be planted 6 in. deep (unlike all other small bulbs which need holes twice as deep as they are tall from base to tip) and 6 in. apart each way. In April its bell flowers about 1 in. across hang on 9-in. arching stems, creamy white, pink, red and purple chequered and mottled in deeper colours. A good companion for this rare British wild flower, which costs about 54p for fifty from any good bulb firm, is *Erythronium dens-canis*. This has rather large red-brown dappled leaves and in March and April, 2-in.-across flowers with four pointed petals that hang from 6-in.-high stems, rather like elfin hats. Space these like fritillarias, plant 3 in. deep, and buy the ordinary mixture of white, yellow, crimson and purple.

These two are good in sun or shade under carpeting alpines with extra leafmould added, but both will thrive in shade because they are woodland bulbs and do well among shrubs, especially azaleas, rhododendrons and other lime-hating species. Shrub borders can suffer from the relatively short flowering seasons of some of the most attractive species, and spaces planted with shade-loving bulbs that prefer to be left alone provide off-season colour.

As Battle Hill at Wisley shows, lilies can carry on the show after the rhododendrons are over, and though many are costly and difficult, some of the easiest are mong the most striking. Consider *Lilium umbellatum* with clusters of trumpets that look upwards from stout 3-ft. stems in June. The best of this race cost 40p or 60p a bulb, they thrive on any soil to which humus (especially leafmould), has been added, and increase so easily that there are only two years to wait from their first autumn to give enough for a blazing show. The modern varieties 'Golden Fleece', bright yellow, 'Orange King', orange with red at the petal tips, and 'Vermilion Brilliant', crimson red, are no more expensive or less hardy than the original species.

These easy lilies are now correctly catalogued as *L. x maculatum* or *L. x hollandicum*, the small 'x' showing they are hybrids.

Dig in good compost, tucking it well down in the trench bottoms, then fork in ½ lb. of coarse bonemeal and about two bucketfuls of leafmould a square yard into the upper layer of the lily bed. Then plant your large onion-sized bulbs 4 in. deep from soil to surface, first giving them a handful of sand to sit on.

This strong race needs no staking, but it is worth pinching off the dead blooms to prevent wasting this strength on setting unwanted seed. Small bulbs will grow where the leaves join the stems and by mid-September they are ready to pick off and plant 2 in. apart along a furrow 1½ in. deep, which should be across a strip of vegetable garden where leafmould and sand have been dug in generously. The following September dig them up and space them 6 in. apart and 8 between rows to allow for hoeing the weeds, and by the next autumn your bulbs will be as large as those you buy, if you have kept them watered in dry weather.

Cut down the stems when these dry-off in October, and cover the lily bed with a 3-in.-thick coat of leafmould, which is all the extra feeding they need. These Umbellatum hybrids are the easiest of all lilies and they can provide a bulk of cut bloom for the house, and a short-lived blaze in many a shady corner. The old-fashioned Tiger Lily, *L. tigrinum splendens* with its salmon-orange turk's cap flowers, needs the same treatment and increases just as easily by leaf joint bulblets. The new Japanese variety, *L. tigrinum Fortuni*, with purple instead of black spots on the petals, will grow up to 7 ft. high, and is a splendid easy lily to have thrusting up through a rhododendron thicket.

There are now a number of hybrid races of lilies that are much hardier than species, which can be grown with Umbellatum treatment, though unfortunately they do not make bulblets. Mid-Century hybrids have upward-looking flower clusters on 3–4-ft. stems in June and July, with a range from yellow and orange to red, and are so far the cheapest and best, but specialist catalogues will show the others as they come down to every gardener's prices.

The autumn display in the shrubbery can be from the two hardy cyclamen, *C. neapolitanum*, pale pink, and the white *C. neapolitanum album*. Their flowers are about $\frac{3}{4}$ in. from the centre to the tips of the turned-back petals, like tiny greenhouse cyclamen on 4-in. stems. They should never be planted with covering carpeters, which strangle them, though they do well in alpine beds and the lower slopes of rock gardens.

Plant them shallowly in the spring if they are bought as dry corms, with the flat surface of the bulb, from which the leaves and flower buds will spring, just on the surface and the round side down. They can also be bought as pot-grown plants from alpine nurseries, and these can go in at any time.

One of the best places to naturalize them, apart from leafy soil in shrubberies, is under trees on lawns, especially cedars, where the grass grows thin with shade. Dig in leafmould and plant them shallowly in colonies, which is how they grow in woods in Italy. The two other species buyable as bulbs are *C. Coum* which flowers crimson, white or pink, according to variety, from December to March, and is best in a cold greenhouse or as a window-sill plant, and *C. repandum*, with crimson flowers from March to May, which can be naturalized with the others but does not flower so freely.

Daffodils are the best of all bulbs for naturalizing, and our wild species grew in pastures and orchards before road and rail transport grew efficient enough to take townsmen out to rob the countryside. Our rarest, *Narcisus obvallaris*, the Tenby Daffodil, like a 1-ft.-high miniature 'King Alfred', cost only about 70p a dozen, and *N. lobularis*, a form of the Lent Lily of Kentish orchards when these began at Woolwich, with a creamy back and a yellow trumpet, grows as large and costs even less.

These tough, early daffodils have smaller, tidier leaves that feed the bulbs enough to finish faster than larger kinds, so that drifts on tree-shaded lawns can be enjoyed in spring yet mown in May. Use only 2–4–D selective weed-killers and between July and September, for other types including ordinary lawn sand (and other times) can treat daffodils as they do dandelions.

Hardy companions for the 'Tenby' one are the all-white *N. cernuus* and two new hybrids: 'February Gold' with lemon petals leaning back from orange-yellow trumpets, and 'March Sunshine' in deep gold and canary yellow. All three grow to a foot and are about 80p a dozen.

Start their colonies by chopping through the turf and driving the spade under, so that a strip rolls back like a stair-carpet 1½ in. thick, leaving bare soil for planting trowel holes 3 in. deep and about 3 apart each way. On poor soils put a tablespoonful of coarse bone-meal for lasting food under the one of sand in the bottom of each hole on which each bulb sits flat end down. Whack the replaced carpet firm over the filled holes and forget the daffodils till you see them every spring.

Never use a dibber for planting, as this makes the hole sides hold water to rot the bulbs, but there is a fine, strong tool like a giant apple-corer to tread into the lawn, taking out holes without back-aches and ejecting the soil with neat turf circles to replace after planting.

This is value in orchards or grassed banks on which large kinds of daffodil can wait till their foliage is at least half-yellowed before the first grass cutting. 'Magnificence' is over in time for May mowing, like an earlier 'King Alfred', but now no dearer—neither are 'Rembrandt', which flowers much longer; pure white 'Beersheba'; and 'Mrs. R. O. Backhouse', with white petals and pale pink trumpets. Dig trowel holes three times as deep as the bulbs are tall—thus, large daffodils will have 4–5 in. of soil over their tips, and small tulips under 2 in.

Straight bulb rows are best for easy sowing of the annuals afterwards. Have them 8 in. apart. Then leave 8 in. between the daffodils, and 6 in. between the tulips, so that both have room to increase.

The ideal annual for stay-put bulb beds is the 'Bush Morning Glory' (like the annual climber, *not* the weed) and the finest is 'Royal Ensign', with rich blue saucers centred with white and gold, flowering from June to October. 'Cambridge Blue' and 'Crimson Monarch' are good contrasting colours. All need thinning 3 in. apart in rows. The same treatment suits the 9-in.-high dwarf godetias, 'Celestial', 'Salmon Prince' and 'Vivid'. The annual chrysanthemum 'Yellow Gem' provides yellow to go with them, and eschscholtzia is also suitable. Both the new scarlet 'Dazzler' and the old orange, pink or yellow can seed themselves. The first pink love-in-a-mist, 'Persian Rose', and the vivid 'Oxford Blue' provide an 18-in.-high mass, and so does 'Royal Bouquet' mixed clarkia—the only one bushy enough for the new system. Other annuals will be found, but they must be long-flowering quick starters, to hide dead bulb foliage and to hold down weeds.

When their show is over, pull up the annuals, and merely handfork out stray weeds, such as dandelions. Then scatter 4 oz. a square yard of bonemeal, and, ideally, spread a 1-in.-thick surface coat of leaf-mould, peat, or good compost without weed seeds, to feed the bulbs for spring and the easy annuals that blaze through summer.

Large ordinary crocuses are better for naturalizing in grass than the alpine species, planted exactly like daffodils, with the same care to let them die down before mowing, and *Eranthis hymalis*, the winter aconite, is even easier, for it flowers sooner, and harvests its foliage off earlier.

The bulb bed under annuals can take all but the smallest of the alpine bed bulbs, and it is also possible for those with a cold frame to raise their own half-hardy annuals to hide the dead foliage even more rapidly than with hardy ones sown ahead. Annuals for this purpose will be discussed in the next chapter, but the basic principles are to get out, or destroy with Amcide, all perennial weeds and to stick to the bulb species that like to stay undisturbed.

The really dry bed on the sunny side of a privet or Lonicera hedge can be made into a bulb border, under eschscholtzias, the most drought-resisting of annuals, which will probably seed themselves year after year, though the ordinary orange variety will predominate very quickly.

The best drought-resisting bulb for this kind of situation is *Triteleia uniflora* (also called *Milla uniflora* and correctly *Brodiaea uniflora*) with 6-in. stems and pale blue star flowers the size of pennies. The bulbs cost about tuppence each, and it often seeds itself. Plant 3 in. deep and 4 in. apart to stay in the ground without lifting even on the worst soil in a London garden, where with leafmould and bonemeal they will thrive and spread.

Their main show is in April and May but they flower on through summer, and in June contrast well with the clusters of yellow stars on 1-ft.-high stems of *Allium moly*. This is a wild garlic and can be dug and eaten for its milder than garlic flavour.

Other attractive Alliums that can also be eaten are *A. azureum*, with clear blue heads in June and July that last well in water and grow up to 18 in. high, *A. Ostrowskianum*, with relatively large pink heads 8 in. to 1 ft. high in July, and *A. pulchellum* up to 2 ft. tall with red violet heads in July and August. All make offsets freely and could be raised among the vegetables for those who like garlic, and cut flowers too.

Though montbretias will grow even in dry shade, provided they have some peat or leafmould, they do better in full sun. Most gardeners regard them as bread-and-butter, or rather 'bread-and-margarine' bulbs, because they leave them year after year in the most awkward corner of the garden and grow only the oldest variety. Unless they are dug up and divided every third year they make too many offsets to flower, because these crowd each other so much that few reach flowering size.

Buy a modern large-flowered mixture in a range of scarlet, orange, yellow and even pink shades, which cost about 60p a dozen, and plant them 3 in. deep and 2 in. apart in March or April, even in the narrowest end bed, but lift them, split them and keep only the largest every third spring. Then replant back after digging in compost or leafmould and bonemeal into their bed. If any of the named varieties can be found, try 'E. A. Bowles', rose pink with a yellow throat, 'Jessie', shrimp pink, 'Gladiator', crimson and white, 'J. A. Fitt', scarlet and dark red and 'George Davidson', the best yellow. All are excellent cut flowers, in bloom from July onwards, and only scarce because few gardeners have ever seen the modern hybrids grown well.

The 'stayput' tulips are the small species usually recommended for rock gardens, but their foliage is rather too bulky for growing under carpeters, so they are best with annuals. The dividing line between small leaves that will wither enough to be cleaned up without harming the alpines, and those that need annuals racing ahead to hide them, is hard to draw, but tulips are definitely over it, and erythroniums near the limit.

The leading race of the tulips that increase when left in, rather than dwindling as large ones will, are the Kaufmanniana hybrids. These grow 6–9 in. high with relatively large flowers that open almost to five-pointed stars and give this new race the name of 'Waterlily Tulips'. 'Corona' is bright yellow with a scarlet centre, 'Shakespeare' is salmon and orange, 'Stresa' is yellow edged with red, and the range of the mixed includes apricot, yellow, crimson and scarlet. Plant them about 6 in. deep to flower in March and April.

The cluster tulips, 'Fusilier' with three to five small scarlet flowers on 6-in. stems, *T. turkestanica* with five to nine creamy white tulips to the 10-in. stem, and *T. tarda* (which catalogues still call *T. dasystemon*) has a more modest two to four white stars with yellow centres, and grows only 6 in. high. Plant these about 3 in. deep and lift them about every three years, or when the show dwindles. As with montbretias, if the offsets crowd each other there can be no room for any to reach flowering size. Replant only the largest at about 6 in. each way spacing, and grow the small ones on as though they were offsets from the ordinary large bedding tulips.

Border tulips, with their tall, straight stems, are the guardsmen of the garden. They look particularly glorious when they are thrusting their way through a carpet of much smaller flowers such as forget-me-nots, which provide the strongest colour contrast of all.

Single Earlies, the first tulips, are the best choice in cases where the parade has to be dismissed early to make room for annuals from boxes. The tallest and straightest of this type is 'Keizerskroon', with a 16-in. stem and a large yellow and scarlet flower in April, while the dark red 'Cassini', the scarlet 'Dr. Plesman', and 'Bellona', the best yellow, are all an inch shorter.

The blooms of lily-flowered tulips are onion-shaped at the base with pointed, spreading petals above. 'Captain Fryatt', which is ruby red, 'Ellen Willmott', yellow, 'Queen of Sheba', orange with red-brown edges, and 'China Pink', are all 20 in. high and make a striking and unusual show in May. The Parrots, which have frilled petal edges and lighter stripes that can include green, also flower in May—the oddest is 'Fantasy', rose-pink and apple-green, and the loveliest is 'Blue Parrot', dark blue-purple, and the nearest yet to a blue tulip.

The largest and latest tulips are the Darwins, which flower in May and even early June. They look very effective with wallflowers in contrasting colours beneath them, and they are ready to be moved out before dahlias are moved in. Those with the most lasting blooms and the strongest, longest stems (28–30 in.) are 'Marshal Haig', scarlet; 'Princess Elizabeth', pink; 'Queen of the Night', deep maroon; 'Scotch Lassie', lavender; and 'The Bishop', purple-blue. Good 2-ft. kinds are 'Paul Richter', deep crimson; 'Rosy Wings', pink; 'Mrs. John Scheepers', yellow; 'Dillenburg', orange: and 'Apeldoorn', scarlet.

Before planting the bulbs, dig in 4 oz. each of fine bonemeal and lime, with a generous bulk of leafmould or compost. Add a scatter of general fertilizer, such as Gunos, for the bedding plants that follow.

The ideal planting time is September, so that the bulbs begin growing roots while the ground is still warm, but those who leave it as late as December can still grow bulbs successfully, provided that they discard the soft ones in any bargain clearance offer. These may well include some of the more expensive varieties that the public has ignored in favour of better known and cheaper kinds.

Plant them in trowel holes that are 5 in. deep and 6 in. to 8 in. apart each way (the tallest tulips need most room). Mark the ends of the staggered rows with temporary labels so that the undercover plants can be put in without the risk of piercing the bulbs or breaking their points.

When the petals fall, snip off the new seed heads—this will save the bulbs' strength. Dig up the finished tulips, keeping plenty of root, and replant them in a shady corner where they can finish growing. Dry the bulbs for storing and sort them out into groups according to size for the following September's beds.

The tiniest bulbs can be planted 4 in. deep and 4 in. apart, with 6 in. between rows, for a cut-flower strip in the kitchen garden (ideally they should follow well-manured potatoes). If the blooms are cut when they have only just opened, with stems that are barely 3 in. long for arranging in short vases, the bulbs will increase in size instead of dwindling. With time, and with good humus, they will grow parade-ground-sized tulips.

Dutch and Spanish iris need drying off and storing for planting in October, exactly like tulips. Dutch iris flower first in late May and early June, and should go in 3 in. deep and 4–6 in. apart each way, in sun or shade, even dry shade—for they will be dug by the time the summer drought begins. Like tulips, the better they are fed the more flowering size bulbs will remain, but they can be cut for bloom without very much loss, provided only the flower stem is taken. If they are planted *earlier* than October they will grow their leaves too early and get these damaged by hard weather in winter, so late planting pays.

The best of the named varieties are 'Blue Champion', mid-blue with a yellow blotch at the tips, 'Golden Harvest', pure yellow; 'King Mauve', the nearest to this colour; 'Wedgwood', a really splendid blue, and white 'Excelsior'. All grow about 15 in. high, and should be lifted and heeled-in like tulips in a shady place when the flowers go over.

Spanish iris need exactly the same treatment and flower about a fortnight late, with 'Cajanus' the best yellow, 'King of the Blues' near-ultramarine with a yellow splash, while 'Prince Henry' is really unusual in purplish brown, bronze and yellow. Both races are cheap and easy, but the offsets are well worth growing on.

The third race of bulbous iris is English, so called because though they also come from the Spanish side of the Pyrenees, some Bristol men brought a few bulbs back in the early seventeenth century and grew them in their gardens long before the others arrived via Holland

and Spain. English iris are rarely grown because they like a fairly moist place in semi-shade with plenty of leafmould, and those who buy them because they flower in July, kill them by giving them Dutch iris conditions.

They could be grown in a shrubbery with the lilies even, though they do well on ordinary soil with some leafmould and bonemeal, and unlike the others they should stay in the ground, digging them only when the clumps become congested, in about four years' time, in September or October, and replanting only the full-sized bulbs at once. The offsets can be planted in rows like tulip offsets or lily bulblets, and it pays to mark the best colours, because English iris can only be bought mixed.

A good mixture should include red-purple, violet, blue, pinky mauve, lavender and white, and the flowers, which are rather like those of Spanish iris, last well in water. It is worth removing the dead blooms to save the strain of ripening seed heads and keep up the size of the bulbs below, though seed can be saved and raised in a cold frame. The bulbs take two years from seed to flowering size.

Another species that suits the same conditions is *Camassia esculenta* which has lavender-blue flowers like slender hyacinths with more open heads of starry florets in May and June, growing about 18 in. high. This too needs leaving undisturbed and planting 3 in. deep and 6 apart each way, like the English iris. It comes from North America and its second name shows that the bulbs were eaten by Red Indians who called it 'Quamash', of which its first name is a corruption.

The last gardener's class of bulbs is those which are planted in the spring because they are not hardy, and dug every autumn to store in a frost-proof shed, unlike the tulips which need a dry one through summer before they spend winter in the open. The most magnificent of these are the Mexican Tiger Flowers or Tigridias, which cost about 60p a dozen and are as hardy as gladioli in dry and sunny borders on any soil.

The fat buds on strong, 18-in. stems, are packed like Sten-gun magazines with folded flowers to fire in a long burst of brilliance from July to early September. Each flower is about 6 in. across—three petals set in cloverleaf formation round a central saucer.

Plant white bedding Alyssum in May for a carpet to set off the vivid contrasts of *Tigridia conchiflora* (with large scarlet spots on bright yellow). *T. grandiflora rubra* (scarlet petals and a yellow saucer spotted with crimson). *T. grandiflora alba* (white with crimson spots),

Ruby Queen (dark red) and *T. pavonia* (mixed in all colour combinations excluding blue or violet).

Dig in compost or leafmould with 4 oz. of fine bonemeal to the square yard before planting the small bulbs 4 in. deep and 6–8 in. apart in April or May, putting sand at the bottom of the trowel holes. They are ready for lifting in autumn when their tall swordlike leaves are half yellow. Dry in the sun and store in a frost-free shed in a box of dry peat.

Gladioli are essentially cut flowers, so the best place for them is in strips across the vegetable garden, on ground that was well manured the previous year. If not, dig in compost during March, with the 4 oz. of bonemeal and 4 oz. of wood ashes a square yard as lasting food, and to provide the extra potash they need anyway to grow the best spikes. On clay soils give them ample hop manure, peat, or leafmould, because they cannot thrust roots through soil that bakes or goes too solid to let in air. This is best in the autumn, so the ground comes rough-dug through the winter, and has time to settle and firm.

Planting can begin with the first week in March in the south, and the last one in the north—for the best way to gain a succession for cutting is by planting at fortnightly intervals, up to the end of May, even only a dozen at a time. Dig the holes 6 in. deep, 1 ft. apart each way for large varieties, and 8 in. for the smaller tribes. On the bottom of each hole spread about $\frac{1}{4}$ in. of sand and sit the end of the corm that has a depression in the middle on this to give the good drainage that removes the risk of rotting especially on clays. Then fill in the hole, so that there is 4 in. between the upper side of the bulb and the surface, but plant them 2 in. deeper on sandy soil, for here they can blow right over if they are too shallow.

When gladioli are planted in herbaceous borders they should go 8 in. apart in fours so they can have a stout cane down the middles and three or four ties of green string to hold them upright. In strips for cut bloom they need a stake, with 18 in. under ground and 3 ft. above it, at the four corners and every 6 ft. between, and stout string or wire round the outsides. Their solid fans of leaves and the weight of the spikes bred on the modern varieties make wind their main problem, though a bed with shelter from the prevailing wind from a wall or hedge may grow the smaller varieties safely for years.

The primulinus gladioli have the smallest florets spaced more widely up the flower spikes which gives them least sail area, so staking can be avoided except in very windy gardens. They are usually about 3 ft. high, and their florets are $2\frac{1}{2}$–3 in. across. No varieties are recommended because there is a constant succession of new ones, and the only satisfactory method of choosing is by going to a flower show or ordering from a catalogue with coloured pictures.

The other wind-resistant group are the miniatures, which are only relatively small, for they are about 30 in. high and have close-set florets like the large varieties. The 'Butterfly' type are the same height, and take their name from the fact that they have a darker marking in a contrasting colour roughly the shape of a butterfly in the throat of the florets which are about the size of those of the primulinus varieties.

The large-flowering varieties are from $3\frac{1}{2}$–$4\frac{1}{2}$ ft. high, from $3\frac{1}{2}$–$4\frac{1}{2}$ in. across the florets, and have about six florets open at a time out of the 14–24 on a spike. They include all colours but pure blue, though there are some very fine deep violets including 'Blue Conqueror' and 'Flying Dutchman'. Again the best way to choose is at a flower show, or in the flower tent of an agricultural one, where specialist firms who plant for succession are displaying them right through to the autumn.

If only the spikes are cut from the middles with at most three leaves from a corm, gladioli last for years without replacement. If the whole plant is cut level with the ground, then the corm will die for lack of leaves from which to gather most of the food for next year's bulb.

Dig the plants by mid-October and remove the cormlets from round each large corm, taking off the rotted remains of the parent one from below it. Then hang the large ones with foliage attached in labelled bunches in a dry shed with plenty of ventilation, for 3–4 weeks until the leaves are dry and brown. Cut off the dead stem, to leave about 3 in. that will eventually wither, and set them out, not touching each other, on trays.

The best type, which also serve for dahlia tubers, is made from frames of 2 in. × 1 in. timber about 1 ft. wide and 3 ft. long with 1-in. mesh wire netting stapled to the 1 in. dimension of the bottom. These provide air circulation all round and are best hoisted with pulleys or laid across rafters under a garage roof, for with a heater under the car sump on frosty nights the roof can be warmed with rising hot air and the electricity or oil may as well warm your bulbs too.

Once, both tender bulbs and fruit were safely stored in lofts warmed by the bodies of horses below, which appear to have maintained the 35°–45° F. temperatures that fit apples and pears, and dahlias, gladioli and tigridias. This temperature in a modern house is secured most easily by those who have lagged between the rafters for insulation when they fit central heating.

Boarding over the rafters and fitting electric light is not only an advantage for searching through trunks and the usual attic junk, but it costs less than lining a shed in the garden for heat insulation, and stored fruit and vegetables can be safe inside, with no need to go out to fetch them in during frost or snow.

Netting storage trays can be hung from the rafters as in a garage, but the Dutch tomato trays with upright 'ears' at the corners which sit one on top of each other, are worth buying and hoarding from the greengrocer. These make ideal chitting trays for potatoes—and as the fruits are eaten, the tulips move in and out, and the gladioli take over, they can be constantly in use.

The smaller gladioli, down to the tiny pea-sized 'spawn', should be stored in these trays and wait until April for planting in 2-in.-deep furrows 8 in. apart. Fill these furrows with a mixture of two parts peat or leafmould to one of sand, and press the cormlets 1 in. deep into it at 3 in. intervals along the rows, covering them with the peat again and a ridge of soil. The object is to make sure that they have ample moisture, and if there is a savage spring drought when the first leaves are up like hopeful grass blades, run the lawn sprinkler on them.

Keep them well weeded and if any of the larger cormlets are unwise enough to flower, pinch out the spikes as soon as the bud shows. Labelling is important because these cormlets will resemble the bulb from which they came exactly, and part of the variation in the price of gladioli is because the expensive and strikingly coloured kinds make the fewest offsets.

The following October dig up the bulbs and sort into those which have reached roughly the size of those sold in shops for planting in borders or cut flower beds, and smaller types to grow on for another year at wider spacing in the rows.

10

Annuals, Biennials and Bedding Plants

Hardy annuals are sown in spring for a show the same summer, half-hardy ones sown earlier in boxes, in frames and greenhouses to plant outside when frost risk is over, and biennials are sown in summer to transplant in the autumn where they are to flower the following season. Bedding plants are a purely garden classification of long-flowering species, like dahlias and geraniums, that need protection through the winter and planting after the bulbs are lifted. This usually includes the half-hardy annuals bought in boxes after raising in heat by nurseries, such as lobelia, petunias, and salpiglossis.

Some of the hardiest annuals gain from sowing in the autumn at bulb planting time, dodging delay from hard weather in spring and making stronger plants that flower earlier and are extra good at hiding the foliage of naturalized bulbs in 'stay put' bulb beds. Sow in standard $\frac{1}{2}$-in.-deep furrows between the rows after the bulbs go in. Labels to mark the rows' end are best, because then everything that appears which is not growing in a line is recognized as a weed. Scattering the seed to produce a 'natural' effect can mean confusion between weeds and annuals when they first appear.

Cornflowers are perhaps the best insurance against horrible springs, and they can be sown as late as mid-October, whereas other autumn annuals need September sowing. Cornflowers can replace traditional wallflowers and forget-me-nots in the bulb border. They flower on from May to September, and hide the dying foliage of daffodils and Dutch and Spanish iris left in, like bulbs in grass.

The bushiest cornflower is the 1-ft.-high *Centaurea cyanus nana* 'Polka Dot' mixture of reds, pinks, blues, lavenders and white. The older kinds—dark blue 'Jubilee Gem', 'Rose Gem' and 'Lilac Lady' —are rather less compact. 'Double Blue', 'Double Pink', 'Carmine Rose' and 'Mauve Queen' grow 3–4 ft. high from autumn sowing and except in sheltered corners need canes with supporting strings between.

Dig in compost if possible, or leafmould with 4 oz. bonemeal to a square yard to feed both bulbs and annuals. Sow in furrows 1 in. deep and 15 in. apart for the tall kinds, 1 ft. apart for 'Polka Dot' sizes.

September sowing brings larkspur, which should be thinned to 15 in., over 4 ft. high for a show at the back of the border and to cut for tall vases in July and August. Choose 'Regal' or 'Supreme' mixtures for maximum height, 'Giant Imperial' and its named varieties for 3-ft. levels.

Love-in-a-mist sown in September grows a sturdy 18 in. without canes, flowering from July to September, spaced 1 ft. apart each way. The new *Nigella hispanica* has less 'mist' and more 'love' than 'Miss Jekyll', with vivid blue flowers 2 in. across, red stamens and larger, shapely seed vessels to dry for winter flower arrangements.

Though clarkia and godetia can be sown in autumn, they race and finish in June, but annual scabious, with its 3–4 ft. of long-stemmed pincushion flowers in blues, violets, reds and pinks, starts in May and finishes with the frosts. Sow ½ in. deep, thinning 1 ft. apart.

Indian Pinks sown at this depth in September make a border or solid carpet at this spacing. The single scarlet 'Bravo', 'Fireball', double, and the many mixtures of *Dianthus sinensis* blaze from June to hard frost and make it perhaps the most rewarding small annual to sow in autumn.

Spring sowing covers the widest range of species, and—for beds where there are no bulbs below—April or March sowing allows the whole batch to go in at once. Even with bulbs, however, spring sowing when the leaves are first up saves a great deal of time, compared with waiting until they are dug.

The candytufts are good bulb-cover for spring sowing, and grow about 9 in. high, with 'Dunnett's Crimson' the darkest red, 'Rose Cardinal', a good deep pink, and the original *Iberis umbellata purpurea* the best dark purple. The tallest is *I. coronaria* 'Giant Empress', which has heads like 2 in. across white hydrangeas, reaching 18 in. None need staking, and sown in rows 6 in. apart and thinned to this much between plants they meet solid, flowering from July to October, provided dead blooms are removed.

Another long-flowering species for the front of an annual border or bulb cover is *Phacelia campanularia* which needs thin sowing and the same spacing as candytuft, growing low and bushy, reaching near

9 in. and producing its royal blue, bell-shaped flowers 1 in. across within eight weeks of sowing.

The most drought-resisting annual is perhaps eschscholtzia, with 'Double Scarlet Glow' or 'Fireflame' the nearest scarlets, 'Carmine Queen' or 'Gloaming' the best pinks, and 'The Mikado' the finest crimson. Once started these will seed themselves, and therefore buy a packet of one of these striking varieties every year, because the ordinary orange will predominate in three seasons.

For a blue to go with them try Viscaria, which has 1-in.-across saucer flowers on arching stems packed into 1-ft.-high clumps from June to August. Sow it at the same spacing and for a drought resistant crimson try *Linum grandiflorum* with heads like the lovely alpine flax but with crimson-scarlet flowers from July to October on 1-ft.-high stems.

The annual chrysanthemums are good sturdy plants for the back of a border, growing up to 2 ft. and with luck not needing staking, especially if the tips are pinched out when the seedlings are 4 in. high after thinning to 6 in. apart each way so they grow bushy. The *Chrysanthemum carinatum*, also called *C. tricolor* varieties flower from June to August, and the best mixture is the 'Court Jesters', with three zones of toning colours on single daisy flowers about 2½ in. across— pinks, reds, yellows, orange and white. 'Lord Beaconsfield' has red and brown zones, 'W. E. Gladstone', copper and scarlet, and 'John Bright' is a pure yellow. 'Cockade' is a striking new one, white with a scarlet zone and a brown centre.

A good blue at their height level is *Echium* 'Blue Bedder' which is between 18 in. and 2 ft., flowering from July to September with thick clusters of cobalt blue bells on hairy branches with leaves rather like those of an anchusa. There is no fear, luckily, of its becoming a nuisance in Britain, though in Australia it is called 'Patterson's Curse' from the gardener named Patterson who let it loose, like rabbits, just by trying what has been called one of our most beautiful annuals in his garden.

Lavateras and malopes are about the best of all annuals for the back of a border, for they need no staking except in windy gardens and are easy on any soil, however poor, with plenty of sun. They are members of the hollyhock family but distantly enough to dodge hollyhock rust, and both grow 3–4 ft. high and flower from June to September. Sow their large seeds in March or April ¼ in. deep and 6 in. apart each way, thinning to 1 ft. apart when all are up. Choose *Lavatera trimestris* 'Loveliness' for deep pink spires, of shallow saucer florets about 4 in. across that look outwards, and *Malope grandiflora* for still deeper pink ones that look upwards from where the leaves join the strong stems.

It is possible to sow whole borders of annuals, and there is one at Wisley every year which is a steady show throughout the summer. It is simply not possible to give descriptions of the many hundreds of hardy annuals alone that there are now in cultivation, so they are listed in Chapter 16 with heights and colours. One of the pleasures of hardy annuals is taking a gamble on unknown names on each season's packets, and trying which suit your taste and your garden. The lists have been restricted to those that are worth growing, for a complicated name can hide a dingy sprawler which is rare because no one orders it a second time.

Annuals that are not short and stocky or very strong-stemmed need staking, and the best method is to break up peasticks and thrust these into the centres of the rings in which they are best sown in the border, or between the rows, so that the twigs save ties. There are a number of wire and plastic staking arrangements but all are expensive and twiggy branches about 2 ft. high are the best way of avoiding drawing the thin stems of annuals into tight bunches, apart from the work of keeping pace with the tying of such fast growing plants.

The secret of growing annuals well is thin sowing, and though it is easy to space large seeds along the row the tinies are difficult. Mix the packetful with about twenty times its bulk of fine bonemeal (better than sand because it weighs about the same as seed, so mixes evenly) and shake it as a 'seed cocktail' in a tin. Then sow it thinly along the standard ½- or ¼-in.-deep furrows where it will show up cream against the dark soil.

If small seeds are sown in circles or spirals these show among the weed seedlings because of their regularity, but the best system is to draw the furrows and sow the patches of each kind in several parallel sections of row. The straight rows between 6–9 in. apart can be hoed between.

Half-hardy annuals are described in Chapter 13, for though most can be sown in the open by mid-May, they have such a short time left for flowering, that those who have no frame should restrict themselves to the limited range grown by nurserymen, and described under bedding plants.

In the same way, those who remember forget-me-nots, sweet williams, canterbury bells and wallflowers only when they see plants for sale, limit their choice to mass circulation varieties. There is time and space in most gardens to rake smooth where the early potatoes were and sow thinly in ½-in.-deep furrows 6 in. apart.

When the seedlings have four true leaves they are ready to go 3 in. apart and 8 in. between rows to allow room for hoeing and growing. All biennials, as these 'sow this year—flower next and finish' plants are called, thrive on this standard treatment.

Wallflowers need their transplanting room trodden firmly, like the brussels sprouts with which they share clubroot, so you should sow and grow on uncabbaged soil. The kinds that must be sown to be seen are 'Golden Monarch', 'Crimson Monarch', 'Scarlet Emperor', 'Ruby Gem', red-purple, 'Hamlet', orange-yellow, 'Rose Queen', real pink, and the new 9-in.-high 'Fair Lady' hybrids, compact and a mixture of all colours but blue.

Fork in 1 lb. of lime to the square yard before sowing, not only because they like it, but to prevent the clubroot. Sow in ½-in.-deep furrows, aiming at over 1 in. between the quite large seeds.

When the seedlings begin to crowd the rows, dig and snip the tips from their long straight roots, so that they grow bushy ones for borders rather than forcing into walls. Then plant them 6 in. apart each way, with 1 lb. lime and 4 oz. wood ashes or 2 oz. muriate of potash to the square yard.

Water them well and pinch out the tips when they start growing again after the move. By October they should be strong and bushy, ready for planting 9 in. apart each way in sun or shade. On any soil.

Canterbury bells are still cups and saucers, single and doubles in pink, white, blue and mauve. 'Dean's Hybrids' are a good mixture, but disappointingly include no reds. They appreciate lime as much as the wallflowers when they are young, because they are *Campanula medium* and a taste for lime runs in the family.

This liking for lime is shared by the Dianthus race, and the biennial sweet william is *D. barbatus*, needing the same spacing and soil treatment as wallflowers. The seed is tiny and needs the bonemeal trick for thin sowing, but it keeps for three years so there is no need to waste by 'using up the packet'. Wallflowers and sweet williams sown early and allowed to grow large become soft and sappy monsters that suffer in hard winters, so never sow biennials before July.

The traditional sweet william varieties are 'Crimson Beauty', 'Pink Beauty' and 'Scarlet Beauty', all growing 18 in. high, but 'Morello' is a large-flowered crimson, 'Giant White' is also large, and the mixture, 'Indian Carpet', has a range of sweet william colours, mostly 'auricula eyed', or white edged which grows only 6 in. tall, ideal under late bulbs such as Camassias. 'Wee Willie' is still smaller, and is an annual used for edging, flowering eight weeks from sowing in a mixture of the same colours, and a change from the alyssum which is sown in the same way, in a series of furrows 2 in. apart so the thin sown seedlings meet in a solid belt quickly.

Forget-me-nots are the traditional ground cover for tulip displays in parks, because their blue is the colour tulips lack, and they too need the standard treatment, in July. 'Blue Ball' or 'Victoria' are the best with tulips, while 'Blue Bird' is rather earlier and is at its best with daffodils dancing over it. The deepest indigo blue of all is 'Compindi', very compact and from 6–9 in. high, making quite a good pot plant if it has a few days to get used to a size 48 pot in the frame. It is excellent under bulbs and in a bed on its own, and will last in water, like 'Royal Blue', the older 9-in.-high variety. 'Carmine King' is the best of the pink varieties, contrasting very well with 'Blue Parrot' tulips or any of the yellow ones.

Forget-me-nots flower early and are finished ready to dig and discard when the tulips are heeled in to harvest off their bulbs, but there are other biennials that will flower the whole summer. One of the most useful of these is the foxglove because it will thrive in shade without demanding excessive moisture. Foxglove seeds are tiny, so cover these with only a sprinkling of soil and flatten the furrow firm with the spade after sowing. Leave their seedlings in the rows till March before moving them where they are to flower. If they go in the dry shade under trees, they need watering at the start to tower and flower in this worst position in any garden.

The Shirley race of foxgloves has giant 'gloves' with up to 7-ft. spires, in colours ranging from white to deep rose with crimson and chocolate spotted throats. 'Excelsior' hybrids are whites, creams, pinks and purples, and 'Sutton's Giant Primrose' and 'Apricot' are named varieties of the same 5-ft. strain. *Digitalis mertonensis* is a 3-ft. companion, with pale strawberry-red gloves nearly 3 in. long, and, like the others, would seed itself once established under trees as easily as wild foxgloves.

Pansies thrive with afternoon sun only and in the north-facing shade of crowded houses, which is why they have been sold in spring from London costers' barrows ever since the 1840's. The original 'Feltham Triumph' mixture of the old, dark pansy colours can still be bought at 50p a dozen from nurseries for planting in beds and over bulbs. They are a better bargain planted in October, to flower from April until autumn, than when bought forced into bloom in the spring.

September is the time to cut down to 1-in. height clumps bought last spring to split and replant for next year only. Pansies are biennials, unlike violas, which have smaller flowers and last for years. These also need a September cut back and split, as they spread thin with age. Put in the new plants or the split roots 6–8 in. apart each way.

Perhaps the finest new pansy is 'Raspberry Rose', with flowers 4 in. across, the colour of ripening raspberries above and port-type red below, with bright gold centres for contrast against the velvet darkness. Sown in July, it flowers from April onwards with 'Pride of Zurich' (clear blue), 'St. Knud' (apricot above, orange below) and the 'Swiss Giant' mixtures (purples, yellows and near pinks).

Newer, but smaller, are 'Clear Crystals' the first yellow centreless, one-coloured pansy in a full colour range of named varieties; 'Perfection Blue', 'Purple Bedder', 'Yellow Gem' and 'Avalanche', white, are compact April starters and autumn finishers. Sow thinly in $\frac{1}{2}$-in.-deep furrows in late July, to grow clumps for autumn planting, or in boxes in cold frame or greenhouse. Cover the seed with a scatter of soil and when a sixpence will cover a seedling, space them wider in more boxes. Ideally, plant them this size 3 in. apart each way in the greenhouse bed to grow much larger for a final move in February or March.

Violas are smaller than pansies, hardier, and longer-lasting, but they need the same uncrowded start in the seed-rows from July sowing and spring moving where they are to flower. Larger plants can be raised by sowing in the frame in March for autumn planting, but transplanted open ground seedlings do just as well.

Though they are excellent bulb cover, especially for the smaller species, they are still better massed under roses, especially the long flowering floribunda class, to hold down the weeds. There is no need to give the soil any special preparation except for the roses, and the seedlings can go out 6–8 in. apart each way in staggered rows. Manure can be spread round the roses without harming the violas which will meet and suppress annual weeds, and have a certain extra value in preventing the rain from splashing back blackspot spores on to the rose foliage.

The best varieties for this purpose are the apricot 'Chantryland', 'Coronation Gold', 'Blue Heaven' and 'Blue Gem'. The smaller pansies, such as the 'Clear Crystals', can be used, but it is better to stick to the older kinds because these are more likely to stay true when they seed themselves. Violas usually live two years, but once they are going in a rose bed on the 'no-digging' principle of leaving the weed seeds lying like sleeping dogs underground, there will be plenty of self-sown seedlings to keep the succession going. Yellows will always predominate, but 'Chantryland' is perhaps the most permanent of the others. Planting out a few blues each year will keep the colour going.

The bedding plant that is a real bargain is the pentstemon, for these once popular bedding plants grown from cuttings and sold in pots are now sold as seedlings in boxes for May planting, at about antirrhinum or aster price, when they give three or four years' display of tall spires of trumpets from July to October.

The usual mixture is 'Scotch Prize' strain, about 18 in. high, in a range of pinks, crimson, scarlet and purples, but 'Sutton's Large-flowered' are nearer 2 ft. with a high proportion of trumpets in contrasting colours. The finest of all is 'Monarch Mixed', reaching 30 in. with large trumpets and a colour range that won an R.H.S. Award of Merit in 1958.

Dig in compost or 4 oz. of fine bonemeal to the square yard before planting the strong seedlings 1 ft. apart each way. In late October, when the flowers finish, remove their dead stems only, for the secret of enjoying a still better display the following summer is *not* to cut the plants down in the autumn. In cold gardens peat or bracken round the stems acts as an added protection.

The old-fashioned, tall antirrhinums (*A. majus*) can also last a second season in a sunny border. These grow up to 3 ft. The rust risk is highest with second-year plants, but the 'Tip-Top' strain of *A. maximum*, in mixed or separate colours, is both tall and immune to rust. No one knows yet if these or the 3-ft. 'Rocket' hybrids will stand our winters as the old kind did in Edwardian gardens. The 'Monarch' rust-immune varieties of ordinary antirrhinum should be bought where rust is common.

Since this rust swept one of the most popular of all bedding annuals from our gardens, the petunia has risen to popularity, and it is always best bought as box stuff because it needs more heat to start it than a cold frame provides, and those who sow in cold greenhouses get their plants too late for a real show. Dig in plenty of leaf-mould and bonemeal or good compost tucked well down in the trench to keep any weedseeds below the surface, because petunias need rather more humus than the usual antirrhinums, stocks and asters.

Extra leafmould pays for scarlet salvias and lobelia, and this was one of the reasons for the success of the mass displays of brilliant bedding plants that delighted our ancestors—they used far more leafmould than we can afford of peat, because they swept and stacked their leaves to make a free supply. Salpiglossis too are leafmould lovers and need heat, so they are worth buying if they can be obtained. They will grow up to 2 ft. high with rather sticky greyish green leaves and the most lovely wide-mouthed trumpet flowers about 2 in. across. Their colours range through crimson, scarlet, pinks, purples, blues and yellows, with veinings of either yellow or a deeper shade, and they last well in water. They need a sunny place and careful staking, but if they were a hardy annual everyone would grow them.

French marigolds bought in boxes provide one of the quickest-to-come and longest shows, planted 8 in. apart each way. The mixtures of brown and yellow are less attractive than the clear yellow 'Golden Ball' and the splendid 'Scarlet Glow' that starts flowering near scarlet and becomes about tangerine orange colour. They flower from June to October and stand drought so well that they are one of the best annuals to plant in tubs, urns and large pots in courtyards. They are particularly popular in riding stables because they are the one bedding plant horses dislike eating.

Plant them with pale 'Blue Cascade' or dark 'Sapphire' trailing lobelia round the edges for tubs, or indigo, dark foliaged 'Crystal Palace' with them in beds. Lobelia is wasted as an edging, for it is far better value in wide drifts that contrast pure and lasting blue with vivid scarlets and strong yellows and oranges. 'Rosamond', the new red lobelia, is rather a dull colour, and nothing like as attractive as the older varieties like 'Cambridge Blue', or 'Mrs. Clibran', with a white eye.

Geraniums are one of the finest bedding plants, starting flowering as soon as they come out of the pots until they are brought into safety from frost. Those who have a greenhouse with any form of heating at all can nurse them through the winter and spring until May, but without winter protection they are an expensive form of bedding. 'Paul Crampel', the traditional scarlet, is only one of the many varieties now available, but because they demand greenhouse space through the winter at modern labour and heating costs, they are always expensive.

Dahlias, however, have overcome the problem by being grown as small tubers, and those who wish to enjoy shaggy cactus, tall decoratives, neat pompoms and all the other classes dear to the dahlia fancier, can buy from the catalogue and store ready to plant at the right season, as though they were bulbs. They can also be bought as pot plants, but it is possible to keep these for later seasons, without a greenhouse, using the technique that suits the seedling races.

The first week in June is the traditional time for planting dahlias, but early May is the season for outdoor sowing. Shilling packets then will bring a late show of the 'bedding' kinds and a splendid display from July until November in the following year from tubers stored like bulbs in a frost-proof shed.

The newest and most striking of the 15–18-in.-high 'Coltness' type is 'Monarch Pink Radiance', with a crimson ring on pink petals. Most seedsmen also sell the older yellow, pink, scarlet, dark red and mixed varieties, with 4-in. single flowers. 'Unwin's Advance' is the leading double-flowered mixture. 'Early Bird' is another good one. 'Queen of Moorlands' has dark copper foliage that contrasts with its pinks, yellows and bright reds. All have stiff stems that need no staking and need no dead-flower removals as do the Coltness kinds, but are rather taller and last better when cut for the house.

Dig in compost, peat or leafmould before sowing or planting, with 2 oz. of sulphate of potash or 4 oz. of wood ashes to the square yard. Repeat the potash as a surface dressing in August and water it in, or use a liquid tomato manure at that time for this improves the keeping quality of the tubers.

Sow groups of three seeds $\frac{1}{2}$ in. deep and 1 ft. apart and pull out the weaker two from each set. Once started in soil warmed by May sun, they grow fast to flower first in August, though buying greenhouse-grown plants means a quicker show to replace lost shrubs.

Ignore autumn frosts that merely scorch the leaves; they leave the dahlias bravely flowering. Wait for a week after a hard one that blackens the foliage dead and then dig the tubers, so that they have time to ripen for keeping. Then cut the stems 2 in. short for bedding kinds and 6 in. for large varieties.

Shake off spare soil, washing only for solid mud, and isolate any fork-pierced or grazed tubers, dusting sulphur on the cuts. Then stand them on wire netting or slats across bricks to dry slowly in the shed. In a fortnight they will be ready to set in a single layer, stems up and not touching one another, on 3 in. of dry coal ashes or peat in boxes deep enough for another 3 in. over them.

Mid-April is soon enough to sprout dahlias like potatoes before planting. Dig them out of the ashes and stand them on moist peat with a little over the tubers in boxes, with light and more warmth. Window-sills or sheds in spring will provide this.

Plant them in mid-May 6 in. deep and 15–18 in. apart, dividing the clusters of tubers into bunches of three fat roots each, with growing shoots at the stem ends for a July start.

11

Perennials for Beds and Borders

The traditional herbaceous border, so called because it 'borders' a lawn or path on which the viewer walks, slopes upwards from perhaps 6-in.-high dwarf Michaelmas daisies in front to 6-ft. delphiniums contrasting with the clipped evergreen hedge behind them. Very fine specimens of this type of border can be seen at Wisley, planted for a succession of flowering times so that there are no complete blanks at any height, from about April to November.

The taller the plants at the back, the wider must the border be, for the plants must come down in irregular steps so that those in front can hide the bare stems or cut-out flower foliage of those behind, and flower in their turn. A border going up to 6 ft. at the back demands at least 10 ft. of width, ideally 12, so the average semi-detached garden would only have room for one, if it had no central path, because the background hedge would take about 4 ft.

The yew hedges of Wisley and other great gardens do more than provide dark green to contrast with vivid spires of hollyhocks or delphiniums. They help reduce the need for staking by sheltering the tall plants from summer gales, and because they are slow, their roots do not rob, as those of privet do. Use a 'privet wall' as described earlier, where a border has a hedge behind, and plant no closer than 2 ft. to it to allow for getting behind and clipping.

One way round the height problem in small gardens, is a triangle border. This slopes up into a corner, between house and the next door fence, between two hedges or anywhere that offers shelter from behind and a view from the front. Chopping the corner off a front lawn to give one decent-sized bed rather than four narrow ones round the edges makes a good triangular perennial or shrub border possible, with room to plant for succession.

Perennials need planning, far more than alpines, for miniature borders, because height is so much more important, and Plan 3 shows the basic principles of border design. At the back is *Malva alcea fastigata* which flowers all the way up the sturdy 4-ft. stems with shallow rose pink cups more than 2 in. across from early July to late October. It needs no staking except in very windy gardens, and two staggered rows 15 in. apart each way can be used as a 'hedge' against an open fence to act as a windbreak for the back of a border, provided the next step down in bloom contrasts blue or yellow with this strong pink.

Assuming that this border is a right-angled triangle from taking a corner off with 8-ft. sides, three malvas 15 in. apart fill the peak section marked (1). The next 'step' down shows three *Anchusa* 'Lodden Royalist' for a glorious blue from May to August at least 1 ft. shorter, and three *Rudbeckia fulgida* with grey-green leaves and vivid orange-yellow daisies with black centres from August to October. Both rarely need staking, and contrast well with the pink mallow and each other.

The third step where the bed is wider takes four plants each of *Aster* 'Sir Winston Churchill', a 2–2½-ft.-high Michaelmas daisy to flower in September and October, which serves to hide the finished anchusa behind it; *Doronicum* 'Golden Bunch', with large yellow daisies from May to July; and *Salvia superba* 'May Night' with violet spires from July to September, which contrast with the Rudbeckia behind it.

The front row begins with *Geranium Wallichianum* 'Buxton's Blue', with 2 in. across cranesbill flowers, blue with white centres from July till October. Next comes *Heuchera* 'Red Spangles', with bright coral-red, round, florets from May to July. *Solidago* 'Queenie', the 9-in.-high dwarf goldenrod then provides bright yellow in August and September. Finally *Pulmonaria angustifolia* 'Munstead Blue', 6–9 in. high and flowering from March to May, the earliest of all.

This particular triangle is planned to grow without staking if it has shelter from two sides, though the anchusa and the salvia may need it. The smaller the garden the greater the advantage from species with long-flowering seasons, because though the eye can skim over the gaps and see the blaze further down the long border, every plant shows in a small one.

Many other triangle beds can be planned with the lists in Chapter 16 and it is also very effective to use the front for naturalized bulbs with bedding plants or annuals between. Lobelia in a wide sheet, not a mere edging, is about the most effective, for long lasting pure blue, to go with yellows, reds, pinks and whites in the 6–9-in. bottom step of the triangle.

The best herbaceous border planting times are from September to early November, and from mid-February to April, and the first step is a thorough dig-over to remove perennial weed roots. Never use a hired rotary cultivator where either perennial or shrub borders are to be planted because the machine will chop up couch grass and convolvulus roots to convenient-sized root cuttings to grow masses more weeds.

In a dry summer, when it is possible to rotavate three or four times to get rid of couch, dig over for a final search before planting but, otherwise use ammonium sulphamate a month before the planting season, or dig carefully in the old-fashioned way.

When the ground is fairly clean, dig under half a barrow-load of compost a square yard, with this much leafmould plus 8 oz. of fine bonemeal as an alternative. Well-rotted farmyard manure is nearly as good as compost, because perennials need slowly released plant foods, well balanced and with ample humus, but with deep-litter poultry manure (straw-based, see Chapter 14 for accounts of manures and compost making) or municipal compost, both of which are low in potash, spread 4 oz. a square yard of wood ashes to level it up.

Compost should go well down in the bottom of the trench so that if it is not too well made and contains weedseeds still alive these will be safely under the surface. There is less need to be as careful with leafmould or peat which is a rather expensive substitute for the humus that is free for thinking ahead and stacking the autumn leaf harvest.

Plant with a trowel, digging out a hole large enough to spread the roots. For fibrous-rooted perennials dig round and relatively shallow holes with mounds in the middle so that the crown of the plant can sit on it and the roots spread down and outwards—the trick for putting in strawberry plants. Cover the roots with soil, and if the weather at planting time is dry, fill up the hole from a canful of water beside you, before putting back the last of the soil and firming it. This 'puddling in' should not be done on heavy clays, where the soil should be well firmed round the plants before watering. Non-fibrous-rooted perennials like mallows should have a hole deep enough to take the long roots without their having to curl round at the bottom.

Because the rain is going to wash away some of the soil, aim to put the plants about 2 in. deeper than the soil marks show they grew in the nursery, except for those which have foliage at planting time (like pyrethrums), which should go in only as deep as they grew. After planting and firming dig over the bed shallowly, not deeper than 4 in., to break up all the packed areas where the ground has been trodden and where the rain could gather and freeze in winter.

During the first summer hoe between the plants as often as possible, for with ample space between it is easy to kill the rapidly germinating seedling weeds. The next year there will be fewer and it is possible, with enough leafmould or peat, to suppress them with a surface mulch. Leafmould which has had time to break down to barely ¼ in.-square pieces is ideal, because it has little sail area to blow about the garden if it dries, as raw leaves will. The old custom of digging between the herbaceous border plants in autumn and spring, for tidiness, brought more weedseeds to the surface at every digging, but a 2-in. coat of leafmould each autumn or in spring about April provides both a build-up of humus and weed control. Lawn-mowings on the surface are unsightly and can harbour slugs, but it is safe to treat the back rows as though it were raspberries or blackcurrants and put on a coat in April, unless it includes delphiniums, whose new shoots are the slugs' delight.

The principles of taking time to clear the perennial weeds, and digging in ample humus for moisture retaining and slowly-released plant foods, apply to all borders, and all those described here begin in the same way; though some plants, such as paeonies, need more humus.

Small gardens cannot afford to run their herbaceous borders too high at the back and Plan 4 has the tallest plants in the middle of its 36 ft. of length going up to a maximum of 5 ft., so it can be 9 rather than 12 ft. wide. This includes the 'Belladonna' type delphiniums which flower rather longer than the large-flowered kinds and leave less of a gap when they finish.

Those who love the tall kinds čan use them at the back to replace the 'Belladonnas', for the thick-foliaged kinds have been placed in front to hide the holes that even 'Lamartine' leaves.

Lupins are even worse gap leavers, but this trouble can be reduced by removing the spikes as soon as these are over, so that there is some secondary growth with small spikes and some foliage to fill in; but, like delphiniums, they should be used sparingly. The man whose front garden is a blaze of Russell lupins in May and June has little to show for the rest of the year.

This applies still more to Oriental poppies. *Papaver orientale*, with brilliant short-lived flowers but furry and floppy foliage, monopolizes large areas of border, while the deep roots are hard to kill. Pyrethrums are a valuable reinforcement for the reds, crimsons and pinks in May and June but they also are floppy. The secret is to stake them really early so that they grow up 'in harness', for once the stems are bent they stay sprawling.

This large border has a whole back row that will need staking, especially if there is no hedge or wall behind to break the wind. These are the strongest growers and should be planted in threes, set in triangles with 2-ft. sides, alternately two at the back and front, in the middles of their larger divisions.

The next two rows of spaces take fours, planted in squares with 18-in. sides, and the front row fives, in five-of-diamonds formation, 15 in. from corner to corner, bearing in mind that though some have tall flowers (for example, the heucheras) their clumps are low. It will be noticed that the 'steps' are not regular. The border tends to rise in the middle, and longer borders can be planted with a series of bays of lower-growing perennials and headlands of tall ones coming forward. The heights given are approximate—the lower one is usual in a dry year.

The plants are chosen to stand drought in full sun, but where there is some moisture, large quantities of humus such as leafmould can be dug in to hold it, or if the border has afternoon sun only, other species can be added as in alpine borders.

The monardas or bergamots are good 3-ft.-high perennials flowering from June to August, and though they need staking they are both tough and showy. 'Cambridge Scarlet' is the familiar red one, but 'Mahogany' is a real crimson, 'Croftway Pink' quite a good shade, and 'Sunset', the new red-purple, a really good plant which should reach a great many gardens as it is as easy to increase by division as the older varieties.

Border phlox, as distinct from the annual *P. Drummondi* and the alpine races, also needs humus and moderate moisture. These grow 2½–3 ft. and perhaps the best are 'Caroline van den Berg', the nearest to blue, 'Otley Purple', a near blue-purple, 'Professor Went', a crimson one, 'Signal', orange-red, 'Sir John Falstaff', salmon-pink, 'Mies Copijn', pale pink, and 'Mother of Pearl', white. The old white variety 'Mia Ruys' is a short one, 1–1½ ft., which fits in well at a lower level. All flower from July to August.

Schizostylis are like dainty gladioli, which need no staking and thrive in full sun, with humus, growing from creeping rhizomes or surface roots like small irises, not bulbs. They flower in October and November when the border has mainly Michaelmas daisies on show, and last well when cut, once the clump is well established. 'Mrs.

Hegarty' is rose pink, 'Viscountess Byng' a soft one, and the old *Schizostylis coccinea* bright red. All need hunting for round the nurseries old-fashioned enough to grow a wide selection of species, unlike the garden-centre type aiming to stock only best sellers. Gardeners should buy the popular kinds from firms which also list the unusual, because they will be the best even if they are not the cheapest, just as the grocer who will order nut butter for a vegetarian will also sell the best bacon, because he takes the trouble to consider even his awkward customers.

North-facing borders which have shelter and humus suit *Dicentra formosa*, with ferny foliage and flowers like small pink lockets in May and June, sometimes for longer, about 18 in. high. There is a small one, *D. eximia*, about 1 ft. high with the same arching sprays of redder lockets, and the lovely *D. spectabilis*, with red and white 'bleeding hearts' that give it its popular name, about 2 ft. high, needing staking because the stems are soft, but making a fine show for a shady corner.

With them have *Heucherella* 'Bridget Bloom', perhaps the only really long-flowering perennial for shade, with pink and white plumes about 18 in. high from May to October. Give it humus and some bonemeal on a soil that does not bake hard in summer, and it will spread and thrive as one of the most outstanding recent perennials, a cross between a Tiarella and a Heuchera.

An ideal front-of-the-border plant for this kind of bed is *Omphalodes cappadocica*, which has creeping stems, mats of pale green leaves, and 6-in. sprays of forget-me-not flowers from April to June, and may flower again in the autumn. Though it can be increased easily from division it does not run all over the place and invade its neighbours. As a contrast have *Adonis vernalis*, with ferny foliage and buttercup flowers on 6–9-in. stems in April and May, but do not disturb it once it is established. It can die down in August, though still perfectly healthy, and risk being dug up by tidy gardeners. A taller late-flowering perennial for the same position is *Cynoglossum nervosum*, with a succession of forget-me-not flowers from June to August, 1½–2 ft. high, and rising from a sturdy clump.

The shade that provides the problem for most gardens is dry shade under trees, for though shade from buildings is easy, tree roots rob the soil of moisture. Diverting water from roofs or paths can bring even more voracious tree roots, and privet walls of various types are about the best way round, supplemented with hoeing. The only real solution is to choose plants sufficiently tough to do their best in a position where they are found in Nature, and to hope for a brief flowering in spring before the leaves close in.

Plan 5 illustrates a full-scale herbaceous border for such a position, assuming that it is not too desperately dry. Aquilegias, though excellent in the open border for May and June display, especially the 3-ft.-high 'McKana' hybrids, will endure shade, like the many cultivated foxgloves. The Japanese anemones (now *A. hupehensis*, not *A. japonica*), will also take this kind of shade, provided that they have ample leafmould to hold on to the moisture, and so will *Campanula lactiflora*. The tall *Tricyrtis stolonifera* is valuable for late colour and worth watering to keep it growing. It has purple flowers about 2 in. across, on the lines of small lilies, from August to October. Its popular name is Japanese Toad Lily, which is rather a handicap, for it is a lovely thing thrusting up stems each year from underground roots that need plenty of peat and leafmould, for it is by nature a woodland species. The most drought-tolerant real lily to go with it is *Lilium umbellatum*.

Towards the front of the border come the reliable drought resisters, and if the bed is really dry concentrate on the two front rows from clumps 10 to 22 in the table. The epimediums are particularly valuable, with almost evergreen leaves rather like those of Berberis, which should be cut back early in March so the new green foliage can get away. Removing the old leaves with shears then lets the small flowers—rather like short-spurred aquilegias up to ten on a branching stem about 1 ft. high—show to the best advantage from April to June. Those who have a large area of dry shade could well plant an all-epimedium bed and collect the many species and hybrids as though they were roses or helianthemums. The autumn tints of the foliage are quite striking, though this only shows when the plants are established, for the best time to move and split them is in July and August.

The Vinca (periwinkles) group are also entirely drought-proof and are the traditional ground-cover for London gardens crammed with trees. Pulmonaria (lungwort: our native species, *P. officinalis*, was once used by herbalists for chest complaints) is almost as tough, and 'Munstead Blue' is the best value in flowers for space. Like the Ajuga it will do even better in an ordinary border. The yellow deadnettle with silver-leaf edges, *Lamium galeobdolon variegatum* will stand more drought than the more usual purple kind.

Perhaps the toughest ground-cover plant for dry shade under trees is *Pachysandra terminalis* with insignificant flowers but shiny evergreen foliage on wiry stems rather like a creeping box (it belongs to the same family as box edging *Buxus sempervirens*) which should be planted 6 in. apart each way for weed-excluding foliage under the worst conditions. The other shrubby solution is *Hypericum calycinum* or 'Rose of Sharon', which will have large yellow flowers when once established. Plant 1 ft. apart, ideally in autumn, so that it will get some rain to start it when the trees are bare.

Irises planted under trees, as they often are in London gardens, are merely space-fillers with tidy evergreen sword leaves and rare mauve flowers. They can never flower well without some sunlight on their fat surface roots called 'rhizomes', so regard them as foliage-only plants in dry shade; but if they have morning or afternoon sun only, the odds on flowers go up, though in full sun they show at their short and splendid best in June.

Though irises can be planted as clumps in long borders, they are really best in beds on their own, and even where they are filling in an awkward corner, there is no reason to stick to the very ordinary blues and occasional yellows found in most gardens. The bargains are the new American varieties that appeared in the early 1950s and have now come down to the 42p and 60p each class because these will be the strongest-growing, since they will have made most rhizomes to divide, while kinds still expensive are usually slow and less tough.

A modern selection should include 'Blue Valley', clear bright blue; 'Deep Velvet', dark red purple; 'Elizabeth Noble', pale lavender and deep purple; 'Firecracker', burgundy red; 'Flamely', bright red and garnet-brown; 'Indiana Night', dark blue-purple; 'Lady of Shalott', rose pink; 'Mattie Gates', clear yellow; 'Ola Kala', orange; 'Pink Cameo', clear pale pink; 'Quechee', ruby red; 'Redwynne', deep crimson; 'Royal Sovereign', light orange; 'Snow Flurry', white; 'South Pacific', pale blue; 'Starshine', cream and white; 'Sunbeam', canary yellow; 'Vice-Regal', bronze and purple.

If you plant them in spring or autumn they will suffer a setback, so order in June for July or August delivery; they will be growing strongly after flowering and ready to take hold of new soil and establish themselves before winter brings snow and snails. The best answer for these snails in old or new beds is watering with Fertosan slug and snail destroyer in early autumn or late spring.

Start by digging in two good bucketfuls of compost, leafmould or hop-manure to a square yard, adding 4 oz. each of coarse bone-meal and wood ashes on poor soils. On chalky ones scatter 2 oz. to a square yard of iron sulphate at planting time to correct the likely shortage of essential iron through its being locked up by the lime.

Plant in clumps of three, in triangles with 8-in. sides, each clump 1 ft. apart. For each iris dig two shallow holes 1 in. apart, then sit the rhizomes on the ridges between the holes with their roots going down each side. Cover these with firmed soil and pack it round to leave the top half of the rhizome bare to the sun.

If you plant irises deeply they will sulk for years, but this shallow planting makes every rhizome flower, starting with one each next June and building up to a show that goes on for six more summers. Then it is time to lift, split and replant with more good humus and plant foods, and perhaps a few still more striking varieties, by then down to a price within reach of every gardener.

The Hemerocallis or day lily is far more tolerant of shade than the border iris and though its individual flowers do not last much longer than a day (hence the popular name) the small lily-like trumpets in clusters open steadily from June to August. They will thrive on any ordinary soil, with extra humus in dry shade, and should be planted 2 ft. apart each way. They take some time to get established and are not at their best till the third season. The pale green foliage, rather like that of a red-hot-poker, should only be trimmed and the old tattered leaves are removed in the spring; for, as with so many perennials, they are a winter protection. A day lily bed stays put year after year, so it is a good idea to give a spring top dressing between the plants of deep-litter poultry compost (which will hold no weed seeds) or well rotted farmyard manure, about every other year.

The Hemerocallis race has been entirely altered by the arrival of a flood of new hybrids from America. As a complete change from the rather dingy oranges and yellows of the past, plant 'Black Prince', deep maroon with a yellow centre, 'Hiawatha', coppery red, 'Margaret Perry', tangerine orange, 'Morocco Red', ruby purple, 'Night Hawk', pure yellow, 'Pink Interlude', bright pink, 'Salmon Sheen', salmon pink and 'Tysoe', bright cardinal red. They are quite easily increased by splitting the clumps in autumn and spring, so eventually the more expensive new varieties will come down in price, or rather other prices will rise so much that they will be relatively cheaper. They flower far better in full sun, but they are so tough that even these new varieties can be grown in the sooty corners of town gardens in part shade, where they appreciate the same anti-slug measures as the equally long-suffering London irises.

Paeonies do best in a bed on their own or in permanent groups (like lilies) on the front of a shrub border, for they must not be disturbed. Unlike most herbaceous plants, which need lifting and splitting every five years (like Michaelmas daisies, heleniums and most fibrous-rooted plants), or lupins which die in five or six seasons, they can last as long as fifty years in the same place.

Though all herbaceous borders could do with double-digging, paeonies insist on it for success. Dig out the soil 8 in. deep, which is one spade depth, along a 2-ft.-wide strip, and wheel this to the other end of the plot. Then dig out 1 ft. of the subsoil below and wheel this to the end, heaping it separately. Fork up the bottom of this last 1-ft.-wide trench and spread 2 in. of compost along it, plus lime at the rate of 8 oz. a square yard. Then fork the second foot of lower soil on top of it, and add more compost, leafmould or manure, plus a scattering of fine bonemeal. Now fork the first foot of undisturbed topsoil across on to it, dig the bottom of the next low trench, add the compost and lime, then fork over the lower layer and repeat the process.

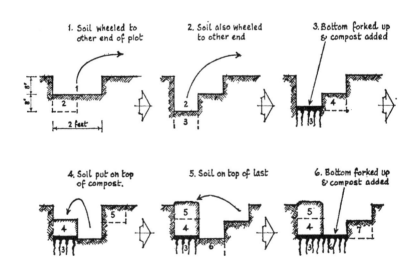

Fig. 12. Old-fashioned double trenching for paeonies and other perennials that appreciate deep cultivation.

This complex operation, easier to do than describe, illustrated in Fig. 12, is old-fashioned double trenching, which improves drainage and provides the depth of soil that paeonies need. With time and energy a whole border can be dug this way, and though it is just as much hard work as it sounds, it only has to be done once, and if your paeonies grow happily for fifty years, it is worth it. 'No-digging' gardeners who insist that none is necessary, only surface mulching, should realize that though Nature grows paeonies without digging in parts of Red China, these are not all that common even in their native country, because they grow only where there is good drainage.

The old-fashioned scented double paeonies come from southern Europe, and also need good drainage. They flower in May and should always be grown with the modern June-flowering Chinese varieties (*P. sinensis* hybrids), to extend the season. Both groups need the same treatment and grow about 3 ft. high, so they are best in groups along the front of shrubberies, and their rise to a craze in the 1960's comes from large gardens largely turning over to shrubs, not because they are value for space in small gardens.

The best of the old-fashioned varieties are *P. officinalis alba plena*, double white; *P. officinalis rubra plena*, deep crimson; and *P. lobata*, 'Sunshine', salmon flame and really worth finding, for it is now rare in cultivation. There are now over a hundred new Chinese paeonies and the best way to choose is on a trip to Chelsea Flower Show, which is just right for their flowering season. So many differ only slightly in colour, however, that only a few give the full range. 'Albert Crousse' is bright pink with a deeper centre, 'Bunker Hill' is crimson, 'Canary' is creamy white deepening to a yellow centre, 'Duchesse de Nemours' is white and sweetly scented, 'Lady Alexandra Duff' is pale pink, 'Lady Bramwell' carmine pink, and 'Solange', salmon pink.

Plant them deeply, with the tips of the fat pink or white buds in the crowns 3 in. below the surface, and ideally in September or February. They will cost at least 75p each, and it never pays to buy them cheaply because these may be split-offs from old clumps, which may die and in any event should spend two years growing in the nursery. Good plants should give something like a show in the third summer after planting. Because they stay a long time in the same bed they need well-rotted manure or compost, to be forked in shallowly round them about every three years.

The wet corner in sun or shade provides an opportunity to grow primulas, not the 'Wanda' sort beloved of birds, but the wet, easy, lordly ones that tower at every Chelsea Flower Show. Like rhododendrons and heathers, they incite everyone who sees them, especially

those with dry and chalky gardens, to buy them, try them, and kill
them.

The primula bog was invented in the 1930's to give a greater water
allowance to a small area of a chalky garden from the gutter or
eaves' drip of a garage or shed, off a cement path, or even by diverting the summer flow from the downpipe of a house roof.

Dig out the bed 18 in. deep, keeping the surface soil separate, and
mix four parts of sandy subsoil, or three of sand to one of fine coal
ashes, to one part cement. Make this to porridge stiffness, and spread
it 2 in. thick on the bottom and smooth flat. When this has set, build
a wall round it almost to ground level with brickends, hard rubbish
and cement. Leave 2-in. gaps between the stones at the bottom of the
wall to let out water, and a larger gap about half-way down the wall
to take the drain inlet which should have small stones around it.

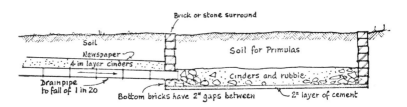

Fig. 13. Primula Bog, using drainage from paths and shed roofs to grow
moisture-loving species in dry gardens.

The drain can be of glazed earthenware or metal pipes leading
from the downpipe of a shed or greenhouse, or small trenches filled
with stones and bottomed with a V-shaped trough of cement so that
water gathered from a path trickles to the primula bed.

Start filling with 3 in. of small rubble and cover with three parts of
topsoil and one of leafmould or peat, with an added part of sand for
soakaways on clay, and 1 lb. each of bone- and fishmeal to a barrow-
load where the surface soil is poor.

A rather easier method is to dig out the bed as before but cover the
bottom with a sheet of black polythene, after taking great care to remove any sharp stones, and to have it slightly higher in the middle
than the sides so that there is no risk of a stagnant pocket of water
staying permanently underground. Do not use polythene at the sides,
for the bottom alone will hold quite enough. Filling and general

treatment are exactly the same. Polythene, which never decays, can also be used for pool making, but here the weight of the water pushing it against a sharp stone can produce sudden leaks. Those who need a small rainwater tank can make one easily, provided that they avoid sharp corners and make a rounded pool with the sides sloping gently to the centre. Heap 3 in. of soil on top of the upper edges of the sheet before laying turf on top.

The primula bog is not a pond, it is merely a bed where the water stays rather longer before draining away, and though wet corners of the garden will make them naturally, these are inclined to grow rushes, docks and grasses that will swamp the plants, and to be too wet in winter when primulas are dormant. One way to avoid this is to bring the soakaway drain up to the side of the house drain and tie a section of motor-car inner tube over the spout of the downpipe with the rest of it leading to the drain. A polythene bag with the bottom cut off will also serve though it is neater to buy an extra elbow pipe that a builder can fit so that it can be removed for the winter like the easy temporary expedients.

The first primulas to flower are *P. rosea* 'Delight' with deep pink cluster flowers up to 9 in. high in April and May, and *P. denticulata* with drumstick-shaped flowers on stout stems up to 1 ft. high. The original species is pale lilac, but 'Pritchard's Ruby' is crimson purple and 'Taylor's Violet' the best deep blue purple. They flower in March and April, starting before the long leaves are full sized, and the many varieties are worth collecting. They can be increased by division, for the named kinds do not come true from seed.

The bed will blaze in May and June. Start with smaller kinds in front, planting about 9 in. apart each way. 'Asthore' hybrids are a good mixture of yellow, apricot, pink and mauve, with *P. Beesiana*, lilac and *P. Bulleyana*, orange, at the 12–18-in. level.

The tallest for the back are *P. pulverulenta*, with up to twelve tiers of magenta flowers on 3-ft. stems: the glorious salmon-pink variety, 'Bartley Strain'; *P. helodoxa*, with smaller rich yellow tiers; and *P. Wilsoni*, tall and purple. With them have *P. Florindae* with giant golden cowslip heads on 1-yd.-high stalks in July and later. The most magnificent are the *P. japonica* hybrids, 'Millar's Crimson', 'Postford White' and the pink shades called 'japonica rosea'.

The water-loving irises, flowering in May and June with colours primulas lack, and extending the season, also serve to provide an evergreen background of tall straight leaves. These do not need their rhizomes on the surface and they can manage with less sun than the border varieties. But they must have summer moisture, without which they fail to flower, and do their best with sunshine by the waterside.

The most usual variety is *Iris siberica* 'Perry's Blue' with smaller and more butterfly-like flowers than the border kinds on 3–5-ft. stems in May and June. With it plant 'Eric the Red', a real red-purple, 'Tropic Night', a dark violet, and 'Dragonfly', pale blue, though there are many other varieties in various blue shades. Add *I. laevigata* 'Rose Queen', for a 2–3-ft.-high rose pink flowering in June and July, with the *I. kaempferi* varieties.

These Japanese irises have very small 'standards', as the upward pointing parts of the iris flower are called, and large wide 'falls' that spread out almost flat. Though they are usually sold mixed, it is worth watching catalogues for 'Purple Splendour', deep violet, Hendersoni, a red-purple double, 'Cassandra', rosy lilac, 'La Nuit', plum purple, 'Morning Mist', white, and 'Janus', lavender-blue. For a pure blue to flower with them have the original *I. laevigata* which is scarcer than 'Rose Queen'.

There are some taller moisture-lovers which can extend the flowering season of the damp corner still further, planted behind the iris, with the primulas towards the front. The tallest is *Ligularia clivorum* 'Othello' with stout 4-ft. spikes of 2-in.-across, orange daisy-flowers from July to September, rising from a clump of big purple, heart-shaped leaves that can be 18 in. across.

With this massive creature have the tall Lysimachia, between 3–4 ft. high, *L. clethroides* with spires of white florets about 6 in. long, rather like those of a buddleia from August to September, *L. euphemerum*, with grey-green foliage and smaller but even more plentiful white spires in July and August and *L. punctata* with spikes of yellow star flowers from June to August. All will tolerate drier conditions and have been planted in normal borders, but they do best in the damp surroundings of the primula bog.

The planting cost of beds and borders can be reduced greatly by planning ahead, for though a large number of named varieties must be bought, a great many can be raised from seed even without a cold frame. With a seedbed in the vegetable garden they are as easy as sweet williams or any other biennial, and can fit in behind early peas or potatoes when they need transplanting.

The secret is to use in rather smaller quantities the John Innes seed soil that gives the alpine border its head start on the weeds, and is now sold in the spring by most chain stores. It is usually dead dry in a polythene bag—so water it with a rose-can and shovel it about till it is evenly damp. Then take out 'V's' with the spade, 3 in. wide and deep, and 1 ft. apart, and fill the holes with the moist soil ready for a ½-in. sowing furrow down the middle of each.

Cover the seeds thinly with the same soil and keep the space between 'V's' hoed through summer, for freedom from weeds does not last long enough to give perennials a lead if new weeds can seed among them.

Sprinkle lime to whiten the furrow bottoms, so that dark seeds show up to make thin sowing easy—4 in. apart for delphiniums so that they can stay in the rows to move when small to their flowering homes in spring.

Tall delphiniums from seed are always mixtures, and 'Pacific' or 'Blackmore and Langdon' strains are both excellent, while the 'Astolat' hybrids are the first *pink* race in deep and pale shades with black centres, growing 4 ft. high. The 'Belladonna' varieties, especially 'Lamartine' and 'Cliveden Blue', will come nearly true from seed, and the first named can be sorted from the mixture because even small seedlings have dark foliage.

Lupins also have large seeds, so does *Malva alcea fastigata*, and wherever seeds are large enough to handle, and room is available, it pays to use this delphinium spacing. Few gardeners, however, can spare this much room in April, May and June when perennials are best sown, and most seeds are too small to handle in this way. So trickle them along the middle of the weedfree zone as thinly as carrot seed, and transplant when they have four strong true leaves, or are 1 in. high.

The limiting factor is how much room can be spared from winter cabbage-tribe crops, but perennials provide a welcome rest from clubroot, for none belong to the order Cruciferae. Where 'Duke of York', the early that can stay in to become a keeping maincrop is grown, this leaves all the potato room cleared in September with just time to plant out the perennials, but all are better moved sooner to have more time ro root well before winter. The seedlings can go 4–6 in. apart and with 8 in. between rows to allow room for hoeing in case any have to stay on until late April, for they are best transplanted with ample watering when they are growing strongly. A few slow starters may need transplanting again to pack them up together to grow on until the following autumn.

Annual, biennial and vegetable varieties are bred to pure lines so that they come nearly 100 per cent true from seed, but named varieties of perennials, as a general rule, will not. Therefore it pays to sow them early with time for the young plants to show a small flower spike, then the washy or unattractive colours can be discarded, or the best colours labelled out of a mixture. It can pay to sow in the frame in March for an early start, and give a sort-through in the summer so that the best are ready for autumn planting.

'Connecticut Yankees', the new race of large flowered delphiniums with the bushy habit of 'Belladonna' but solid spikes in the full colour range of purple, lilac, light and dark blue and lavender, are very easily sorted this way. So is *Aster* 'September Glow', the 4-ft.-high red Michaelmas daisy bred to raise from seed, though the ordinary Amellus and novaeangliae mixtures mean a long wait for the more ordinary colours.

All Dianthus races suitable for border fronts pay to sow early and sort, for even though the first flowers are small, the colour will stay the same. The Allwoodi alpinus, the 'Dwarf Fragrance' carnation mixture, and the 'Old Laced Pinks' are fast starters and it is possible to discard on straggly habit too, as should always be done with helianthemums.

Iris are easy from seed but involve a long wait till they grow to flowering size, though *I. siberica*, *I. Kaempferi* and the ordinary *I. germanica* (the border iris) and the dwarf *I. pumila* with miniature flowers in May on 9-in. stems, can all be raised, but take two years at least to flower, though the waterside races are worth growing to montbretia size and planting out to take their chance.

Heuchera Bressingham hybrids, *Kniphofia* T. and M. Strain, *Scabiosa Caucasica* House's Mixture, and Sidalcea T. and M. Strain, have all had special care in selection, like Russell lupins and the many races of delphinium and dianthus. All are worth raising, with the guiding principle that the slowest and weakest-looking seedling may well bear the finest colour of the lot.

The lists in Chapter 16 have a symbol to indicate those easily raised from seed, and it is worth chancing any of them in the open, for even the smallest seed (or the stalest) may get away well in sun-warmed soil. Anything tiny, or expensive, can be safer in the frame, and starting sowing perennials and alpines as soon as the half-hardy annuals and any early vegetable plants are out, is the best policy. Even in summer there is a gain from the shelter, and a slightly quicker start under glass.

Species differ from hybrids in the fact that seedlings will resemble their parents and not produce a mixture. In some cases the good form in cultivation increased by cuttings or division does not come entirely true. As an example, *Salvia superba* from seed is rather taller (2½ ft.) and not such an intense violet, but a good plant and worth a place in any border.

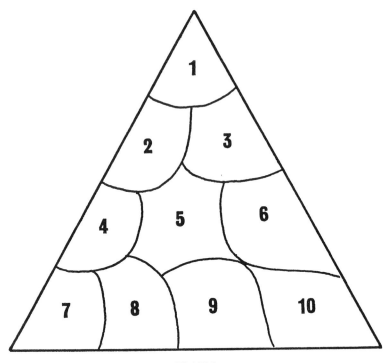

PLAN 3

The Corner Herbaceous Bed

		HEIGHT	COLOUR	SEASON
1	*Malva alcea fastigata*	4 ft.	Pink	July–Oct.
2	*Anchusa* 'Lodden Royalist'	2½–3 ft.	Blue	May–Aug.
3	*Rudbeckia fulgida*	3 ft.	Orange	Aug.–Oct.
4	*Aster* 'Winston Churchill'	2–2½ ft.	Crimson	Sept.–Oct.
5	*Doronicum* 'Golden Bunch'	2–2½ ft.	Yellow	May–July
6	*Salvia superba* 'May Night'	1½–2 ft.	Violet	July–Sept.
7	*Geranium* 'Buxton's Blue'	1 ft.	Blue	July–Oct.
8	*Heuchera* 'Red Spangles'	1 ft.	Red	May–July
9	*Solidago* 'Queenie'	9 in.	Yellow	Aug.–Sept.
10	*Pulmonaria* 'Munstead Blue'	9 in.	Blue	Mar.–May

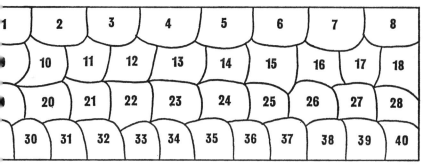

PLAN 4

Herbaceous Border for a Sunny Site

		HEIGHT	COLOUR	SEASON
1	*Heliopsis* 'Golden Plume'	4 ft.	Yellow	June–Aug.
2	*Sidalcea* 'Mrs. Anderson'	4 ft.	Pink	June–Aug.
3	*Delphinium* 'Lamartine'	4 ft.	Dark blue	June–Aug.
4	*Sidalcea* 'Wensleydale'	4 ft.	Red	June–Aug.
5	*Artemisia lactiflora*	4–5 ft.	White	Aug.–Oct.
6	*Helianthus* 'Lodden Gold'	5 ft.	Yellow	July–Aug.
7	*Veronica crinata*	4–5 ft.	Purple	Aug.–Oct.
8	*Phygelius capensis*	4 ft.	Scarlet	July–Oct.
9	*Polygonum amplexicaule*	3 ft.	Red	July–Sept.
10	*Rudbeckia Deamii*	2½–3 ft.	Yellow	July–Oct.
11	*Aster* 'Eventide'	3–3½ ft.	Deep Blue	Sept.–Oct.
12	*Delphinium* 'Cliveden Blue'	3 ft.	Pale Blue	June–Aug.
13	*Kniphofia* 'Royal Standard'	3–3½ ft.	Red and Yellow	June–July
14	*Echinops Rito*	3 ft.	Deep Blue	July–Aug.
15	*Centaurea ruthenica*	3 ft.	Yellow	July–Sept.
16	*Aster amellus* 'Bessie Chapman'	2 ft.	Deep Blue	Aug.–Oct.
17	*Solidago* 'Goldenmosa'	3 ft.	Yellow	Aug–Sept.
18	*Aster* 'Beechwood Triumph'	3 ft.	Red-purple	Sept.–Oct.
19	*Scabiosa* 'Clive Greaves'	2 ft.	Blue	July–Oct.
20	*Lythrum salicifolium* 'Robert'	2 ft.	Pink	June–Aug.
21	*Achillea* 'Moonshine'	2 ft.	Pale Yellow	May–July
22	*Aster* 'Winston Churchill'	2–2½ft.	Deep Red	Sept.–Oct.
23	*Liatris spicata* 'Kobold'	2–3ft.	Purple	July–Aug.
24	*Coreopsis verticillata*	1½–2ft.	Yellow	June–Aug.
25	*Euphorbia epithymoides*	1½–2 ft.	Yellow	April–May
26	*Veronica longiflora*	1½–2 ft.	Blue	June–Aug.
27	*Achillea clypeolata*	2 ft.	Yellow	June–Aug.
28	*Sedum spectabile* 'Carmen'	1½ ft.	Pink	Sept.–Oct.
29	*Armeria* 'Bee's Ruby'	1–1½ ft.	Deep Pink	June–Aug.
30	*Polemonium reptans* 'Blue Pearl'	1 ft.	Blue	May–June
31	*Pulsatilla vulgaris*	1 ft.	Purple	April
32	*Doronicum* 'Miss Mason'	1–1½ ft.	Yellow	April–May
33	*Inula ensifolia*	1 ft.	Yellow	July–Sept.
34	*Dianthus* 'Old Laced Pinks'	1 ft.	Pink to Red	June–Aug.

		HEIGHT	COLOUR	SEASON
35	*Iris pumila* 'Goldfinch'	9 in.	Yellow	April–May
36	*Lindilofia spectabilis*	1 ft.	Blue	May–Aug.
37	*Heuchera* 'Carmen'	1½ ft.	Pink	May–July
38	*Aster* 'Blue Bouquet'	1 ft.	Blue	Sept.–Oct.
39	*Gypsophila* 'Rosy Veil'	1 ft.	Pale Pink	July–Sept.
40	*Stokesia laevis* 'Blue Star'	1 ft.	Blue	July–Oct.

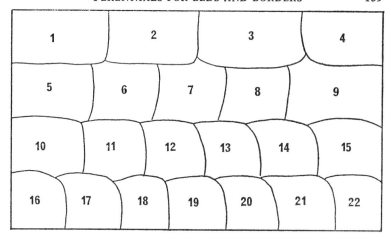

PLAN 5

Herbaceous Border for Shade

		HEIGHT	COLOUR	SEASON
1	*Digitalis ambigua*	2–3 ft.	Yellow	June–Aug.
2	*Aconitum* 'Bressingham Spire'	3 ft.	Blue	July–Aug.
3	*Aquilegia* 'McKana'	3 ft.	Mixed	May–June
4	*Digitalis mertonensis*	3 ft.	Pink	June–Aug.
5	*Aquilegia* 'Mrs. Nicholls'	2½ ft.	Blue	May–June
6	*Anenome hupehensis* 'September Charm'	2 ft.	Pink	Aug.–Sept.
7	*Tricyrtis stolonifera*	2 ft.	Mauve	Aug.–Oct.
8	*Anemone hupehensis* 'Bressingham Glow'	2ft.	Red	Aug.–Sept.
9	*Campanula lactiflora*	2–2½ ft.	Blue	June–Aug.
10	*Epimedium grandiflorum violaceum*	1 ft.	Violet-blue	April–June
11	*Aquilegia* 'Dragonfly'	1½ ft.	Mixed	May–June
12	*Epimedium rubrum*	1 ft.	Crimson.	April–June
13	*Epimedium versicolor sulphureum*	1 ft.	Yellow	April–June
14	*Ajuga pyramidalis*	8 in.	Blue	May–June
15	*Epimedium grandiflorum* 'Rose Queen'	1 ft.	Pink	April–June
16	*Lamium maculatus*	6 in.	Purple	June–Sept.
17	*Vinca minor alba*	6 in.	White	April–Sept.
18	*Vinca minor multiplex*	6 in.	Purple	April–Sept.
19	*Vinca atropurpurea*	6 in.	Lilac	April–Sept.
20	*Vinca major*	1 ft.	Blue	May–Sept.
21	*Lamium galeobdolon*	9 in.	Yellow	April–June
22	*Pulmonaria angustifolia* Munstead Blue'	9 in.	Blue	April–May

12

The Rest of the Roses

The rose is Britain's national flower, and the most popular of roses is 'Frensham', blazing in front gardens where once 'Paul Crampel' geraniums shone in an earlier age. It was the first of the modern floribunda roses, the kind with flowers in clusters that make a show from June onwards into winter. Because it was the first, and a vigorous and free-flowering bright crimson, beating the earlier 'Kirsten' and 'Karen Poulsen', hundreds of gardens still have it.

It is, however, a martyr to mildew, and in some seasons can have it as badly as the old 'Crimson Rambler' of pergolas in the 1930's, and those who do not wish to collect roses as though they were stamps should choose the varieties that resist diseases, grow vigorously, flower freely, and hold their colours in sun and rain.

Most of the older generation of gardeners are convinced that modern roses have no scent compared with those of the past. This is probably partly the effect of thirty years of smoking (and other people's cigarettes, car fumes and the smells of an age of air pollution) but there are new roses as fragrant as any of the old even though we cannot go back and smell them with the fresh nose of a gardener's boy in the 1900's. Let us restrict our choice still further by demanding scent as well as disease-resistance and first-class colour, and the thronging roses of today become quite a small collection.

Floribunda roses can fill the formal beds of a small front garden with a long and trouble-free display, especially if under-planted with violas or the many carpeting plants suggested earlier. They can also, chosen for heights, bank up into almost a 'herbaceous border' for an informal shrub effect, though they are always best planted formally, with straight paths and square, oblong or round beds.

Perhaps the best all-round variety is 'Allgold' (2–2½ ft.) which is a glorious long-flowering, double orange yellow that resists not only mildew but also blackspot, the dreaded fungus disease of roses. The approximate heights will be given in brackets after each kind for help in planting beds with the effect of a gentle dome of colour rather than the steep slope of a perennial border.

Behind 'Allgold' have 'Korona' (2½–3 ft.) which has large, semi-double vivid orange scarlet flowers that fade with age to salmon, and in front have 'Chanelle' (1½–2 ft.) with large clusters of a quiet pink, or 'Plentiful' (2 ft.) a double deep pink scented and very free flowering. A front garden does well with only three varieties of floribunda rose, for the strong colours can 'swear' at each other, though this strong team would make a dozen, all different, for those who prefer a collection.

'Dainty Maid' (3 ft.) is the best single pink mildew resister, and 'Evelyn Dison' (3–3½ ft.) a good tough, tall, double red, while 'Fervid' (3–4 ft.) is a vivid orange red single. 'Paprika' (2–2½ ft.) is a single orange red with a nearly purple centre and 'Pink Parfait' (2½–3 ft.) has large clusters of double flowers, deep pink on the petal outsides and lighter within. 'Saraband' (2–2½ ft.) is a pure scarlet single, and the next best black spot resister to 'Allgold', so these two can make a splash where the disease is about.

'Lili Marlene' (1½–2 ft.) is the best dark red single and 'Orange Sensation' (2–3 ft.) the nearest to a real orange. It is weatherproof, long flowering and tough, with a splendid rich scent, but it will take mildew late in the autumn. The final floribunda is 'The Queen Elizabeth', a giant growing 5 ft. high with deep pink flowers on long stems, a fine hedge rose, but too strong and tall for the ordinary bed. Its best place is at the back of a triangle border for a show from June onwards, with all the flowers on top of the bush, so it is nearer a small tree or shrub than a bedding rose.

Normal-sized roses should be planted 2 ft. apart each way, allowing 1 ft. from the edge of the bed to the planting holes, which gives a guide to how large the bed for how many roses, should be. Bear in mind that they need full sun, hate a position even near trees, much less one under them, and will not thrive in chalky gardens unless the subsoil is dug out and replaced with a more ordinary soil—ideally a clay or loam, which is sandy clay.

Start by digging out the top soil and heaping it to each side of the bed, and if this is on a lawn put down sacks to keep the soil off the grass. Then spread a 4-in.-thick layer of peat or leafmould plus ½ lb. of fine bonemeal and ½ lb. of hoof and horn a square yard on the exposed subsoil and dig this in, tucking it well into the trench bottoms. If a rotary cultivator is available that will work in the small space, churning the humus into the bottom spit to 9-in. depth saves hard work. Then replace the heaped-out soil, and spread a 2-in. layer of peat or leafmould plus 4 oz. each of bonemeal and hoof and horn on it before digging this in. The bed will be now far higher than the surrounding soil, but if the job is done in August or September the ground will have settled by the end of October, which is a good rose planting time. Spring is less desirable, but they can go in up to early April, but October and November are the best months.

To save leafmould and peat which are ideal lasting humus, the lower spreading can be compost, but if this is Municipal (see Chapter 14) add 2 oz. of wood ashes to every pound, because it will be short of potash which roses need; with none available add 2 oz. of sulphate of potash a square yard, or 4 oz. of a seaweed fertilizer.

A 6-ft.-wide bed will take three staggered rows, allowing for 1 ft. each side for mowing and edging room, and the holes should be dug 1 ft. square and 9 in. deep which takes the main roots down to the humus-enriched subsoil.

Most good nurseries send out their roses trimmed, not pruned, with merely the tall growths shortened to prevent the wind rocking them after planting, which is fatal, but if this has not been done, shorten anything longer than 18 in. to reduce the sail area. This leaves plenty to prune off in the spring in case the cold gets in the cut and causes dying back.

Modern roses are budded on briars planted behind a plough, so their roots are roughly 'L' shaped. If any are broken, snip off the damaged parts, and if some are too long to fit the hole, cut them short, do not bend them round. Hold the stem of the rose against the middle of one side of the hole, so that it has its 1 ft. clearance from the end and side of the bed, and extend the roots across the bottom of the hole in a fan. The bulge where the rose was budded can always be seen, and it may even have traces of bast tie showing. This should go 2 in. below the soil surface, and top soil may need to be heaped below it to get the position right, with the spread roots going down to the full 9-in. depth of the hole. Then fill back the soil and firm it round your well and truly planted rose.

Though this sounds a great deal of trouble, when other people trowel them in as quickly as planting bulbs, any rose is going to stay at least twelve years in the same place, and will repay the routine care of giving it a good start. Like almost any gardening operation, it is easier to do than describe.

The following spring they will need pruning, by cutting back the shoots to three or four eyes, or joints where a leaf came off, whichever one points away from the middle of the bush. The next season, merely shorten the shoots that grew the previous summer, taking off only about 3 in. below the flowering growth, and remove any that are weak or broken. In the third spring do this to the strong young smooth-barked shoots, but shorten the ones you left before to two or three eyes. This means that half the bush is pruned hard to grow new shoots for the following season.

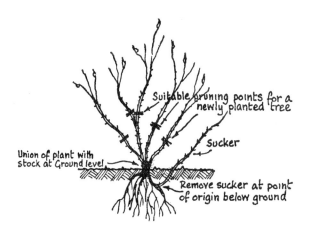

Fig. 14. Pruning a bush rose.

This is the best pruning system for the modern floribunda roses, and it should be done when red-tinted shoots begin to grow at the eyes. When a shoot is cut, winter rain can soak into the pith and the spores of the die-back fungus can enter, starting into growth in the spring when many roses have been lost by autumn pruning. The beginnings of growth show that the tide of spring has turned in your district and your roses are ready to heal and race ahead. If you delay too long there is, of course, some risk of bleeding and you waste the strength of your bushes as they grow shoots that will have to be cut away. The usual time is March or early April, but the new growth is the best guide.

The ideal tool for rose pruning is a knife, because a rose shoot is a hollow tube full of pith, and secateurs crush it. They can be used to take out thick old wood from *rambler* roses in the autumn but not for any young shoots. Always cut at a slant, $\frac{1}{4}$–$\frac{1}{2}$ in. above a bud, and slanting away from it to run off the rain.

Neither knife nor secateurs should be used for 'suckers' which are shoots either from the main stem, but below where it was budded, or direct from the roots. These come straight up out of the ground and have different thorns and foliage because they come from the stock, usually a briar, and if they are left on they will take most of the sap, and the rose will dwindle and die; while if they are cut they make more shoots and become thriving briar bushes. The only safe policy is to dig down beside them to where they join the root, grasp firmly in a gloved hand, and pull them sharply inwards so that they break away with some of the root like a 'heel' cutting. This takes away the shoot buds that have formed round it, and though it may be necessary to put a foot on the root to hold it, or grip the rose stem in the other gloved hand, it is better to take suckers out young at the root, rather than snip them off and have them grow large at the expense of the rose.

Hybrid tea, or 'H.T.' roses, as they are described in catalogues, are planted at the same spacing, in the same way and after the same bed preparation as floribundas, but need different pruning. Cut them back to the third or fourth eye, whichever points outwards in their first spring. The shoots that flower will grow from these eyes, and in the second spring cut them back in their turn to the third or fourth bud, on a routine that is the same every year and lets the bushes grow about 4 in. higher each season.

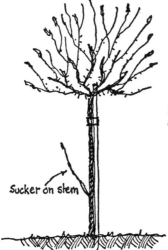

Fig. 15. Standard rose showing sucker on rugosa stem, which should be removed before it ruins the rose above.

Sucker on stem

As a general rule only three flowering shoots will develop on a rose branch each season, and if these are at the top of 1 ft. of left-on shoot the sap will have to pump this distance against increasing resistance as the branch thickens with the plant-equivalent of hardening arteries. If the three shoots are near the ground the rose wastes least energy on pushing sap against gravity to feed high shoots, and fattening old branches, so it has more to spare for flowering.

Those who inherit roses that have never been cut back hard should search for the vestiges of an eye near the bases of half the old shoots and cut them right down to it. Then spread a surface mulch of well-rotted manure and fork it under shallowly, as a tonic. The following spring do the other half, and cut back the new shoots that will have grown from the first branches cut down to the normal three or four eyes. Old roses treated like this either take on a new lease of life, or die and are better on the bonfire, though giving the manure treatment in the spring or summer before the first spring pruning will put up the survival chances even for very old cherished roses.

Normal bushes grow 4–6 in. higher each year so it pays to watch for any new shoots starting low among these annual lengths and to cut these back to single eyes, so they send up a strong shoot. With sufficient of these it is possible to remove the longer and knobbier chains of sections that make up the branches with any weak or badly placed shoots or any dead wood at spring pruning time.

The H.T. is the 'ordinary rose' familiar from chocolate box covers and there are a bewildering number of varieties, but, as with floribundas, those here have been chosen for toughness and mildew resistance. It is possible to collect roses, as I wrote above, like stamps, but the best effect comes from sticking to outstanding varieties in widely different colours. A bed of a dozen different reds will have nothing like such a good effect as one of contrasts.

Perhaps the best all-round light red, or rosy carmine, near the colour of the old 2½d. stamp, is 'Wendy Cussons', a bright red is 'Champs Elysées', while perhaps the finest dark red is 'Ellen Mary', with one of the richest scents of all.

Among the rose pinks, 'Ballet' and 'Eden Rose' are the best for vigour, disease resistance and generous flowering qualities, with 'Pink Favourite' and 'Prima Ballerina' good in the class with the outsides of the petals a deeper shade, while 'Gavotte' is a splendid pale one. 'My Choice' has petals yellow outside and pink within, strong stems, ample scent and is vigorous and free flowering, one of the very best of the modern roses. The other rose of today, as 'Madame

Butterfly' was of yesterday, is 'Super Star', glowing vermilion red, long flowering, fragrant and tough.

Good yellows were scarce in the past but now 'Ellinor LeGrice' is a splendid scented and vigorous deep yellow, while 'Sutter's Gold' is slightly deeper, even more scented, and with naturally fine long stems for cutting. Two paler shades, about hen canary yellow, are 'King's Ransom', and 'Dorothy Peach'. The latter has large, scented, shapely flowers, vigour, and disease-resistance, and looks very like 'Peace', but is smaller and freer flowering. Really outstanding white roses are scarce, and 'Virgo', which is strong and free flowering, but opens out flat as a semi-single, is about the best.

All these varieties can be cut for vases and this improves them, provided the stems are taken fairly short, about 8 in. Those who need length of stem should spread poultry manure between the rows and hose it in, ideally on a special bed for cutting. This is one of the reasons why nurseries show roses having far more stem than is ever available in their customers' gardens.

Length of flowering season with roses is largely gained by taking out the dead blooms, and those who can spare the time to remove the gone-over clusters from their floribundas and H.T.s will be well rewarded. Use kitchen or special garden scissors and snip the bloom off just above the first full-sized rose leaf, not the smaller size nearer the flower. The most essential need for a lasting display of very many summer flowers is not sprays, is not good soil or manures, but someone who cares enough for them to go round with a basket and a pair of scissors.

Standard roses today are nearly always budded on *Rosa rugosa* with slender black stems and slim thorns like those of raspberry canes, not the old-fashioned English Briar dug by gypsies from the hedges. Therefore their first essential is a stout stake, a metal one with a flat plate bolted to the bottom to prevent it blowing over in the wind and generously painted (and allowed to dry) with black or green bitumen paint. This is made to prevent steel rusting in the open and is rather cheaper than ordinary paint.

Unlike standard fruit or ornamental trees which thicken their trunks and stand unsupported, standard roses on rugosa need stakes. all their lives; these must be out all through every winter so wooden stakes have a far greater rotting risk than those for tomatoes, dahlias or runner beans which spend the worst half of the year safe in a dry shed. This applies still more to stakes for weeping standards, which have a rambler instead of a bush rose budded on the top of the tall rugosa stem, and to the posts for pergolas. As the rose grows larger and heavier the stake grows weaker with rotting at ground level.

It is worth buying an earthenware drainpipe, about 3 in. inside diameter and 1½–2 ft. long. Place the pipe upright on its narrow end and fill with sand or ashes topped with a piece of polythene, and then fill the bell-mouthed end with cement, ideally with a piece of crumpled-up wire netting as reinforcement. When it is set, empty out the sand or ashes to leave something like the solid-bottomed drainpipe that stood in front halls to take walking-sticks and umbrellas in the Victorian age. Stand your stakes point down in this and fill up with creosote, leaving them in overnight to soak up all they will. A gallon of creosote in a bucket does not come up high enough, but the drainpipe gives a thorough soaking to the buried and ground-level portion where fungi attack most. The rest of the stake should be creosoted with a brush in the normal way, and the whole allowed 48 hours to dry before use.

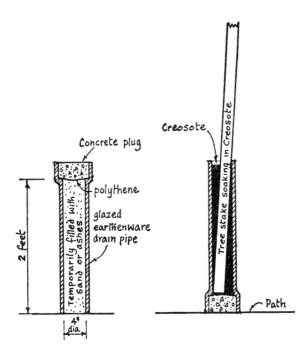

Fig. 16. Soaking tree stakes in creosote for maximum rot resistance.

The stake for a standard rose should go in the hole first and have the roots fitted round it, while replacement stakes should if possible be driven more deeply into the same hole, and tied, like trees, with either patent ties to give as they grow, cloth and string, or nylon stockings, for rugosa stems grow thicker with time though never enough to do without a stake.

All the leading H.T.s and even floribundas can be bought as standards, and their pruning is exactly the same as for bush specimens, but weeping standards need to have their long shoots shortened to half length after planting, and in later years their old wood removed in rotation, and excessively long shoots shortened. They require 'rose trainers' which are like open-wire umbrella frames that fix to the top of the stake so the long trailing shoots can be trained over them. Buy plastic-covered rather than galvanized, for replacing a rusted trainer under the thorns is an awkward job, but nothing like so bad as having a really splendid weeping standard that has got well established and is making a real show, snap off in a gale because the stake rotted. It is hardly necessary to say that all shoots that spring from the stems of standards should be twisted off like the suckers of bush roses before they can starve the rose at the top.

Rambler roses, with smaller flowers in clusters, and climbers which are extra-vigorous trailing forms of bush varieties, can be trained up stout wooden posts or pillars, over arches and trellis, but it is important to realize that they will last longer than their supports and that anything made of larch poles with the bark on is going to rot through at ground level very rapidly, so creosote well.

Their best place is the rose hedge, ideally on plastic-coated chain-link fence, and on the house side. A square trellis is their ideal support, for the ordinary diamond mesh is far too flimsy and awkward to tie on. Buy prepared (planed) 1 in. $\times$ 1$\frac{1}{2}$ in. timber, and cut this to lengths to run as high up the side of the house as the climber will go, and lengths to go across the area. Drill a hole to every 3 ft. of upright and countersink it to take a screw head, then brush on two coats of creosote with care to get it in the screw holes; and leave the timber to dry.

Fix the uprights 8 in. apart to the side of the house, with 2$\frac{1}{2}$-in. screws and Rawlplastic or Rawlplugs, then nail the cross pieces at 8 in. apart intervals all the way up, giving the effect of a large square trellis. The rose shoots can be tied round the cross pieces which stand 1 in. away from the wall and some can be held up by tucking behind them and over them like weaving a basket. Those who have seen a climber go high up a house without flowering until a branch is bent to avoid a window will see that the bending with this system increases flowering. Unlike flimsy trellis this type has the thickness to take the large-headed, heavily galvanized nails used for roofing felt that are ideal for tying climbers. These can be used to zigzag the young shoots where this is possible to increase their flowering ability. This type of trellis can be used for other climbers, but only roses gain by the zig-zag effect.

Tying and training is more important than pruning, and a pair of steps or a short ladder with two stout lengths of wood strutted from below to rest against the wall through the gaps in the rose is an asset for summer tying, and the care of all climbers.

The main tying is at pruning time, between October and November for ramblers and climbers because this consists mainly of cutting out old branches. The long, smooth, green-barked young shoots bear the finest flowers so these should only be shortened when this is abso-lutely necessary. Climbers will send out flower shoots from the older wood, so aim to remove a quarter of the weakest and most elderly branches every fourth year, cutting these back to 2–3 eyes of the base as though they were overgrown bush roses, so that there is always a new supply of long strong young shoots coming on to replace those that are wearing out.

Ramblers need harder pruning on the wall than in a hedge where their branches fill in the gaps by constant tying down. Look for the long branches that have the fewest and shortest new green shoots and cut these out down to the lowest strong side shoot, removing at least a third of the old wood each season. When pruning anything it is worth remembering the Bible: 'To him that hath shall be given, from him that hath not shall be taken away,' for cutting back the weak or over-age shoot to a single eye may make this grow a fine strong shoot to flower full length.

Though the roses recommended for hedges are excellent on house sides there are many more. Among the ramblers that give value in length of flowering season and toughness are 'Danse de Feu' with orange-red flowers about 3 in. across in clusters, and a glorious scent; 'Golden Showers', clear yellow, long-flowering and scented; 'New Dawn', the longest-flowering and most sweetly scented pink; 'Ham-burger Phoenix', a long-flowering bright crimson, well scented, and 'Leverkusen', a large-flowered semi-double, bright yellow and an ideal companion for 'Danse de Feu'.

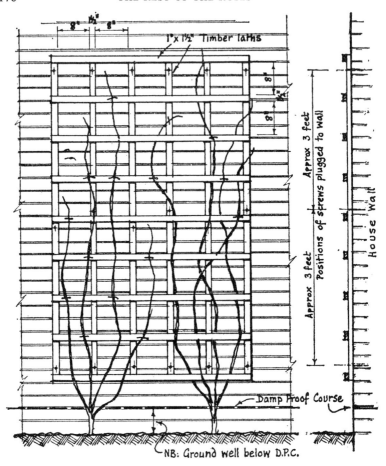

Fig. 17. Strong square trellis to take rambler or climbing roses highest up the house. Note the method of weaving the first young shoots for maximum flowering.

Those who chose 'Zephyrine Drouhin' for scent and thornlessness, with 'Kathleen Harrop' beside it as a pale pink, can add 'Crimson Glory', a deep red, richly scented, semi-double, with large clusters and a long flowering season, for its young shoots are almost without thorns. The three, like all well-scented ramblers, are good on trellis near sitting-room windows so that the fragrance drifts in on summer evenings when the casements are open.

Those who want a rose to look in at their bedroom windows should plant 'American Pillar' with massive clusters of deep pink single flowers with white centres, and prune it down only to the required level, for it is vigorous enough to support a splendid crop of blossom through up to 15 ft. of stem. The only other rose that will succeed near eaves' level is 'Climbing Lady Sylvia', a clear pale pink with fully double and beautifully fragrant flowers. Give it the same minimum pruning as 'American Pillar', tying in the shoots without removing anything until it has gone 12 ft. up, then cutting out only elderly or weak wood above that height. If it is pruned normally hard it grows nothing but more wood, but it is glorious given its head up a house, where it can live twenty years. The bare stem below the flowering top growth will take annual or other not too powerful climbers competing for food and moisture in the bed below.

The other climbers are less powerful and 10 ft. is about their maximum height. 'Guinee' (recommended for hedges) is one of the longest-flowered, perhaps the darkest red rose we have, one of the most deeply scented and really splendid against a white house wall. 'Soldier Boy' is a bright red single, scented, vigorous, and about the longest-flowering rose yet known, for it can start in May and finish in November. 'Climbing Ellinor LeGrice', or 'Golden Dawn', are perhaps the best yellows of this type with a summer and an autumn crop, rather than a long show.

The best roses to cover a trellis or fence for a screen to hide something are the Wichurianas which are very nearly evergreen, and vigorous ramblers that need little pruning. 'Alberic Barbier' has large clusters of pale buff flowers that fade to white, 'Emily Gray' has bigger semi-single buff flowers and larger bronzy foliage which does not hang on so well, and 'William Allan Richardson' has an even better scent, with two crops of buff flowers instead of one. Prune them by taking out the oldest branches if they grow too big for their supporting framework. All three are good cover to trail down rough banks. Other varieties can give the weeds too much of a chance to grow when their leaves are off in winter. 'Alberic Barbier' is the nearest to an evergreen rose.

Newly planted climbers and ramblers, however, need to have their shoots shortened to half, unless this has been done before they leave the nursery, for though these are left on normally, they will produce leaf growth freely and demand food and water that the roots will not be able to supply in the first summer. The bush rose is cut back hard because it has less strength, but even an 'American Pillar' is handicapped by being trained whole up the wall. When almost any woody plant is moved, its income from cut roots falls drastically, so those who feel, 'I mustn't be too hard on it when it has just been planted' should think of their rambler roses as though they were human. They will have to spend their first summer after moving house with a smaller pay packet. Cut back the shoot equivalent to a cut in smoking, a missed summer holiday, or a postponed new T.V., and they will get established all the quicker.

The narrow beds where ramblers grow need exactly the same preparation as beds for bush roses, but those against houses need more, for the higher a rose goes the more foliage it will have that must be breathing out water through every summer. Often, too, this bed will be very dry and full of builders' rubbish.

First fork out the top spit which should be good soil, but may be merely a thin layer spread to hide the rubbish. If the next spade depth is reasonable, shovel this back too, going down level with the side of the house. Then dig out and wheel away the lower subsoil, dig humus, bonemeal and hoof and horn into the bottom layer before shovelling back the next spit, plus humus and bonemeal, and the final top soil.

The object of wheeling away the worst bottom soil and adding an extra humus dressing is to ensure that the bed when it settles will be lower than the damp course, instead of raised against the house. This will make it possible to run a hose in the bed which should be at least 1 in. below path or lawn level. One way of making sure that your ramblers and climbers have a good start is by burying a large flowerpot beside each, which can be filled with water two or three times on a summer evening to get the moisture right down to the roots by the traditional trick used for dahlias and tomatoes.

After the second season the pot watering will no longer be necessary but those who have good farmyard manure available should spread it 1 in. thick on the 3 square feet round the base of their tall climbing and rambler roses in spring. This is as good a policy for hard-working roses as it is for fruit trees.

13

The Garden Frame

The cold frame described in Chapter 2 is very much more useful to beginners than a greenhouse, and far more value than the dark and dripping lean-to conservatory against so many old town houses. Though there are now metal and fibre glass frames these are almost always inferior to wooden, because their designers try to make them look 'modern' rather than fit for the job that gardeners need them for.

From the end of September until late May the task of the lights will be to let the sunlight through the glass and hold in the heat radiating back again, for this passes through rather less easily. In summer this heat can build up and scorch seedlings, so the lights need shading with a coat of whitewash on the inside (where rain will not wash it off) to be removed in September when it is no longer needed.

A metal frame, with glass sides and lights hinged in the middle, lets in too much light, and gets too hot in summer, while it will always be awkward to shade. Cheap asbestos or expensive fibre glass frames are often made with large, loose panes of glass fitted across them instead of lights. These cannot be propped up for ventilation in summer and the panes can blow off and smash, apart from the breakage risk in handling them.

Though polythene and other plastics are useful for emergency repairs, they are unsuitable for covering frame lights, for they yellow in sunlight, grow green algae, and sag in the middle so that the condensation moisture gathers there and drips steadily on some unlucky plant, instead of trickling to the lower side of the frame out of harm's way, as it does with an ordinary glazed light. The worst 'glass substitute' is the type reinforced with thin wire net, for this rusts and cuts down the light more drastically than ever.

There is no real substitute for glass, which is cheap, easily replaceable, lasting and easily cleaned. The fine siftings from coal ashes are an excellent abrasive for removing whitewash from the inside of glassed lights, and town soot off the outsides, used with hot water and a scrubbing brush.

Site your frame and provide drainage below it as described in Chapter 2, remembering that it will need a path along the low side in front, and space at the back so that the lights can be slid back and tilted up. A standard cedarwood cold frame, 6 ft. long and 4 ft. wide, with two lights 4 ft. by 3 ft. costing about £20 (1974) will often hold more plants than the smallest size of greenhouse, because the path area is outside, and there is no temptation to use it as an extra shed by wasting its more expensive space for storing pots and spare seed trays.

It is also very much more cheaply heated with so much less air-space inside, and glass surface, than a greenhouse, and apart from convenience in going out to open the lights or to water, siting the frame near the house is easiest for electricity.

This is by far the best frame-heating method, and if one already has Night Storage central heating, the frame supply can be from the same meter and use this cheap off-peak supply, for frames need heating mostly at night. The question is whether the advantage is worth the investment of the cost of the gadgetry, for between April and September the sun will make an unheated frame as hot as a heated one. Where it is desired to keep geraniums, fuchsias, heliotrope and other bedding plants through the winter to save buying new each year, a heated frame can earn its keep, but otherwise this is only useful for quite a short time in spring, when heat makes it possible to raise bedding plants and tomatoes.

There are many electric propagators on the market, consisting of a metal or plastic box containing heating elements in which a seed tray will fit with a plastic dome on top of it. These cost about £5 each and though they get hot enough inside to germinate tomatoes, cucumbers, lobelia, petunias, salvias, salpiglossis and tobacco plants as early as February, they hold only one box at a time, and when the seedlings are up they have to move into the relatively cold frame.

This type of gadget is ideal to use inside a heated greenhouse to provide a small area of extra warmth for seedlings or cuttings, like leaf cuttings of begonias or African violets, or the seedlings listed later which need real heat to start them early. It is less suitable for a frame, which needs something simple to warm its relatively small airspace enough to winter a few part-hardy plants, and to start seedlings moderately early and grow them on.

The greatest advantage an amateur gardener can get from his

frame is in raising his own tomato plants, for though he can buy the box or two of petunias or lobelia he needs from a local nursery, no nursery or garden centre will stock tomato varieties bred to ripen early outside. They prefer to sell surplus greenhouse varieties, which ripen at least three weeks later than outdoor kinds, have less taste, and ripen less well between wadding in a dark drawer when picked green at the end of the season.

He does not, however, need his plants till the second week in May —if he can accumulate enough large cardboard boxes to fit over his plants at night if frost threatens—or the first week in June, and he can do this with quite simple heating, if he sows in March when most of the work will be done by the rising tide of spring.

The bottom heat to warm seed boxes into life can come from a 20-ft., 75-watt soil-warming cable, heavily insulated with plastic, which should be coiled round under one of the lights and buried 1 in. deep in the ash drainage layer. This needs no transformer and it can be connected to a socket in the frame side to take a three-pin plug leading waterproof electric cable to a 13-amp fuse plug indoors through a hole drilled in a window-frame, unless there is an outside supply for potting shed or workshop.

It is always advisable to have any electrical gadgets installed by the electricity company, as it is not only risky to tamper with a 240-volt mains supply when you are standing on wet soil, but you can easily cost yourself a considerable sum in making a metal fence 'live', or wasting current electrolyzing water to oxygen and hydrogen with leakage from a poor connection. If you are using the Night Storage system which halves the current cost you must have the company's men to connect through the house to the separate meter.

A soil-warming cable of this size costs about £7, and heating the air inside the frame costs about the same. It is possible to hang a second cable round the sides and ends inside the frame, but even if a 40-ft. cable is looped round, this is only 150 watts and not enough to hold a hard frost. The best and safest space heaters for a small frame are tubular ones.

These look like hot-water pipes but are 2-in. diameter, rustless aluminium alloy tubes with resistance wires round mica or fireclay inside. One 6 ft. long to go along the back, complete with brackets to mount it low on the wooden side, costs about £6; and as these take 60 watts a foot, this gives you 360, which should keep frost out of the geraniums, and keep tomato plants growing happily.

These two heaters between them will use about as much current as

half of one-bar electric fire when they are on. They would pay to connect to the off-peak rate meter if one was fitted already, but not if one
must be installed for them as there is a quarterly charge of about £2
on meters. Here a small thermostat is better value, costing about £3
to buy outright, which will cut off the current on warm nights or
when the sun comes out hot in the middle of the day.

The routine of frame management is the same whether it is heated
or not, and the electric heating is only on until about April or mid-
May if tomato or cucumber plants are grown. The tubular heaters
need no maintenance, but just stay fixed at the back, yet it pays to
dig up the soil-warming cable, unplug it and coil it up to hang in
safety, not in a box, because sharp bends can crack the insulation.

All seed trays are prepared in the same way, but today these are
frequently plastic. These nest nicely into each other, but they should
be lifted by both ends, because they are bendable and the soil can be
squeezed away from the sides to leave a permanent slot down which
water drains, so the box never gets properly watered.

Wooden seed trays now cost about 20p each; kipper boxes at
5p are good substitutes, but strong, small cardboard boxes can
usually be obtained free from sweetshops. They should not be longer
than 15 in., wider than 8, or deeper than 4. Corrugated or flimsy
cardboard is useless.

Buy a $\frac{1}{2}$- or $\frac{1}{4}$-in. hollow-head punch from an ironmonger and
hammer out drainage holes, roughly one every 3 in., with the bottom
held against firm wood; this is neater, easier and does less to weaken
the box than jabbing with scissors. Paint the boxes with Brunswick
black to dry waterproof and last one season. On a flat surface the
water cannot escape through the holes, so the boxes should stand on
the fine gravel on greenhouse staging; but the ash layer in a frame
provides ample drainage.

Start with a layer of cinders or small stones on the box bottoms,
then fill level with 2 in. of soil. John Innes compost is easily bought in
bags, but is usually so dry that it needs watering and shovelling about
till just damp enough to cling together when gripped and to firm
evenly in the box with the fingers.

Smooth the surface and flatten with a block of wood so that the
seeds—sown thinly, aiming at $\frac{1}{2}$ in. for each—lie equally deep. Hide
them only with fine soil, then water with the rose on, taking care that
the box is level so that the seeds do not wash to one end; there should
be a $\frac{1}{4}$ in. of room for water.

This standard system serves for tomato seeds, and the varieties that are worth the installation of heating for growing are firstly 'Harbinger', with the finest flavour of all and at least a fortnight's faster ripening than 'Moneymaker' or any other greenhouse kind, even the new hybrids; and it is the perfect 'drawer ripener'. In good seasons their first picking can be in mid-July and in an average, half the crop can be picked before 10th September.

The other variety is 'Outdoor Girl', which is a week or ten days faster still, and is often the only outdoor variety to ripen any fruit in the open in really cold, wet summers. This is a very short-jointed kind, needing straw under the bottom trusses to keep the lowest fruits off the ground, and inclined to ripen all together in October. The third choice tomato is 'Ailsa Craig', which will ripen nearly as well off the plant as 'Harbinger', but is not so early in the open. This is the best for those without a heated frame for it can often be bought as a plant, as it is without the thin skin that makes 'Harbinger' a poor traveller, and therefore useless commercially, though splendid where its only journey is up the garden path.

In sodden Septembers it is 'Harbinger's' superior ripening ability from green that converts outdoor tomatoes from a gamble into a storing crop like apples. They should keep until January, and then those bottled in brine from September picking can take over. 'Outdoor Girl', because its fruit runs smaller, and can come on all together in the autumn, is a rather better bottling tomato.

The longer tomatoes stay unpicked in wet autumns, the greater the risk of blight, brown rot and moulds, so snatch a day when the fruit is dry and pick everything down to pullet's-egg size. Think of their skins as egg shells, easily 'smashed' by bruising or by the removal of stalks, which let in the bacteria of decay.

The best method of ripening is in a drawer in a not-too-warm bedroom. You need 3 yd. of draper's wadding (normally used for lining dressing-gowns) for a drawer 2 ft. long. At 18p a yard for 18-in. width it is cheaper than cotton wool and does not catch in stalks.

Lay it on the drawer and set out the greenest tomatoes, stalks up and not touching: fold over 2 ft. more and add a layer of riper tomatoes, finishing with a final fold of wadding. The wadding holds the humidity the tomatoes need and a normal bedroom will give the 54–56° temperature for slow ripening. Pick them over every other day to remove those that are ripe and throw away failures. At the end of the season fold up the wadding—it lasts for years.

If the tomatoes are sown thinly and stand over the soil-warming cable they should be up in about ten days, with their long seed leaves held together by the seed case. When they have thrown this off, and two small real tomato-shape leaves can be seen in the middle, it is time to pot them. There are many kinds of pot today, plastic, paper and compressed peat, but the original clay type have the advantage that they can be used over and over again, and these are the wisest choice for tomatoes.

John Innes No. 1 potting soil is best for them, and with only a dozen or two it is worth buying for potting, but a mixture of one part of sand, two of leafmould and three of good loam grew tomatoes well before the John Innes recipe or soil sterilization were invented. If there is a stack of turf at the bottom of the garden, piled grass side down to rot, this will be good loam after it has been stacked a year. The pots will, however, need weeding, for home-made mixtures are without the great advantage of sterilization to kill the weed seeds.

Toss a few chips of broken pot, small stones or little cinders into the bottom of the pot, then a handful of soil, and hold the seedling tomato in the middle, taking care not to squeeze the tender stem, and arranging the spread of its roots 1 in. below the pot rim. Then fill in with soil and firm it over the roots till the young plant stands upright, water it with a fine rose, using water with the chill off (add a bit to the can from hot-water tap or even kettle, or stand the can in the frame if there is room, to keep the shock of mains-cold water off the leaves) and stand it at the back next to the heater and over the soil-warming wires.

The back two rows will always be warmest and the tomatoes can be spread along there, with watering more and more as they start to grow, and spaced wider apart as their leaves spread. Later they can move to the front, and finally out under whatever protection can be afforded. 'Harbinger' is a good cold greenhouse kind, for planting in early May, and anyone who sold his to neighbours would have a circle of clamouring customers by the following spring. Though tomato seeds are few in the packet, most gardeners need about a couple of dozen at the most; so it should be remembered that those bought one winter can be spread over the three springs that follow. There is no gain in sowing thickly to 'use up the packet'.

Cucumbers also need heat to start them, and the cooler kinds that suit amateur gardeners are rarely buyable. Cucumbers and tomatoes are awkward companions, for tomatoes want the greenhouse windows open for fresh air, and cucumbers need them shut for moist heat. The answer is a cooler cucumber, and the Japanese climbing variety will share a small greenhouse with tomatoes, and is hardy enough for a sheltered sunny border in the open, or a frame that is not required for summer seed and cutting raising.

Unlike ridge kinds grown in the open like marrows, it has a real cucumber flavour, and though the fruits are miniatures of 6 or 8 in. long they make up on quantity compared with fewer monsters from varieties that are happier hotter. Plants are scarce but seed is easily raised in April without heat, or sown in March with soil-warming cable in a frame.

Sow edgeways and $\frac{1}{2}$ in. deep, one in each clay or card pot, then water once and cover with newspaper till all are up and wearing their seed cases like hats. Replace the paper at night if frost threatens and keep them watered as they grow, with always a little from the hot tap to take the chill off cold canfuls.

Dig holes 1 ft. square and deep, spaced 3 ft. between centres for outdoor planting, and fill these with 9 in. of compost or manure, or trodden lawn mowings with fish-meal or poultry guano mixed in generously to give the rich feeding and moisture-holding humus cucumbers need outdoors. Put back 6 in. of soil, mounding in to allow for sinking as the mowings decay, ready for planting a fortnight later in early June.

Plant with a trowel, leaving the soil unbroken round the roots, and water well. Then set a tripod of beansticks or dahlia stakes over each. When the shoots spread, tie one to each stick and they will climb with strong tendrils, but tie again if shoots flop, for the modern variety has larger fruit than the Japanese original. In the greenhouse dig the manure in about a week before planting 30 in. apart when the seedlings are 1 ft. long.

Thrust in a cane by each plant to lead them to strings tied from wire to wire at 6-in. intervals up to the roof ridge. Ordinary kinds grow side branches, which should be cut shorter after the second flower which has a small cucumber behind it, for they can rear two on a shoot, but in frames with less room shorten to one only.

The Japanese variety needs shortening only if it invades tomato territory, and its fruits hang small and many for least tying and trouble—the coolest cucumber of all.

Ridge cucumber seedlings are sown singly the same way, and so are marrows, but though these appreciate a heated start, they are just as easy in a cold frame. The object here is to sow them and have them growing fast ready to move outside when frost risk is over. If they are sown too early they may be hard, yellow-green and flowering before the weather is fit for them. A wide-mouthed polythene bag, spread on sticks, is a frost protection that can stay on through the daytime, though the cardboard box trick for outdoor tomatoes serves also for ridge cucumbers and marrows. It pays to keep a gardening diary so that you have a rough guide to the sowing dates that suit your local conditions.

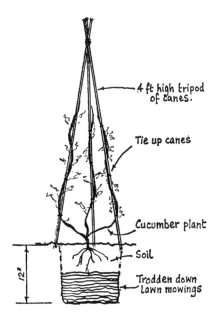

Fig. 18. Japanese outdoor cucumber on tripod above lawn-mowing humus holder.

Cabbages and cauliflowers also pay for sowing in February in the cold frame, or a heated one for an even quicker start. This is because only the most common kinds are sold at the time when most people need them. 'Summer Monarch', the fast round cabbage that is bred for eating raw in salads, with a fine nutty flavour that makes it rather better value in a small garden than lettuce, is well worth sowing under glass, and 'Early Snowball' cauliflowers, large enough to plant by April, will be ready for eating by July.

Sow them like the tomatoes, and, though their seed is not large and flat, if it can have the same roughly 1-in.-apart spacing the plants will grow strong and sturdy without handling until they can go outside. Because small brown seeds are hard to see against brown soil, whiten the flattened surface with lime which the cabbage tribe like anyway, and the seeds will stand out clearly so that any too close can be moved with a pencil point. Cabbage tribe seed keeps six years, so thin sowing pays.

Where tomatoes and the bedding plants that want heat are raised as well as cabbages that go out at least two months sooner, there is a need for more 'hardening-off room'. This is somewhere that provides easier conditions than the open for acclimatization, and releases room in the frame where everything is demanding more space.

A good way round this problem is by fixing one side of a piece of clear polythene 2 ft. wide to the side of a shed with 1-in. nails through a strip of sawn timber like builders' lath or a dahlia stake and securing the other side in the same way to a long and fairly heavy stake. Level the ground beside the shed, or spread ashes if it runs beside a cambered path, set out the boxes for hardening and lay the stake along their outsides so the polythene stretches like a lean-to tent over them. The condensation will run down the inside, rain or even eaves' drip down the outside, and two stout door hooks in the shed side, with eyes in the stake, will hold the temporary polythene shelter flat against the shed at watering times. Ends of some kind are essential. Wooden triangles, or temporary piles of loose bricks are better than triangular frames covered with polythene, for these will be light and blow off, but the polythene is gripped all the way along by the *sawn* surface of the nailed-through timber, so it will not flap and tear away as it will from drawing-pins.

The flower seeds that require real heat to start are all tiny, and are best sown mixed with fine bonemeal as recommended for the finer perennial seeds. Prepare the boxes as for tomatoes and sow the mixture thinly, with a very thin soil covering. With all fine seeds it is best to stand the boxes or pots in a container of water and let them stand and soak till the soil surface is damp, then set them level outside to drain before standing them in the frame. Take care that they sit level, and label each one with the date, for this helps to build up your knowledge of how early or late you can sow something in your particular frame in your district and get away with it. All frames vary according to shelter, but still more by district and season.

When the seedlings are up and their true leaves are showing clearly, as well as their round-ended seed leaves or 'cotyledons', prepare other boxes, firming the soil and flattening them like those for seed sowing. Their soil need not be John Innes potting soil, for bedding plants can manage on a weaker mixture. Four parts of garden soil to one of sand and peat or leafmould will be good enough for most bedding plants.

Make a small dibber from some non-splintering wood. The point and 3 in. of a wooden knitting-needle (sizes one to five) is ideal. Round off the flat cut surface with sandpaper to prevent getting blisters from this essential tool in the operation of 'pricking out'.

First use the dibber to make a row of holes about $\frac{1}{2}$ in. in from the side of the seed tray, then hold your first seedling over the middle of the first hole with the roots hanging down inside, and firm the soil back round it with the dibber point so it stands upright. Lobelia are tiny seedlings and can go in bunches of three, with seven rows of ten to a standard seed tray, and this spacing, or seven rows of nine, making five dozen and three spares to a box, is about standard in the nursery trade where millions of seedlings are pricked out annually.

When the box is filled, water it carefully or soak it from below and put it back in the frame to recover. The seeds that need heat, especially lobelia and petunias, have seedlings on the tender side and these appreciate a week above the warming wires if they are sown in February, up in a fortnight, and pricked out in March. Then they can move over to the unheated part of the frame, in April to the polythene-covered 'annexe' to harden off, and be finally planted in May. Those who wish to grow them without heat should wait till early April when there is heat enough in sunlight to start them; and carry out the same routine, but with planting in June.

However few seeds there may seem to be in a packet, if they are thinly sown they will fill box after box, and one of the most important lessons to learn is to throw things away. Petunias should be planted finally 9 in. apart each way, lobelia 6 in., and salpiglossis 1 ft. Salvias are larger and best treated like tomato plants, potting in size 60 (3-in.) pots, with final planting in May, 1 ft. apart each way.

Because spring frame space is limited, the bedding annuals should be chosen on the same principle as the vegetable plants. Raise the kinds that are scarce, or new, or too expensive to buy enough to make a real show.

One of the most rewarding of the heat-demanding annuals is heliotrope, which is very rarely sold, though the modern dark blue purples are perhaps the most splendidly scented of all bedding plants. These were once raised expensively from cuttings as lobelia and salvias were, but 'Lemoine's Giant', a strong dark blue, or 'Madame Bruant', deep violet with a white eye, are among the newer French hybrids bred to flower well the first year from seed.

Sow them with the other heat-lovers in February, and they should be up in a fortnight, ready to pot in 60s when they are 1 in. across the leaves. Pinch out the growing points when the young plants are 4 in. high, so they grow side shoots which should themselves be pinched back when they reach this length. They should be hardened off in April ready to plant 12 in. apart in May.

Zinnias need this treatment, with the large seeds sown $\frac{1}{4}$ in. deep in March, and the seedlings potted as soon as they can be handled, and stopped to make them grow bushy when they are 3 in. high. This gaudy bedding plant has lost favour since the need to cut costs made nurserymen grow it in boxes where it sulks from root damage. Though the dahlia-flowered hybrids are rather stiff and formal, the new 'Pompoms' (Z. pumila hybrids) are compact and about 1 ft. high. 'Pink Buttons', salmon, and 'Red Buttons', scarlet, have $1\frac{1}{2}$-in.-across double flowers, and 'Thumbelina' hybrids in yellow, pink, scarlet, orange, white and even lavender have flowers this size on neat bushes 6 in. high. They should be hardened off in May and planted out at the end of the month about 1 ft. apart, or closer with plenty, to flower until September ends.

The same routine suits verbenas, which can be pricked out in boxes in six rows of eight because they are larger than most bedding plant seedlings, hardened off and planted 1 ft. apart spacing in early May. The compacta type with medium blue 'Amethyst', coral-pink 'Compliment', salmon-pink 'Miss Susie Double', scarlet 'Dazzler', and 'Splendour', purple with a white eye, are 7-in.-high bushes, while the Giant or Mammoth types are 1 ft. high and their larger flowerheads make excellent cut flowers. They flower from June right on till October, and though they are perennials, they make the best show in their first summer, so it never pays to keep them a second season.

The last of the heated frame demanders are vegetables. Though celery plants can usually be bought quite easily, they can be sown thinly in a box over the soil-warming wires as February ends, and pricked out six rows of eight in a seed tray when their true leaves are $\frac{1}{2}$ in. long, ready to harden off and plant in early June. 'Golden Self-blanching' is the early one which needs no trenches or earthing up, but is killed by frost about October, while there are many other white and green varieties that last for winter salads till about January. 'American Winter Green' is one of the newer varieties, and 'Standard Bearer', an almost red 'pink' celery. The turnip-rooted celery, or celeriac, with the stem base swollen to cut up for cooking as a celery-flavour root vegetable, or for soups, is grown exactly the same way, but is hardier, and can be sown without heat in March.

Though those without warmth can sow these more tender bedding plants in late March or even early April when sun heat will replace electricity, this brings them very late. Without heat it is best to stick to the hardier kinds that will only be slightly smaller for their colder start.

The bushy annual *Phlox nana compacta* varieties are particularly good sown in late February or early March. They could be called 'Russell Phlox Drummondii' with new colours and habit, growing 9 in. high with stems that need no staking, and flower heads like border phloxes but flatter and neater.

There are mixtures, but 'Fireball', scarlet; 'Snowball', white; 'Meteor', salmon pink; 'Rose Cardinal', rose pink; 'Isabellina', buff-yellow, and 'Dark Blue', give the full colour-range so far, for window-boxes, tubs or beds. Here they go 8 in. apart each way to mass solid for least weeding, and as well as replacing antirrhinums for the rust-ridden, they can sow outside in April as a change from clarkia, though flowering later than from boxes.

Prick them out to the standard sixty-three a box spacing that suits the mass of bedding plants. Antirrhinums are excellent from March sowing, with a wide range of varieties, and the new rust-resistant kinds now make it possible for gardeners to enjoy them as they did in the 1930's. Asters are perhaps the most popular of all bedding plants, and the easiest to buy, but if they are raised at home, use steam-sterilized John Innes potting soil to prick them out in, as well as the seed soil for sowing, because this beats the wilt disease that can slaughter them at seedling stage. This applies also to stocks (Matthiola) of all varieties, especially the ten-week bedding type, because they suffer from damp-off fungus, which can be treated with Cheshunt Compound, buyable at any really good garden shop, but is best avoided by sticking to John Innes for all seed sowings.

Alyssum for edging, both ordinary white and 'Pink Heather' and purple 'Royal Carpet', are among the easiest from March sowing, and so are the longest-flowered bedding plants of all, the French and African marigolds. These have quite large, slender seeds, and it pays to use lime on the surface as for cauliflowers and to space them with a dibber point so that they need no pricking out. Plant them 6–8 in. apart each way in early May, and they will blaze till October.

There are a number of annuals that resent the root breakage from digging out of the boxes, so they are usually sown where they are to flower. March sowing in small pots or cheap peat or cardboard ones brings flowers sooner and gives them time to wait under glass till spring flowers finish, and yet move out of the cold greenhouse before tomato plants move in.

Each pot needs some small cinders in the bottom for drainage, then filling and firming to within $\frac{1}{2}$ in. of the rim with John Innes seed compost or four parts sifted garden soil to one each of peat and sand. Flatten the firmed soil with a round bottle-bottom, sow a pinch of seed or set three large ones in a penny's space in the middle and cover with soil to matchstick thickness.

Water to the brim to start the seed, then only when the soil is dry, and thin the seedlings to the best in each pot when they are growing strongly. As they grow larger they need more water, but if cardboard pots are handled, the soil can squeeze from the side and let waterings waste. So stand the pots on coal slack grit in the shallow trays obtainable from the greengrocer. Move them outside to harden and back when frost threatens.

Balsams (Impatiens) do well this way; both the tall camellia-flowered types and the new 6-in. dwarfs, 'Salmon Rose' and 'Leigritza', are good annuals to flower in shade. Tall annual kinds gain most, especially the 4-ft. 'Gloriosa' daisies with flowers 6 in. across in shades of yellow, orange, and brown.

As the sunlight strengthens through April and the frame begins to warm up in the middle of the day, the lights should be propped open to lower the temperature. Those who are interested can get a maximum and minimum thermometer and hang it on one end to be set each morning, and see how the temperature has been. It should range between 55°–65° F., though inside, next to the warming wires, it should be 60°–65° F.

A cold frame temperature will always go down at night and warm up by noon, so begin by propping the lights open about 2 in. for two hours in the middle of the day, and increase the openings as the mid-day temperatures rise. A useful prop is a piece of 2 in. × 4 in. timber 8 in. long, which can be used three ways as a prop, and the best way to obtain a couple of short pieces of this is to ask on a building site when the carpenters are putting the roof on. A timely tip will secure a store, cut accurately to size by a craftsman, from the odd ends.

A blazing May might bring scorching sunlight, but through this month, even with tomatoes, the lights can be slid right back in day-time and replaced at night to keep the frost out. Finally, when the bedding plants are cleared, the tomatoes and outdoor cucumbers planted and the lights whitewashed on the insides, the frame is ready for the next phase of its three-stage programme for the year.

If the frame is only going to be needed to nurse a few geraniums through the winter, it can be filled with a mixture of two parts each of soil and leafmould and one of sand, firmed and levelled to within 3 in. of the glass on the other side. Then plant three Japanese or ridge cucumber plants along the back of the frame, assuming it is a standard 6 ft. × 4 ft. size. Trim them as suggested earlier, and give plenty of water, keeping a temperature of 60°–65° F., by propping open the lights if it gets too hot at midday. Water well, and damp down the leaves with a rosed can on hot days, giving twice-weekly waterings with a proprietary liquid manure when the cucumbers are seen lurking among the leaves.

It is likely that by August and September there will be more cucumbers than any family can eat. These small Japanese cucumbers are excellent pickled like gherkins, and those who prefer pickled to fresh cucumbers can give themselves a large crop by constant picking as soon as the fruits reach 3 in. long.

Where there are no bedding plants like geraniums or fuchsias to keep through the winter, the soil can be left in after the cucumbers finish as September ends, to grow a crop of lettuce. Sow 'Winter Density' (cos) or 'Trocadero Improved' (cabbage) in early August in the open, and move the thinly sown plants—about 1 in. across the spread leaves—into the frame, spacing the cos kind 6 in. apart each way, and the cabbage kinds 8. If they are packed closer they are more inclined to rot each other. Both kinds will heart up under glass, but need careful watering between the plants to keep them moving, for Botrytis disease can strike if they get dry. Heat can be turned on to keep them moving in the autumn, but there is room for so few relatively that all will be eaten by the time the soil is shovelled out to clear the ashes ready for the first sowings of spring.

Unless a frame is made without a drainage layer, which makes it unsuitable for bedding plants and other seedlings and cuttings. it will not grow tomatoes well. They gain only about a week compared with planting under cardboard boxes or other protection, and they grow too tall to benefit from the lights in summer.

The best second stage is growing the many seedling herbaceous plants, alpines, and shrubs, which could be sown in the open, but grow away far faster under glass, and the many others with tiny seeds that are safer sown in the frame in boxes or pots.

There will usually be far fewer in the packets of these than bedding plants, and they may take a long time to come up. Large flowerpots are very much better for seedlings to wait about in than boxes, and the best are sizes 24 or 32 (8½- or 6-in. diameter), which are now little used by nurserymen for chrysanthemum growing, and are well worth buying cheaply to store. Shallow clay pans are even better but usually more expensive.

Fill the pot half full with small coke or cinders, as rather better drainage material than broken flowerpots, and the other half with John Innes seed soil, firmed and levelled with a flat bottle-bottom to leave 1 in. below the rim. Then sow on the flattened surface and cover with a ¼ in. or less of fine soil. A small sieve made by tacking perforated zinc to a wooden frame about 6 in. square is ideal.

A useful trick for those who attempt seeds that may be slow germinating because they are stale, like gentians or rhododendrons, is to sift coal dust through the perforated zinc sieve, wash it under the tap to remove the finest dust, let it dry in the sun and sift it again over the seed. The tarriness of the coal dust prevents the growth of moss and liverwort on the soil surface. This is extra useful for seeds of species that hate lime, such as members of the Erica family.

Opening any seed packet for the first time is a surprise, and those who take a chance on a catalogue and order shrubs, alpines or perennials for an exciting gamble on unfamiliar names, have a series of shocks. Some packets will hold about nine monsters, and others only a pinch of snuff. The last needs fine bonemeal mixing and then thin sowing, while any seed large enough to handle should be spaced out to 1 in. apart or more.

These seedlings will be far ahead of any sown in May in the open. They gain from the heat—controlled by the shading—and the protection from wind, as well as by watering from below and water when they need it only, not the droughts and thunderstorms that some summers can bring. If they are sown thinly enough they need no pricking out, and the fastest growers can go out as suggested earlier where the early potatoes have released room, in August or September, with a watered start.

Those who do not wish to grow bedding plants can sow perennials, alpines and shrubs in the spring for May and June planting, which gives a chance for some to flower and be discarded. At the other end of the season, there is no point in planting seedlings later than mid-September because they will not have time to make many roots before winter.

These are best potted into 60s and stood back into the frame to keep growing through the winter. As all should be hardy there is little gain from running the heater, but the warmth that the glass will hoard from even winter sunlight will keep them moving, with watering only when they are dry, so they can be moved out into a hardening-off shelter in late February and March, ready for planting when they have got used to colder conditions. The polythene lean-to 'shedside shelter' can be hooked up in the daytime and lowered at night to give the same effect as that of a frame with lights gradually propped open, because by planting-time spring seeds will clamour for sowing.

One of the problems of seed frames in summer is ants, which get in through the drainage holes and nest among the roots. The best way of getting rid of them is by mixing equal parts of icing sugar and borax thoroughly and sprinkling this inside the frame where the ants are likely to find it. Borax is a poison so should be kept away from children, though it was once allowed in sausages as a food preservative. However, it is cheap and effective against ants and many other modern food additives may well have new spheres of usefulness as pesticides.

Among the perennials that can be sown in July and August are pentstemons and antirrhinums. The last are perennials on the borderline of hardiness, and if potted in September or October and grown through the winter with stoppings to keep them bushy, they will make good plants for an early start the next season. This allows a choice of varieties, but pentstemons can be bought as bedding plants and left in as directed earlier.

Those who take a crop of new hardy seedlings every summer add great interest to their gardening, and however rare or difficult a plant may be by repute, it is worth a gamble if it sounds good and you have a place for it. Even if only one or two survive these may be all there is room for, and no one today can afford to experiment to find plants that are permanent acquisitions in a garden on any scale, except from seed. Chapter 16 contains lists of perennials and shrubs which are 'odds-on' gambles from seed.

Species will come true from seed, but hybrids and varieties will not, and the only way to increase named varieties of anything is by 'vegetative means'—division, cutting and root-cuttings. Most divisions can be made in the open ground, the traditional way of increasing herbaceous plants, but in October it is possible to grow a large stock of aubrietia and other alpines by potting divisions.

Take three strands of aubrietia, bunch the heads together, cut off about 6 in. of stem, and pot them firmly in 60s with the leaf rosette sitting firmly on the soil surface. Water well to start them, and then only if they are dry. Under the washed clean lights of the frame they will have rooted enough to plant by April. This easy method suits the mossy saxifrages, and most carpeters, including thymes, can be potted as fragments with some roots to keep growing through the winter, enough for spring planting.

Only a few cuttings will root in the open ground, like the hard-wooded ones of forsythia, and the majority need a frame. A cutting is usually a short length of growing (not flowering) shoot and it must live on in saturated sand in the frame, like a cut flower in water, taking up moisture through the stem until it grows new roots. If it economizes on water by 'flagging' to reduce the size of the pores which throw out water into the atmosphere, it risks rotting, and the object of the frame is to have so much water in the air inside it that the cutting is not driven to dangerous economies. Mist propagators supply this moisture in a fine spray controlled automatically, but this is only worth using on a commercial nursery, and gardeners with cold frames can use the slower and easier methods of the past.

Among the easiest of all alpines from cutting are helianthemums, and those who intend to enlarge their helianthemum bed can raise several thousand in a standard 6 ft. × 4 ft. frame in a single summer. It also pays to buy a collection for autumn planting, cut them back after flowering, and propagate enough to turn even single specimens into drifts of colour. Choose young shoots without flower buds and take them off between the third and fourth joint down from the tip. Then remove the bottom pair of leaves close to the stem-sides and cut through the severed stem again cleanly, just below the joint. This is the standard cutting 'making' procedure, and with small ones like those of most alpines, used razor blades are ideal, but a really sharp knife is needed for geraniums (or rather zonal pelargoniums), which have the thickest of all soft wooded cuttings.

The first helianthemum cuttings can be taken when the plants are flowering in late May and June, selecting sizeable shoots and leaving more to come on for successive batches, for they take only a month to root. Those who only wish to raise a few dozen replacements can use the simplest 'frame' of all—the polythene propagating pot.

Fill a size 24 pot with a third its depth of cinders, 1 in. of soil and then sand firmed and levelled to within $1\frac{1}{2}$ in. of the pot rim. Then use a pricking-out dibber to make a hole deep enough to take the cutting down to its first pair of left-on leaves, and firm it with two strokes of the dibber point. Insert the cuttings in two rings round the edge of the pot, ideally just not touching each other.

Water them thoroughly with a rosed can, which washes the sand firm and level, and cover with a square of polythene large enough to secure under the rim of the pot with a large rubber band. Stand the pots level on a path in sheltered shade and place small pebbles in the middle of the polythene covers. The moisture condensing on the underside trickles to the middle and drops where there are no cuttings every evening, as a 'self-watering' device that uses deliberately the sagging that will over-water plants under a polythene-covered frame light.

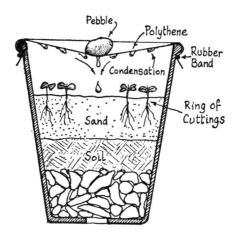

Fig. 19. Polythene-covered pot for propagating
alpines without a cold frame.

Some water will be lost through the drainage hole, but unless the cuttings appear to be flopping flat instead of standing up, stiff, green and strong, they will need no watering for the first fortnight. Then remove the rubber band and dig one up with the dibber point to see if it has roots. Replace it, and if it has, give rather more water and put the polythene back. After another fortnight they should be ready to have the now growing tips pinched out, and be moved to a polythene lean-to, without covers on the pots.

Six weeks from insertion they should be rooted well, having reached the soil layer on top of the cinders, and made a few starting side shoots. They are then ready to be tipped out of the pots with care so most of the sand can be used again, and transplanted 4 in. apart in rows, with room to hoe between. These should be watered to start them on in drought and kept weeded so they become sturdy plants ready to move to the alpine bed or border in the autumn. They should be dug up with plenty of soil and planted in a hole large enough for this soil ball to fit in without breaking. If a frame is available, they can be potted and will grow faster to better plants, but it is possible to grow helianthemums, alpine phlox (using 2-in.-long shoot tips with leaves removed from the bottom two joints), *Veronica rupestris* in all varieties and *Polygonum vaccinifolium*. These are certain to do well with this 'no-frame' method, but others can be tried, and though losses may be higher, the answer is to insert more cuttings. One out of ten is impossibly unprofitable commercially, but those who only *need* one to replace a plant that is past its best, will be satisfied.

Cuttings require entirely different conditions to seedlings or potted plants, for they need the frame closed to keep the humidity high, while seedlings require ventilation and far less moisture. With only a few batches of cuttings it is worth using the polythene pots even if a frame is available, and the cuttings can take advantage of the extra heat and shelter if they stand among the seedpans.

On the other hand the method wastes room with round pots and only two rings of cuttings in each, and is only suitable for the easier alpines, though it does save watering and attention for them. A better way is to divide the frame in half with polythene nailed through a wooden slat to the central light runner (with care not to interfere with sliding the lights) at the top, and to a length of 2 in. × 3 in. timber standing across the frame on the ashes. If one side has a soil-warming cable this division is a help to those who raise tomato plants or other tender seedlings by concentrating the heat on the one side that needs it most.

When it is time to change over to cuttings, fill one side 3 in. deep with sand which the 2 in. × 3 in. crosspiece will prevent from bulging and slipping under the polythene. Firm it and level it as though it were a pot or box of seed soil, and insert the cuttings across it in rows 1 in. apart with labels to tell the varieties. Do not insert cuttings in the 3–6 in. of room next to the low side of the frame, for the water trickling down the light can soak them too much.

Water well after insertion and keep the shaded lights closed, if possible watering them every morning in hot weather. The indication that they need it is dry sand grains on the surface between the cuttings. This type of cutting raising is much quicker, and a great many will be rooted in three to four weeks. Pot them in John Innes seed soil (which suits alpines) or a mixture of seven parts loam, four sifted leafmould or peat, and three sand. For helianthemums and the easier alpines one can use ordinary garden soil in place of loam, provided that this is not heavy clay or hungry town-garden soil.

The potted cuttings should go into the non-sand side with the lights kept closed for the first four days after potting and then opened a bit more each day, till the cuttings are growing happily in about a fortnight, and are ready to move out to make room for the next batch.

As alpines, shrubs and perennials are hardy they can move to a plunge-bed where they can keep growing larger until planting time. Plunge-beds are made ideally where they have sun for part of the day only, by digging out the soil to a depth of 3 in. to make a sunk bed 2–3 ft. wide and any convenient length. Fill this with fine coke, or boiler ash, rather than ashes from open coal fires which are inferior in drainage qualities, and surround it with 3-in.-wide sawn planks on edge nailed to 2 in. × 2 in. corner posts with extras every 3–4 ft. along the sides. Spread a fillet of ashes against one end, then press the first row of pots into it, and another generous fillet of ashes against their sides and squeeze the next row in. This fills the spaces between the pots with ashes that hold the water, checking evaporation from the pot sides, while the end and side planks keep off the drying winds, as well as preventing the plants blowing or knocking over.

Like the millions of alpines grown in plunge-beds every year, they can be watered with a thorough soaking each week, or more often in hot dry weather, either with an overhead irrigator as used for lawns or a hose with a can rose on the end. The plants can spend the winter in the plunge-beds growing on until spring, but they will need re-plunging after any roots that have grown through the drainage holes have been scraped off with the trowel edge if they must wait longer than about eight months. There is of course a great advantage in avoiding the handicap of broken roots from transplanting open-ground-raised alpines by growing them in pots, which is why most nurseries grow their plants this way.

A few alpines and many shrubs are difficult to root from the soft cuttings in summer that are easiest to obtain. It pays to use this method for slow-growing species because it is easy to take half a dozen tips from non-flowering shoots, in spring for autumn-flowering ones, in late summer for spring flowers, without missing them.

For these a rooting hormone is advisable, and Seradix B, strength 4 for shrubs, and 1 for alpines and herbaceous plants, is excellent. It is a powder into which the cutting tips are dipped before insertion, and multiplies the odds on success enormously, especially for *Lithospermum* 'Heavenly Blue' and the small species of rhododendrons and daphnes. There is a gain in using it for *Aethionema* 'Warley Rose' and any alpine of which you have only a few cuttings because it grows slowly, but not for helianthemums and other very easy species.

Plants, it seems, convey their 'instructions' through chemicals in the sap, and these hormones are only present at certain seasons in some species, like Lithospermum which root easily only in July, or in small amounts, as in gypsophila. Seradix is one of these that has been synthesized, and it always produces a thick web of roots, whatever the habit of the plant. So in effect one is 'telling' the cutting to root with a faked message. This chemical is indolyl butyric acid, and although another hormone, naphthalene acetic acid, is used in some proprietary rooting preparations, this makes fewer and thicker roots that are more easily broken when digging the cuttings from the sand or potting.

Seradix is especially useful for the herbaceous plants that need to have cuttings taken in the spring from the shoots that appear first above ground, like delphiniums, gypsophila and lupins, for the more that are taken and wasted, the fewer flowers there will be on the parent clumps later in the year.

The best place for these is the heated side of the cold frame, with the sand added over the soil-warming cable. Dig up the delphinium clumps that are thrusting their pale green shoot tips through the soil and remove any shoots that are 3 in. long and can be taken off with a portion of the main root, called a 'heel', to block the hollow, pith-filled stem, as with rose cuttings.

Then replant the clump. If this operation is done in March or early April the robbed delphinium will flower normally. Lupins cannot be dug up like this for they have deep roots that are easily damaged, so dig away the soil round the shoots that are just appearing and take them off as near the roots as possible. Then remove all but the stiff, upright pointed leaf in the middle when 'making' them with a clean cut through below one of the close-together joints near the root. Gypsophila are easy. Remove the shoots above ground when they have three joints, make them like helianthemums by removing the lowest pair of leaves, but shorten the others by roughly half—quickest done by holding the leaves and snipping straight across with garden scissors, missing of course the growing middle point.

Dip these in the fine pink powder that is Seradix B, strength 1, and insert like ordinary alpine cuttings—but about 1½ in. of stem should go underground because they are larger and heavier. Without soil-warming cables they will root, but not so well, or not with such a high proportion of successes. When their centres begin to grow, re-move those that are rooted, and pot to grow on first in the other side of the frame, and then its 'annexe', ready for planting in a nursery bed in the open about June, and then in their final homes in the border in the autumn. This method is particularly useful for lupins, because named varieties of these do not live longer than about five years, and replacements are comparatively costly.

Only those plants which have roots of which small fragments will grow can be raised from root cuttings—couch grass and convolvulus would be ideal subjects if anyone wanted to raise a few million quickly. Prepare a pot or pan as for seedlings, but fill equal parts of sand and seed soil to within 2 in. of the rim. Then dig up an *Anemone japonica* plant in the spring when it is starting to grow, and remove some of the thicker roots before replanting. Cut these into lengths 2 in. long and lay them flat on the soil surface, covering with a further 1 in. of the sandy soil. Even matchstick-thick roots will grow as root cuttings and will be ready to pot by May and grow on in the plunge-bed to transplant to the permanent homes the following spring.

Other perennials suitable for root cuttings in exactly the same way are anchusas (but not *A. caespitosa*) and *Primula denticulata* in all named varieties (some of which are lovely, and this is the only way to increase them true to colour), and oriental poppies, and border phloxes. The alpine that grows from root cuttings is *Morisia hypogea*, which should be dug up during the summer and have one or two of its longer roots removed, and then be replanted, watered and given a temporary shade with small pieces of Cupressus branch.

Fill the pot completely with the sand and soil mixture, and flatten it down to 1 in. below the rim. Then make 1-in.-long sections of Morisia root and insert these upright in dibber holes with the tops level with the surface. Put them in as they are cut off so that you remember which end of the root is 'top'—the nearest to the parent plant—which is quite easy to forget.

Morisia is the only root cutting that prefers to be upright, and it has another odd habit. It comes from the seashore of Corsica, and looks rather like a tiny and refined dandelion with a ring of stemless yellow flowers round its rosette for a good deal of the summer. As these flowers go over they form growing points instead of seed pods, and thrust these down into the ground, with such force that if morisias are planted on a clay that bakes hard they will force themselves out of the ground as they struggle to push their seeds underground. These seeds rarely ripen in this country, and since root cuttings are so easy few gardeners try for them.

Pans or pots of sandy soil like those used for Morisia root cuttings are best for small cuttings that are slow to root, like those of Kabschia saxifrages, *Armeria caespitosa*, the dwarf thrift, and other tiny treasures. Insert them after they have finished flowering, and keep them in the cutting pan in the frame until autumn, when they should be ready to go three in a pot and winter in the frame. Here they stay until the spring congestion, when they may be moved to the plunge-beds. They are fully hardy, and their native mountains can give them far fiercer winters, but the frame keeps them growing ready for planting about the second week of May.

This type of sand and soil pot is the best wintering device for Mimulus. These are not fully hardy and the many lovely named varieties that will not come true from seed, like 'Whitcroft Scarlet', are hardier as cuttings than plants, which moreover take much more room. Insert a batch of cuttings in early October, about three joints each, water them well to start with and then give them water only if they are very dry. Pot them in March ready to plant in late April, taking more cuttings in the same sand mixture, for they root easily in a fortnight, ready to pot and plant out soon afterwards.

Bedding geraniums are also hardier as cuttings than plants, and will root easily in a frame, provided that the cuttings are taken early enough. In late July or early August look round the plants flowering in the beds and take cuttings about 3 in. long of shoots that will not be missed, pinching out the buds in the growing points. Remove the lower leaves and cut through the thick stem as near $\frac{1}{8}$ in. below the bottom joint as possible.

Then spread the cuttings on newspapers in the sun to wilt till the stems are flabby, which may seem 'cruel' but it is the best way of helping these thick and awkward cuttings to root, for they gain no benefit from hormones, or, rather, both those so far synthesized give a 'message' they ignore. Then pot them for half their length into small 60 pots of John Innes seed soil, pressing the thumbs on both sides of the stems and banging them firm on the potting bench. Once the sound of nurserymen potting scarlet 'Paul Crampel' geraniums sounded like the then newly invented Maxim gun.

Stand these in the frame, water them well once, then keep the lights closed until they begin to root, which shows when the small leaf in the middle grows round, furry and firm again. Water sparingly until the roots show when they are inverted and knocked out of the pots for a look. Keep them with little water through the winter in these small pots, but in March repot them into size 48 (3½-in. diameter) pots and stand them on the warming wires. Pinch out the tips so they grow bushy, or if they are very tall, take cuttings from the tips to pot as before and stand on the wires. They will be ready to plant in May when the risk of frost is over.

The alternative is to dig up the geraniums that have flowered continuously from May till October and to cut them back drastically, shortening the shoots to leave them only about 8 in. from cut ends to where the stem ends among the roots that still show the shape of the pot. Trim these back a bit and pot them in 60s, water, stand them at the back of the frame and water to start them, but keep them dry through the winter, until in March they can be potted and stood above the warming wires.

The ivy-leaved geraniums, popular for hanging baskets, can be cut back and potted in the same way, but their cuttings need no wilting and root very easily. The trailing stems can be cut into two joint sections, the lower leaf of each is removed, and they are potted firmly like the ordinary type. A growing point should form where the upper leaf joins the stem, and though cuttings from the tips make good plants quickest, two-joint ones mean far more plants quickly.

Fuchsias too can be cut back and potted to grow slowly through the winter, but the best way to keep a stock is by selecting soft side shoots about 1 in. long from the branches in June and rooting these in pans filled with sandy soil for potting in September and growing through the winter like slow-starting seedlings in the frame. Even if they lose their leaves in an unheated frame, they will recover and grow ahead in spring for late April or early May planting.

Heliotrope, marguerite daisies and the sturdy calceolarias with their yellow or brown purse flowers can all be wintered by cutting them back hard, potting in 60s and growing with little water but plenty of light in a frame with a tubular heater or even a soil warming cable only, potting them to larger pots in spring.

This of course means a room problem, for the larger pots need space between them, and as none of these tender bedding plants move out till May, they compete for space with seedlings. Geraniums, however, flower well in winter, and fuchsias start in spring, so the sunny window-sills of the house can act as an extension of the frame. The cottage window-sills of the past grew a very wide range of pot plants because of the high humidity from the kettle steaming on the hob, and because their oil lamps were less hard on foliage than the gaslight that limited their 'betters' to aspidistras. So put a bowl of water on electric radiators to add water vapour slowly, and concentrate the plants on bedroom or other window-sills where there is less heat. 50°–55° F. is plenty and it does not matter if the temperature does go down at night to even 35° F., so long as there is plenty of light. Conventional 'houseplants' are mainly shade-lovers from tropical forests and grow far better for Continentals and Americans who run their central heating at least 10° F. hotter than we like.

Another winter crop for a cold frame are bulbs, which can be brought on to near flowering stage with a tubular heater and brought in to flower rather earlier than those on the traditional linen cupboard and bulb fibre routine. Prepared and Roman hyacinths, single early tulips, and all the bulbs sold for growing in bowls with fibre can be grown with soil in pots in the frame, but can be planted to finish growing like those lifted to make room for bedding plants, and stored for planting in the open the next season. Daffodils, as an example, that have had this modest forcing in frames are excellent for naturalizing.

Pot your bulbs in size 48 or larger pots, or pottery bowls with drainage holes in the bottoms, using a tomato potting soil or John Innes on top of a few cinders in the bottom for drainage. August and September are the best months, or as soon as the bulbs can be bought, and after potting and watering they should stand on a solid surface (so that worms have no opportunity to get in through the drainage holes) and be covered 3 in. deep in ashes. It is worth making an ash stack about 1 ft. high and flat-topped so that the sulphur washes out, for this kind of job—saving the coarse cinders for drainage material.

When inspection shows that the roots are well round the pots and the leaves are beginning to thrust up into the ashes, which will be about October, the bulbs will be ready to bring into the frame and warm with the electric heating. When they are in bud they can be brought into the house in succession and all should be ready by the time the bedding plants and tomatoes need the room.

There are a number of pot plants that can be raised in the cold frame and one of the easiest is the Solanum or 'Winter Cherry'. Save the berries from one bought at Christmas, and extract the seed in April ready to sow in a box, and pot two in a 60 when they are about 2 in. along the willow-shaped leaves. Pinch out the tips to make them bushy, and pot into 48s when bedding plants going out leave room in the frame for them to stand spaced out; they stay until the end of June, when they should be transferred to the plunge-bed, with the ash bottom scraped away to take the taller pots. Keep them well watered and bring them back into the frame in October to ripen their berries by Christmas time.

Another even easier is the French marigold, potted three in a 48 from the batches raised for bedding or from a later sowing in July to make bushy plants for the autumn. So long as they are on a sunny window-sill and not in shade they are very easy pot plants, but the best varieties are the 'Petite', or 'Miniature' or 'Pygmy' races which grow 6 in. high, because they will always be taller in pots.

It is not possible to give full accounts of the many pot plants that a modestly heated frame will raise for the house, and the reader is referred to *Growing Pot Plants from Seed* by H. G. Witham Fogg (Faber and Faber, 18s.) for really detailed information.

14

Finding the Fertility

It is the vegetable garden that needs the richest manure and compost, for with greedy crops fitting one behind the other, there is more need to keep a large sum on 'current account'. Think of the soil as a bank of fertility with the top 8 in. busily earning and spending, with money turning over fast, and Friday's pay cheque half spent by Saturday night and banked by the butchers and grocers on Monday morning. Lower down, where the tree roots spread, is cash on deposit, which is only 'spendable' when the leaves fall and rot to leafmould, or the prunings and sawn boughs release potassium in their ashes as 'interest' on the long-term stock in the wood that may wait a century in an oak to return the minerals its tap root drew from perhaps 20 ft. down.

Alpines, herbaceous plants, trees, shrubs and almost all ornamental crops feed slowly, and leafmould is one of their best sources of humus. For in addition to the plant foods of which nitrogen, potassium, phosphorus and calcium are needed in most quantity, all crops must have humus, which does more than provide a moisture-retaining sponge for thirsty soils. It is partly broken down vegetable matter, and taking it down a stage further provides the power that 'drives' everything in the soil from bacteria and fungi to earthworms.

Almost all the energy in the world today (nuclear energy and water and wind power are the exceptions) comes from the 4 per cent of sunlight falling on the living leaves and turning carbon-dioxide into sugars and starches by the process known as 'photosynthesis' on which all life depends. Coal, oil and petrol are merely the fossilized sunlight of the past, and the energy with which we dig comes from the sun via the leaves of our crops, via livestock, or from the sunlight on the fenceless meadows of the sea where the tiny floating plants called 'plankton' pasture the beginnings of the chains of eaters and eaten that provide our fish.

Plant foods are made available by bacteria, and we need humus to feed our willing and unpaid helpers, and to provide the conditions they need. The humus from the compost heap is the most quickly available; that from the leafmould heap is slowest, and good gardeners make both. In the past head gardeners would buy only beech or oak leafmould, because these held the most tannin, for it is the tannic acid in leaves that makes them decay slowly, which is a very great asset on sandy soils. Peat also had its plant foods locked up by tannin, and so of course has leather, which is why old boots take years to decay in compost heaps.

Autumn brings the scent of burning leaves in most gardens from the smoke of wasted humus, because we have forgotten the value of leafmould as made for nearly 200 years at the Royal Botanic Gardens, Kew. Most large parks make it, and at Kew it is used for choice by men who appreciate its qualities, which are as different from those of compost as butter is from cheese.

Leafmould needs no activator and no turning, merely limited space, time, and not only the leaves you would burn anyway but those you can collect most easily. For the council roadman can often be persuaded to empty his barrow in your garden. If you have a dark, dry, out-of-the-way corner where nothing will grow, it might just as well hold your leafmould heap.

Level off the site and drive in stout posts at the corners, with extra posts every 4 ft., and staple wire netting round them, with one end free so it can be hooked shut like a gate. The object is to stop the leaves blowing round the garden, and it can be moved on to another heap each year. The leaves go in as they are gathered, with no layers of anything, needing care only to pick out any dead branches and not to tread them too much. Pack your cube of leaves so that it is filled solid, and if it is under trees, water it occasionally in summer and Nature will do the job of making humus as efficiently as in a thick drift of leaves on the forest floor.

The following autumn the material will be ready for use. From 5 cubic yards of loose leaves as swept, making a stack 9 ft. long, 3 ft. wide and 3 ft. high, you get roughly a ton of humus, or 2 cubic yards. Compost shrinks much more; approximately 6 cubic yards of green material make 1 cubic yard—but a leafmould mound is not a compost heap. It is low in nitrogen, 0·4 per cent against 2·1 per cent in good compost, and high in potash and phosphates, but only in very slowly-available forms. The real value is in the lignins and hemicelluloses which make the most lasting humus of all. Dug into any humus-starved garden, with 4 oz. of lime to the square yard, to give alkaline 'bread' for the soil bacteria to begin their meal of vegetable 'cheese' (made by fungi which like acid conditions) it is good food for the soil.

It is not a manure, it is not a fertilizer, but an ideal shrub, tree and herbaceous plant food—slow, lasting and safe, which makes your compost go further. The very best bargain for anyone with a heavy clay soil would be to pay the cartage cost of leaves by the lorry-load from his local council's street trees, to use by the ton, when they mature, an investment like National Savings Certificates.

	Beech leafmould per cent	Rhodo-dendron peat per cent	Farmyard manure per cent
Ash	17·7	9·25	—
Nitrogen	1·8	1·2	2·2
Phosphoric acid	0·1	0·15	1·6
Potash	0·15	0·1	2·0
Moisture	12·05	13·1	—

The table shows what is there, but not the humus. There is very little difference between leafmould and peat, which is usually 'leaf-mould' from water plants, so far as chemicals are concerned. The question is one of cost, for a single bale of sedge peat costs about £2 to cover a space 15 ft. wide and 20 long, 2 in. deep. Spread between the rows after sowing, or on top of lime, and with the cabbage tribe, especially for brussels sprouts, with no digging at all, it stops winter rain puddling the clay, and suppresses weeds, also allowing picking or cutting without trampling. Leafmould does the same job for the cost of just thinking ahead and a little trouble. It is by far the best way of lightening clay with humus because you can use enough every year to make a real difference. Use it with lime and perseverance.

The earliest use for an autumn-made heap is in the following spring when the first lawn-mowings are ready. Spread the part-rotted leaves in a 2-in. layer under newly planted fruit trees and bushes, and add 2 in. of mowings on top, which will hold the leaves down to finish decaying without blowing. This trick can be used in a new garden or a neglected one, with 3 in. of leaves (plus mowings to prevent blowing) to suppress weeds and rot ready for digging under in the autumn.

Fallen autumn leaves are both a tree's defence against competing grass and a top dressing. This suggests that a gardener can use the leaves he has to sweep up from the lawn to feed his young apples, pears, plums and cherries.

On a commercial scale organic fruit growers aiming at the best fruit with the fewest sprays do this with the 'birds' nests' of straw and mowings which they build round the tree trunks, but this method is too untidy for gardeners.

For a neater garden version you need for each tree 11 ft. of 1-in. mesh, 1-ft. wide, wire-netting painted with black bitumen paint to make it last. Cut off 2 ft., join it into a circle round the tree, with the bottom buried 2 in. There will be about a 3-in. space between the netting and the tree and stake in the middle.

Then make a wider circle (or square) round the tree with 3 yd. of netting. Fill the space between the two circles with dead leaves of any kind; the inner circle is left empty to prevent the stem from rooting into rotting leaves and suffering when the heap is removed after four years. As the leaves sink, top up with more, and cap with 1 in. of burnt bonfire earth, which adds some helpful potash and prevents the leaves from blowing away. This starts off the young tree with as much leafmould as it would have shed itself in fifteen years.

Leafmould feeds slowly, and for tired old trees half can be replaced with manure; but this is too rich for youth. Fruit farmers' compost is ideal, made by filling the space with straw or dry bracken (never wood-wool), sprinkling $\frac{1}{2}$ lb. of dried sludge or 4 oz. of nitro-chalk among it and capping with bonfire soil. Use short canes to hold the inner wire away from the tree, for if the gap is lost country mice will nest in straw and nibble the bark destructively. Both types serve also as rabbit guards.

There is another way using baled straw, bought at pet shops in towns or more cheaply in the country. Half a bale does one tree. Cut the string and take the compressed bale apart in 2-in.-thick 'tiles', building them in three layers round the tree and a few inches away from it, with sludge or nitro-chalk between each layer. No inner circle of netting is needed, only a low outer ring of netting or $\frac{1}{4}$-in.-thick painted boards nailed to corner posts to prevent the straw from blowing away.

The nitro-chalk ($\frac{1}{2}$ lb. for each tree), provides nitrogen for the bacteria that rot the straw and leaves lime that is so useful for stone fruit. In chalky gardens use always sludge for apples and pears, for too much lime can rob them of magnesium.

Re-christening the rubbish heap does not make compost, for this cannot heat well enough to kill the weed seeds that will come up like a forest wherever bad compost is used. The best way to hold the heat from the bacterial action that turns garden rubbish into better manure than townsmen can buy, is to use a Compost Box, which is also the tidiest method for small gardens.

The semi-detached type with one compartment ready to use or rotting and the other filling as rubbish accumulates, is best, but it must be built. Compost boxes, even the long 'terrace' of compartments as shown in our first photograph, are far more easily made than any shed, but those offered for sale are made with useless, open slat, sides. Making your own involves only straight sawing and driving nails home into strong timber. The cost will be less than that of a load of inferior manure.

One with compartments 3 ft. square and high takes 200 ft. of $\frac{1}{2}$ in. × 4 in. sawn planks and six 4-ft. lengths of 2 in. × $1\frac{1}{2}$ in. timber. Saw enough planks into 3-ft. lengths for the two ends and the middle, and 6-ft. lengths for the back, then creosote the lot and leave them to dry, including the 2 in. × $1\frac{1}{2}$ in. uprights.

Lay three of these uprights 1 yd. apart and nail the 6-ft. planks to their upper 3 ft. Then nail the 3-ft. planks at one end to the upper 3 ft. of the three remaining uprights. Dig six holes at the corners of 2-yd. squares, fit the three uprights on the back into the back three and ram the soil firm round them. Put the upright of the first end in its hole, replace and firm the soil round it, and nail the loose ends of the 3-ft. planks to the corner upright, holding a brick on the inside to take the shock of hammering.

When the middle and second end are fitted in this way, you have a strong wooden letter 'E' made of two bottomless and topless boxes. Now saw some of the spare planks lengthways and nail a piece upright about $\frac{3}{4}$ in. away inside the outer 2 in. × $1\frac{1}{2}$ in. posts to make slots for the loose board fronts of the two compartments to slide down. Three are needed on the middle one to make slots on both sides. Creosote these and the front boards, and when all have had a week to dry, paint with black bitumen paint to prevent the creosote warming out of the wood and acting as a disinfectant to stop the beneficial bacteria of decay, which are entirely distinct from those of disease.

An alternative is to replace the 2 in. × $1\frac{1}{2}$ in. timber with 2 in. × 1 in., nailing three pieces edgeways to the back and two flatways to the ends and middle. Holes drilled top and bottom will take slender 4-in. bolts which can be removed to take the box apart, for it is a tenant's fixture like a portable shed and packs flat to go on the van on moving days.

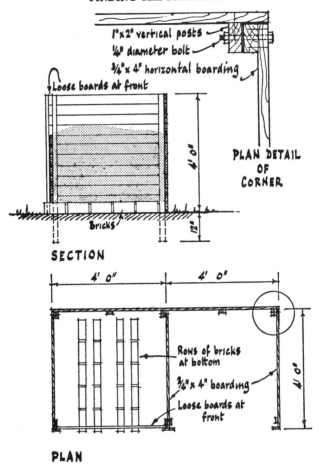

Fig. 20. Section, plan and details of compost box. Note the brick air channels below for maximum heating.

It is not essential to have a box for compost. A heap in the open, however, will not decay at the sides and always rots best away from the prevailing wind, so site a boxless heap in a sheltered place. Remove the top and chop down the sides till you come to rotted compost in the middle, and use the undecayed outsides to start another heap, or turn the heap 'sides to middle' after about six weeks.

On the floor of each compartment lay two double rows of brick-ends, with the ends of these rows coming out under the bottom front boards, as shown in the second photograph. This is to supply the air, for lack of which the proper bacteria will not be able to work. It is lack of air, and acid decay, that put out the 'bacterial bonfire' in a heap of lawn mowings so that it stays a smelly slippery mess.

Cover the bricks with tough and stemmy rubbish to keep finer materials from blocking the air channels and then put on the first 8-in.-thick layer of weeds, lawn mowings and garden waste, with kitchen refuse in the middle where dogs and birds cannot reach it. Then scatter enough dried sludge, Gunos (dried poultry manure) or fishmeal to darken the surface, as quickly available food for rapid bacterial increase, add another layer and whiten this with slaked lime to stop the heap becoming too acid. Add another layer of material, then the manure or 'activator', more material and lime again, layer by layer, for the heap will sink as it heats and filling goes on till sinking stops.

Summer heaps are ready in 2–3 months and both compartments of the box filled solid by the end of November mean about 2 tons of humus by April. The test of readiness is worms moving in, and this is why living earth, not dead concrete, should bottom the compost boxes.

This system is called the 'Indore' (Not 'indoor') after the research station at Indore in India where it was developed by the late Sir Albert Howard. It can be done with any animal manure as an acti-vator, but these are scarce in towns and many proprietary makes are sold by garden shops. Fertosan Standard and Myco are sold in packets and need dissolving in water like Q.R., another well-known brand, while Fertosan Special in a tin with a sprinkler top is made especially for lawn mowings and sappy rubbish.

The easiest is Alginure, in a tube or tin, because it can be stoppered and parked by the heap ready for whenever enough rubbish has ac-cumulated to finish a layer. This needs no lime, merely small dabs of the black jelly, about $\frac{1}{2}$-in. square, in five-of-diamonds formation on each layer.

This jelly is made from seaweed and is, like the Agar jelly used by bacteriologists, a first-class bacteria food. They grow so fast that they can release the nutriments they need to keep going from the compost material. There is a powder seaweed preparation, Marinure, which is merely scattered on the layers, just enough to darken the surface, about 2 oz. a square yard of layer, and neither needs lime layers except for heaps that are mostly lawn-mowings.

Once a heap is made it is little trouble, but it can stop decaying and dry till it is only fit for burning for lack of moisture in drought. So water your heap, either with the hose or a rosed can. A heap the size of the one described would need about four canfuls a compartment if it got dry enough to stop heating.

Both in drought and wherever there is any difficulty in getting a compost heap to heat, watering with bedroom slops acts like magic in starting quick decay. Many successful heaps have been made using this old-fashioned 'activator' and lime layers. During the winter heaps can lose plant foods from continued rain so a black polythene cover over the top of the box is the answer. Covering the heap with polythene completely makes it too damp from condensation and a home for slugs, apart from excluding air from the sides. This is why corrugated iron or asbestos are not good compost box materials.

Another problem is excessive quantities of soil in the heap, for there is not enough heat in sappy weeds to cook weed seeds and roots inside cold clods. Some proprietary activators suggest soil layers, but these layers should always be a mere scattering. Their object is to provide a starting stock of bacteria, but there are so many thousands of these even in the soil clinging to a groundsel root that where a heap includes weeds, this soil on the roots is enough.

Woody material like brussels sprouts and cabbage stumps is best crushed before it goes in, and this can either be done with the garden roller on concrete, or by spreading the hard rubbish near the garage drive-in, where a few weeks' car traffic will reduce even privet hedge clippings to rottable refuse. Fruit tree and rose prunings, like wood shavings, should not be put in the compost heap. Kitchen refuse, especially vegetable peelings, tea-leaves and vacuum-cleaner dust (but excluding only bones, plastics and metal milk bottle tops) can all go in, with no more than 10 per cent of paper—the kitchen waste paper, not the great bulk of Sunday supplements plain and coloured.

It is possible to 'take the temperature' of a compost heap with a metal-sheathed thermometer thrust in, of the kind used by mushroom growers. A good well-made heap in summer should hold over 120° F. for about a week, which is enough to destroy the eggs of most pests and the spores of most plant diseases (the spores of Rusts are killed at 115° F.) as well as weed seeds.

Compost does not need to be put on in ounces like a chemical, but a bucketful to a square yard is a fair dressing, though the more you can dig in the better. Unlike farmyard manure it can be put on with lime, and it can be dug in even just before sowing a root crop without making the roots grow coarse and forky.

Roughly speaking it is a better balanced farmyard manure, for it has always more available potash, as the comparative analysis table below shows. Peat has the moisture-retaining power alone, compost has plant foods too, and other qualities that add up to a healthy garden soil.

	Nitrogen per cent	Phosphate per cent	Potash per cent	Moisture per cent
Farmyard manure	0·64	0·23	0·32	76·0
Indore compost	0·5	0·27	0·81	76·0
Spent mushroom compost	0·86	0·63	0·67	53·14
Alginure compost	0·48	0·63	0·63	76·0
Peat deep-litter	4·4	1·9	0·65	17·7
Straw deep-litter	0·93	1·63	1·0	50·2
Pig manure	0·48	0·58	0·36	76·0
Cow manure	0·44	0·12	0·04	86·0

The material that is sold expensively as 'Composted Stable Manure' is spent mushroom compost, and very good value as a source of humus with balanced plant foods near ordinary compost, as shown in the table. It should not be used for rhododendrons or other lime-hating shrubs because it contains gypsum which becomes lime enough to be awkward. Those who can buy it from a mushroom grower direct by the lorry load have a bargain, for buying anything in small quantities becomes increasingly costly as transport costs and loading labour costs soar higher and higher.

Farmyard manure today contains very little horse manure, for it is mostly pig and cow. With any choice get pig, for from the table it is obvious that this has the best balance of nitrogen and potash of any animal manure. The ideal is more potash than nitrogen, and this is the quality compost has and one of the reasons why it is far the best. It is a good idea to start off a new garden with a full lorry load delivered after the ground is cleared, and to have it rotavated in, for no one begins with enough compost material for a heap and it will need time to decay. The old 'well rotted horse manure' is a thing of the past, but those who are lucky enough to have some should use it, making an Indore heap with manure layers even 2 in. thick. Any manure delivered when it cannot be used should be stacked with compostable refuse, but not any likely to contain weed seeds, for a bulk of manure will have too much moisture to reach full heat, even though it may steam.

Deep-litter poultry manure from under broilers is a bad bargain, because it does not stay down long enough for the bacteria to use up the fierce nitrogen of poultry droppings in composting the woody material of the litter. Layers' houses stay decaying for a year and make good manure from straw or peat, but not from sawdust or shavings. These will contain wood ends which are fragments of wood that provide too little working surface for the bacteria to finish the job in the time. When they are dug in the soil bacteria will try to go on rotting them down and take up nitrogen from the soil to make up their bodies—the well-known problem of 'nitrogen robbery', which means a fall in crop from manuring, not a gain.

Peat litter is best because it is driest, and the last column in the table shows how much of the cost of cartage will be spent hauling water. The bacteria have broken down some of the peat, releasing some potash, but the litter has held on to most of the nitrogen. Some of the peat has stayed as extra humus and the whole load will be free from weed seeds.

A full load would be a fine start for a new garden, but it is as well to remember that the flower garden needs less rich feeding than the cabbage patch. On a poor sand it would be excellent and the peat would provide moisture-retaining power until leafmould and compost could be made. On subsoil or a worn-out town garden soil, a really generous dressing of peat deep litter followed by green manure crops as recommended to follow wet sludges (see p. 215) would build up a lasting store of fertility.

Straw deep litter is the easiest to obtain, and it is far better to buy a full load from one of the manure dealers who advertise in country local papers than to pay just as much for a small car trailer load of pony manure that is mostly straw. This deep-litter manure will be rotted already, for it will have been a year in the house, and it is worth insisting on this, because a dealer can often supply some that has been down even longer, till it has rotted down to a crumbling, dark brown. This is the best buy, especially for reclaiming subsoil or on heavy clays.

The drawback for individual gardens is the size of load that brings the price down to £3 a ton for the quality that is sold only in bulk and mainly to market gardeners, who spread 20–40 tons an acre every five years and buy only the best because it pays. The average semi-detached garden has room for about 3 tons this often, spread 2–3 in. deep under the bush fruit and on the ground ready to dig, and stacked as a reserve for the summer.

The answer is neighbour co-operation, sharing the bill for an 8- or 10-ton load on the basis of thirty good barrow loads—enough for 120 square yards—as roughly a ton.

The manure that should never be bought is from battery hens, which is plain poultry droppings with their nitrogen as ammonium carbonate unconverted by the deep-litter bacteria, wet and smelly and responsible for the bad reputation that poultry manure has among gardeners. The only way to use it would be in layers in an Indore heap. This applies also to the crude animal droppings from other factory farming methods such as slatted-floor veal calves and 'sweatbox' pigs.

Rabbit droppings make a good Indore heap activator, and so do those of sheep or goats, while pigeon droppings are about twice as 'strong' as battery poultry manure and usable only as an activator. Using any of these odd animal manures if they are available in quantity is best as extra thick layers in Indore heaps. Wheat straw is the best value in potash for composting—1 per cent—with barley about half as good, while dry bracken is merely 0·11 per cent. This is because bracken returns its potassium to store in the roots in the autumn when the fronds die down, and the real value comes from cutting it for composting in June, July or August when it can be over 2 per cent and rots rather better.

Both types of deep-litter poultry manure need a potash balancer if they are to be used for potatoes or any potash-demanding crop, and the most readily available one is wood ashes.

Coal, coke and anthracite ashes contain so little plant food that they can make poor soils poorer still. But the ashes that glow in our gardens on 5th November are a different matter altogether—they are full of richness. Cover them the same night with a dustbin lid or other fireproof shelter to prevent rain wasting the richness away before next morning.

Hardwoods have the greatest potassium content; thin branches and prunings contain more than tree trunks. The record for potassium is held by oak twigs with 40 per cent. Old furniture has about 20 per cent, and poplar has least with 3 per cent. Ashes from the average mixed bonfire contain about 12 per cent. The composition of all wood ashes includes about 33 per cent lime, 1 – 4 per cent phosphorus and 2 – 10 per cent of magnesium oxide.

Sift out the sparkler wires, the remains of the Guy's boots and other unburnt rubbish, and pack the cold grey ashes into tins which have lids—the ashes contain $\frac{1}{2}$ – 2 per cent sodium which can attract damp.

Onions and beetroot appreciate sodium, but large quantities should not be dug into heavy clays which can be made sticky by the salt. Lucky gardeners with unlimited ash from wood fires should use it in place of lime layers in compost heaps, and the standard 4 oz. a square yard is safe for all soils, including clays. All beans are potash greedy. So are onions, tomatoes, potatoes and gooseberries, and it is worth burning winter prunings separately to add to November's hoard for sharing among them in spring.

The magnesium oxide in wood ashes provides a small supply of this essential trace element, which is an important ingredient of chlorophyll, but locked up in the soil by excessive liming, or in chalky gardens. It is also made unavailable to plants by too much potassium on its own, and this is why the most common symptom of its lack is tomato leaves turning yellow while their veins stay green. This is usually regarded as virus trouble or the result of too much watering, but the remedy is 1 oz. a square yard of Epsom salts (magnesium sulphate; cattle grade is cheapest and good enough for gardens) on the tomato border, watered in.

Gooseberry leaves show red leaf margins, blackcurrants purple patches in the leaf middles, apples, pears and cherries have brown patches between the leaf veins, and potatoes have both leaf yellowing *and* brown patches. These can be mistaken for potato blight, but they are always between the veins and never extend to the edge of the leaf, and are accompanied by pale green leaves that turn yellow except for their veins. This condition is so common that whenever you think a 'virus' has struck suddenly, try either Epsom salts on the surface, or dissolved at the rate of 1 oz. in a 2-gallon can and watered on 2 square yards. If this solution is sprayed on the foliage, it can be taken in direct through the leaves by 'foliar feeding' which is a more certain way of correcting trace element deficiencies in large orchards than by spreading a mineral.

Another use for Epsom salts at this strength is to cancel out lime when azaleas, ericas, gentians, magnolias, rhododendrons and other lime-hating species show through their yellowing foliage and general unhappiness that calcium is creeping in despite peat and leafmould. The action is one of base exchange and the swap over with calcium carbonate leaves insoluble calcium sulphate which is harmless to lime-haters, and magnesium carbonate which they rather like. They can also suffer from calcium locking up the iron they need and the new iron sequestrene supplies this not only for lime-haters but for roses, which can suffer with yellowed leaves from iron shortage on limy soils.

Wood ashes used in quantity for many years can supply too much sodium as common salt, which is appreciated in moderation by most root crops especially beet. The trouble only occurs on clay which excess salt makes permanently sticky by converting it to a 'sodium clay' which is what the sea leaves after flooding the land. The Dutch remedy is gypsum which was also used in England when potash-demanding hops in Kent were supplied from an almost all-wood-burning London for centuries. Dig in ½ lb. a square yard in the autumn or spring, or, ideally, spread it through the top 6 in. with a rotary cultivator. The effect in making the clay more crumbly and less soggy should show in about three weeks, and a gypsum dressing is always worth trying for it can do no harm if excess salt even in the remote past is not the cause of stickiness. It is a hydrated calcium sulphate, a ground rock that is burnt to make plaster of Paris.

Those who garden with chemicals can give their soils so much calcium, nitrogen, phosphorus and potassium that these main plant foods get in each other's way like highly paid fitters, turners, moulders and boiler makers in an engineering works waiting idly in darkness for an electrician to fit a new main fuse. Potassium and calcium locking each other up and together putting magnesium out of root-reach is only part of the story. All nitrogen fertilizers lock up copper; sulphate of ammonia can combine with lime to make insoluble gypsum; and nitrate of soda can make clay sticky faster than wood ashes will, apart from 'burning' lettuces when used to excess. Phosphorus is not a locker up of plant foods and this is most easily available in organic fertilizers.

If plant foods are supplied in organic mixture form, with their trace elements, they 'work harder' and far less of them grows our crops, especially in the flower garden where most species are slow growing and we need their flowering rather than weight of foliage, seeds or roots. Therefore composts, manures, wood ashes, lime at need, and such slowly-acting organic substances as bonemeal are all the gardener needs. Though magnesium shortage is easily corrected, the garden answer to most of the others is compost or manure which will contain the trace element that should do the trick. One of the reasons why so many 'organic gardeners' say that 'compost banishes all plant diseases' is because they do not know the difference between mineral deficiency symptoms, like 'green back' in tomatoes from magnesium shortage, and genuine plant diseases.

A very valuable source of humus, trace elements and lightening material for heavy soils is Municipal Compost, which is made by several English and Scottish councils from dustbin refuse and sewage sludge. A full list of these, together with prices and analyses, will be found in *Fertility Finder* published by The Henry Doubleday Research Association, Bocking, Braintree, Essex (24p post free). This also includes the dried sewage sludge sold by many more councils all over Britain, which is both richer in plant foods and cheaper, especially because it has a far higher chance of being near enough for delivery by council lorry. The table gives some typical analysis figures with other manures for comparison.

	Water per cent	Nitrogen per cent	Phosphoric Acid per cent	Potash per cent	Organic matter per cent
Farmyard manure					
Rothamsted Average	76·0	0·64	0·23	0·32	23·31
Municipal Compost					
(Midlothian)	30·0	0·97	0·36	0·19	18·90
Municipal Compost					
(Radcliffe)	27·52	0·62	0·44	0·47	27·36
Dried sludge					
(Isleworth)	10·0	3·0	2·0	Trace	50·0
(West Kent)	36·1	1·74	1·80	0·04	32·5

Municipal Compost is always more expensive, but a good one is richer than farmyard manure, and the Radcliffe (near Manchester) has a rather better proportion of potash. They will have heated up in the composting process enough to kill all weed seeds, especially those of tomatoes which can come up like a forest from a wet sludge. Dry ones are also weed- and tomato-seed-free, and these are usually 20 per cent or less moisture.

The greatest value from Municipal Compost, however, is in its trace elements, which include boron, copper, iron, cobalt, manganese, magnesium, titanium, molybdenum and zinc. Any worked-out garden soil could do with a load of manure *and* one of Municipal Compost, especially on a heavy clay. The mineral portion of the compost is very finely ground ashes, glass, china and even plastics, making a lasting 'sand' effect, and releasing its minerals slowly, which is what the soil requires, for if there is more than a trace of a trace element it can be as dangerous as an excess of a chemical fertilizer.

Municipal Compost is clean to handle, and about as dry as normal soil, ideal for spreading between herbaceous plants, shrubs and vegetable crops as a combined food and weed suppressor. As is not the case with peat, which is often recommended for this job, its plant foods are available, not locked up by the tannins; but it is not such a good moisture retainer, because of its sandier texture. A ton is roughly 1½ cubic yards, which will cover 27 square yards 2 in. deep, going rather further than a bale of peat, which covers only 21, and at a very much greater cost.

Compost is not a concentrated fertilizer, like dried sludge; it is a source of humus and lightening material, so that it pays to use it in greater quantities but less often. Just as a market gardener or farmer will plough in 20 tons of dung an acre every five years, the amateur gardener could buy a lorry-load of Municipal Compost to raise his humus level high in a single season, and then keep up the level with his own compost heap.

The Midlothian Compost has an excellent leaflet, recommending the working in of 6 lb. a square yard for onions during the spring; a ½-in. layer in the bottom of potato trenches (covered with 1 in. of soil); 4 lb. a square yard for cabbage and for herbaceous borders. The best advice is to buy as much as you can afford and use it generously in a new garden, or one that starts low in humus, to give your soil a flying start instead of waiting to build it up slowly as compost material accumulates.

All the recommended composts are Ph. 7·4, which is neutral, so they can be used for lime-hating plants. One of the problems with rhododendrons, camellias and other shrubs with the same tastes is that though they need peat they also require normal feeding. A top dressing of Municipal Compost is therefore helpful to them, even in the Scottish gardens where they thrive.

The grittiness of this compost, compared with home-made, and its freedom from weed seeds, make it an excellent product for mixing with potting soil. Add 1 part to 7 of ordinary garden soil (unless this is heavy clay) for pricking out seedlings and for most potting.

Dried sludges are used extensively on football pitches and golf courses, and these are the best and cheapest lawn food. Where the sand in lawn sand is conspicuously 'coals to Newcastle', the humus from the sludge improves the structure of the soil and holds moisture, as well as supplying the tonic effect of the nitrogen. The normal dressing is ½ lb. a square yard in September or in February and March, with a summer application in June or thereabouts. Sludge at £1 a hundredweight is better value than lawn sand at £4. Where the problem is clover—as on a sports ground—the answer is a sludge-based 'lawn sand' or rather, 'lawn sludge' which is sold at an extra charge by some councils.

The standard recipe is: 10 parts by weight of a fine grade sludge, 7 parts sulphate of ammonia, and 3 parts sulphate of iron. Sprinkle this on the crowns of daisies, plantains and dandelions, or spread it at the rate of 4–6 oz. a square yard where the lawn is very weedy. This destroys the weeds with the 'burning' effect of the two sulphates, and is rather more effective against pearlwort than modern selective weed-killers, which make the grass unsafe to use for compost, or for mulching between bush fruit, for the next two mowings. Sludge instead of sand makes the grass grow fast to cover the bare patches.

On clay, or where a lawn does not need feeding, use 10 parts of sand instead of sludge, which makes ordinary lawn sand.

Sludges are a good compost heap activator but slow starting, for they have been heat sterilized, which destroys any risk of disease bacteria, but kills the useful ones too. There will probably be enough available in the soil of weed roots to heat the heap success-fully but in the event of trouble, go back to a fresh manure or one of the proprietary activators.

Another use for these dry sludges is as a general garden fertilizer, and they can be balanced for using on tomatoes, potatoes and other potash-demanding crops by adding 4 oz. of sifted wood ashes to every pound of sludge. Half a pound per square yard is a good regular dressing for roses, herbaceous borders, and any part of the garden that is not particularly greedy. This is the best use for the very small amount of wood ashes from prunings and woody rubbish that there should be in the modern garden, for everything else gives better value in the compost heap.

Though this mixture will provide a general diet, and is excellent under gooseberries which are avid for potash, any good dry sludge is better used alone for blackcurrants and raspberries. Spread it between the rows at the rate of 1 lb. per square yard in early April, before you spread the first mulch of moisture-retaining lawn mow-ings.

Most councils who sell a sludge worth buying produce a booklet of directions, and the gardener should always ask for one, as its existence is a sign of proper pride in the local sludge. These booklets are usually written by the park superintendent or by representatives of local allotment societies pooling their experience. They recom-mend planting fruit trees with 2 lb. of dry sludge in the bottom of the hole, advise about $\frac{1}{2}$ lb. to a rose bush, and furnish many other useful hints.

Those who are starting lawns on poor soil should rake 2–4 lb. of dried sludge per square yard into the top 2 in. to give the grass a flying start, but this should be a 15 per cent moisture or drier sludge, if the lawn is to be sown. A thriving crop of tomato seedlings can swamp new-sown grass, though even wet sludge is safe under new-laid turf.

Wet sludges are useful because they are cheap and contain a high proportion of readily available nitrogen for reclaiming subsoil or poor and pebbly mixtures. 'Cheap' is, however, a relative term for it; as an example, the West Kent sludge in the table costs exactly the same as a local straw deep litter poultry manure: the better potash balance and higher quality humus from the straw makes this far better value. Sludges are essentially for those who cannot buy any manure from a farmyard, or even one from deep litter houses.

Adding a manure with 3 per cent nitrogen, like the Isleworth sludge made by the Middlesex County Council, will give a flying start to green manure crops which will take up this nitrogen and convert it to a better grade humus when dug in. Spread a 2-in.-thick layer of a wet sludge, or a $\frac{1}{4}$ in. one of a dry type, and rotavate it in, before sowing common mustard, which is cheaper by the pound than in salad packets, at the rate of $\frac{1}{2}$ oz. a square yard, and it will grow a crop worth digging in within eight weeks. The seed stays good for three years so there is no need to sow as thick as salad to use it up—aim at a seed to every square inch.

Rake the dug grould level, scatter the seed evenly and rake again to cover it lightly. Watering once or twice with a lawn sprinkler gives a flying start to what will look like a forest of rather slim tomato plants.

And, like a forest, it will kill out the weeds below it before they seed, growing 4, 6 or even 10 in. high according to weather and time; for it must be dug in by mid-September, and in bud, not flower. At this tomato-plant size it tucks neatly in the digging trenches which become long, narrow 'compost heaps' which rot without trouble or turning.

Two green manure crops offering more bulk to dig in, and a club-root-destroying rest from the cabbage tribe, are annual blue lupin for sandy soils, and buckwheat for any, including heavy clay. Both have large seeds, which should be sown about every 3 in. along 1-in.-deep furrows. An ounce will give 50 ft. of rows 8 in. apart, with a mass of foliage 3 ft. high.

The lupin should be rolled or trodden down before its tree-lupin-like flowers show blue, and the buckwheat when it has odd green tassels among its large pointed leaves and thick stems. Leave a row to seed, for the lupin is a pure blue, and the pink buckwheat flowers are good bee fodder, and the ripe seed can be fed to cage-birds or poultry.

These are summer green manure crops and are best as spring sown 'sludge tamers', though it is possible to dig them in about July and sown again to secure more humus, and make the bed ready for autumn planting with shrubs or herbaceous plants. Both can be used to fill in unwanted summer space in the vegetable garden, for though some gardeners talk of 'making friends with weeds', chickweed and groundsel seed so fast that one can easily dig in trouble, while green manure crops are slow seeders, well under control.

Except where a garden is too large for its owner, or is being started from scratch, summer green manure crops are at the expense of others we wish to grow. Hungarian Grazing Rye is bred to grow cattle fodder through colder winters than ours, and though it can be sown in spring and dug under in August before it goes stemmy and grows 'ears', it is the finest gardeners' green manure crop to sow between August and early October and dig under in spring. It can follow even maincrop potatoes without loss of cropping space.

Autumn digging, with manure or compost dug in and the big clods of earth left on the surface to be broken down by the frost, is a good gardener's tradition. But not all gardens have the heavy clay that gains from weathering: the fertility of the sandy soils and 'soot and pebble mixtures' of cities and suburbs can be washed away in the winter.

Rake the dug ground smooth and sow 1 oz. of rye for a square yard in the same way that you would sow a lawn. Scatter soil over it and roll firm. (At 50p a pound it is cheaper than rye grass and grows more bulk in the time.)

Mild southern winters can mean a carpet of weeds by spring after autumn digging, but the rye keeps ahead of them and, by April, can be over 1 ft. high from the earlier sowings. Tread the rye down and dig it in with a sharp spade in April. If you do this, the soil will gain humus not only from the foliage but still more from the rotted roots. Gardeners who use a scythe or rough-grass cutter can mow for compost material and still have the root humus when this annual rye dies in August.

Because winter tares have the advantage of pea-tribe root bacteria, which gathers free nitrogen from the air, they can be dug in later, but they are less efficient weed suppressors. Sow them between August and October (or from March to May to dig under in July or autumn) in ½-in.-deep furrows. The rows should be placed 6 in. apart; 3 in. between the larger seeds.

Sandy soils that suffer from drought, and easily dug town garden soils, gain by old-fashioned double-digging—but with a difference. Wheel the top 6 in. of the first 1-ft.-wide strip to the other end of the plot. Then dig the exposed subsoil, treading fresh swept leaves into the trenches. Spread any compost, leafmould or manure on the dug surface and fork the next strip of topsoil over it. Fill the last one with the wheeled soil.

This variation of the old method provides a layer of moisture-holding humus below normal digging level. It is worth renewing every three years. Like leafmould which has been stacked behind wire netting for next year's digging, it saves fertility which is too often burnt in autumn bonfires—the gardener's most wasteful tradition.

Shoddy is wool waste. Once it was used to make inferior cloth; now it is sold to fruit farmers as the cheapest and most hard-wearing manure for new plantings, especially raspberries, rhubarb and black-currants.

All these need to be fed with nitrogen, not quickly from chemicals, but slowly as they grow. Shoddy contains about five times as much nitrogen as good farmyard manure and it is particularly suitable for town gardens as it is readily available, clean and odourless, and it rots to humus, improving clays and holding moisture on sandy soils.

Some second-hand furniture shops sell bargain humus, for old mattresses, which are normally burnt, are often stuffed with about ½ cwt. of wool shoddy, and a gardener can take his pick for about 20p. Before buying, pull out a lump of stuffing and light it. If it splutters, melts and burns away completely it is wool shoddy: a steady bright flame and ash that keeps its shape means cotton and a very bad bargain. Cotton *takes* nitrogen for its decay instead of giving more to garden fertility.

For tomatoes, the cabbage tribe, french and runner beans, spread the shoddy at roughly 1 lb. a square yard, tucking it well down in the bottom of the trench. For peas or potatoes, spread 1 lb. to every 3 ft. of trench. A 2-in. layer on the bottom of holes for tree or shrub planting provides slow nitrogen to go with slow phosphates from bonemeal.

But sooner or later the supply of vintage mattresses will run out; interior springs hold no humus, and nylon, Terylene and other man-made fibres are useless in shoddy, for they will not even decay in compost heaps.

Bonemeal is the best lasting feed for all trees and shrubs, and it should be used in two grades. Fine bonemeal presents the largest working surface to the bacteria that make plant foods available so they release it more rapidly, while coarse has only a fraction of the area so can last ten years slowly doling out its nitrogen and phosphates. Fishmeal is also a phosphate fertilizer, but far richer and quick-acting, with from 6–9 per cent nitrogen and 10–20 per cent phosphoric acid; so it can be used as a compost heap activator, but it is very much more expensive than sludge. There are brands to which 10 per cent of potash has been added to make them better balanced, and these can be used for tomatoes and potatoes for those who have no compost. Dried blood is entirely a nitrogen fertilizer, useful as a quick tonic for lettuces but too costly for a compost heap activator. Dried poultry manure, however, is very good value at £2 per 56 lb., for the heat of drying tames its nitrogen and reduces its amount until it is more in step with its potash. It is the nearest yet to an all-organic general fertilizer with nearly an F.Y.M. balance.

There are very few organic sources of potash, and one is dried seaweed. The best-known make, Marinure, averages 2·9 per cent nitrogen, 0·3 per cent phosphorus and 2·0 per cent potash, with an excellent balance for tomatoes and a host of trace elements thrown in. There are a number of foliar sprays made of seaweeds, but these use the emergency feeding system of the plant rather than its roots. Though a man can be fed through a tube, he is much better off eating the normal way, and weekly sprayings are more work than digging once.

The other regular source of potash for those who garden without chemicals is Comfrey. Roughly five barrowloads of soft sappy weeds make one of finished compost, so gardeners rarely have enough, but five of cut comfrey foliage make four, and are so rich in plant foods that they are 'instant compost', ready-made without a heap.

Comfrey is a perennial and is grown from offsets in a permanent bed like rhubarb. It needs full sun and thrives on clay, but any soil is really adequate except for solid peat or chalk.

The best variety is 'Bocking No. 14' because it is richest in potash, is earliest with a first cut ready in April for maincrop potatoes, and has thin stems that wilt easily. 'Bocking No. 4', the kind grown for cooking like spinach, has thick stems that may sprout and grow where they are unwanted if used as 'compost'.

Dig out perennial weed roots, especially the wicked white ones of couch grass, and dig in manure or ½ lb. of Gunos, dried sludge, or fishmeal to the square yard. Then plant the offsets 2 ft. apart with their growing points just peeping. Ideally, this should be done between March and August, so that the plants become established for a full cutting season in the following year.

In the ten years since this new use for comfrey was discovered, gardeners have found that a dozen established plants yield about 2 cwt. of foliage a summer in four to five cuts with the last about October. That one can be used for digging into onion beds or where early potatoes are to be planted.

Comfrey is ready to cut when it is 1 ft. in height. Lop it off 1 in. from ground level with shears or a knife and leave it overnight to wilt till the stems are limp. Cutting every six weeks gives the highest yield, but most gardeners make their cuts to fit in with the crops that need most potash.

Thus the first can be spread like manure under seed potatoes at the rate of 1–1½ lb. a foot of trench: the next dug in before planting outdoor tomatoes or sowing french or runner beans; and the third placed under lawn mowings between raspberries, gooseberries, or red currants.

Wilted comfrey has about the same plant foods as good farmyard manure, but more than twice the potash (1·19 per cent against 0·5 per cent).

Though it gathers minerals with roots deep as a tree's, it needs lime and nitrogen to grow its heavy yield of foliage. Every other autumn give the bed ½ lb. of lime a square yard dug in with the autumn clean-up. This is usually all the weeding it needs once it is growing fast.

Each spring spread 1 lb. a square yard of dried sludge as the cheapest nitrogen. Poultry-keepers can give it fresh manure, for comfrey can take it in cruder form than any other crop. In exchange, it grows far more bulk of a better balanced manure than town gardeners can ever buy.

15

Disease and Pest Control with Fewest Poisons

The pests and diseases of fruit and vegetables concern also the flower gardener, for many attack their ornamental relations, while still more, like black millipedes and wireworms, appear to like expensive lilies as much as they do potatoes. As this book is not concerned solely with the flower garden but is written to act as a companion to the writer's *Down to Earth Fruit and Vegetable Growing* (Faber and Faber), this chapter covers pests and diseases for both ends of the garden.

It is easy enough, by reading the directions on the tins and bottles in any garden shop, to find out how to cure almost anything. It is also easy to spend more than the retail value of any crop your small garden has room for, as it is very likely that by the time you need the rest of the tinful it will have rusted through the side. So many gardens have potting shed shelves like hypochondriacs' medicine cupboards, that this chapter will deal with how to have a healthy garden without spending fortunes on poisoning birds, bees and, in the long run, your family.

One of the main incentives for growing fruit and vegetables today, is not only the superior flavour of compost grown produce, but its safety. All pesticides begin as safe as thalidomide was until it was found out, and no writer recommending modern chemicals is safe from having the one he recommended, on the best authority, banned, and off the market before his second edition.

An example is Fluoracetamide, which is now prohibited, except for poisoning sewer rats far from dwelling houses, since the Smarden and Merthyr Tydfil disasters. In the 1960 edition of *Horticultural Pests—Detection and Control* by the late G. Fox-Wilson of Wisley (Crosby Lockwood), it is stated that, 'The lowest concentrations can be used with perfect safety on non-edible plants for the control of aphides and it has also been found effective against Blackcurrant Gall Mite on non-fruiting bushes.' But later editions of

220

this excellent work will have references to this recommended poison deleted.

Another disadvantage of modern synthetic insecticides, especially the organo-chlorine and organo-phosphorus compounds, is that pests develop immunity to them. Though D.D.T. has nearly wiped out the malaria mosquito, this was only because it was used intensively and quickly, and in Australia D.D.T.-proof houseflies are now a serious problem.

Carrot and cabbage root flies are developing immunities to R.H.C., lindane, aldrin and dieldrin, and it is possible that before the wild life protection bodies, especially the Royal Society for the Protection of Birds, can get all organo-chlorine compounds banned, they will no longer be in use. They will have been replaced by still more powerful poisons in an 'arms race' that profits only the chemical manufacturer.

This is of course controversial, but the gardener has no need to balance the views of disagreeing scientists. He can return to older methods which served for centuries of British gardening, and at least be sure that he is not spending the summer poisoning the birds he feeds in the winter.

As we saw, in the last chapter, there are comparatively few plant diseases, compared with disabilities that arise from mineral deficiencies; and better feeding is the answer for most mysteries. These are commonest with tomatoes because most gardens have only one sunny and sheltered bed, so tomatoes are grown here year after year. Quite a few more problems vanish when a soil is well drained and reasonably fed. As an example, the Chocolate Spot fungus of beans does not attack unless the soil is low in potash, and with the normal rotation of vegetable crops it is possible to avoid others. The classic example of evasion by crops rotation is the modern method of growing onions from sets. This defeats the Onion Fly completely. Further, the onion bed is now rotated round the garden, thus avoiding Downy Mildew, Grey Mould Fungus and Soft Rot, which lived on from spores in the permanent onion beds of the past.

The diseases that remain are real problems, and the worst is Potato Blight, *Phytophthora infestans*, which killed more people in the Irish potato famine of the 1840's (when chemical fertilizers had not left Rothamsted, which began working on them in 1841) than nuclear weapons have achieved so far. This blight attacks both potatoes and tomatoes in dull, cold summers, and there is no evidence that balanced feeding or ample humus is any defence. In the garden, however, it is less severe than on farms because though the spores can blow and spread fast across a district of potato fields, this is less easy with streets and non-potato-growing gardens isolating infected plots.

One way round is by growing 'Pentland Dell', the new blight-resistant variety, which is not 100 per cent immune, but with the odds that garden crops have on missing infection it carries almost complete protection. It is a heavy-yielding, white skinned, floury variety, rather like 'Majestic', and far better both on flavour and resistance than the old 'Doctor McIntosh' which was a poor yielder, except in wet seasons, and rather tasteless. Maris Peer and Maris Page are second earlies that can be lifted for scraping as new potatoes, like Duke of York, but blight resistant.

Another way is by growing the early varieties that will reach full size and keep like maincrops, so that one kind serves both purposes. Digging them in August or September gives more growing time for the cabbage tribe crops that follow it. Favourite varieties for this purpose are 'Duke of York', for those who prefer a yellow and waxy potato that holds its shape for frying, and 'Stormont Dawn' which is white and floury, with a taste that delights those who prefer this type.

These two can evade blight in years when it strikes late, because when the distinctive dark brown patches appear at the edges and tips of the leaves, they will have almost finished growing their crop. Do not wait for the haulm to blacken and become an evil-smelling mess. Cut it off at ground level and compost it, which is perfectly safe and is easier than burning wet potato foliage in the wet years that favour blight. Wait a fortnight before lifting so that the spores lying on the surface do not contaminate the potatoes as they are dug so that they go rotten in storage, and you will save the crop and have a larger one than if your variety was one that did not reach full size till October.

It is hardly worth a gardener's while to spray with Bordeaux Mixture as a preventative, especially as in bad blight years there is usually enough rain to wash the copper sulphate mixture off the leaves as often as it goes on. Because tomatoes have Potato Blight far worse than potatoes, for there are no immune kinds and no possible evasive action, it pays to spray outdoor plants if there is blight in the district.

Bordeaux Mixture is the standard copper sulphate fungicide and this is best bought ready ground for mixing with water according to the directions on the tin. For complete prevention spray once a fortnight from mid-July onwards in the south, mid-August in the north, and spray again if it rains within two days of spraying. Only start when the potatoes catch it in your district however, since most gardens miss it except in really bad seasons.

Peach Leaf Curl not only attacks peaches and their ornamental relations like 'Clara Meyer', but almonds and other members of the prunus tribe. The answer for this one, Peach Leaf Blister, Peach Mildew and Peach Canker, is spraying just before the buds start to swell, in February or March according to district and season, with Burgundy Mixture. Since this has been replaced by the organo-phosphorus compounds developed from from nerve gases which were fortunately not used in the Second World War, gardeners should make their own.

Dissolve 3 oz. of copper sulphate in a gallon of hot water in a plastic bucket and leave it overnight to cool. Stir 4 oz. of washing soda (sodium carbonate) into a gallon of cold water, than mix the two. This mixture should never be sprayed on anything with leaves on; it is a powerful fungicide for killing spores, and a proprietary wetting agent can be added to help it get into bark cracks. Spread paper or polythene to keep it off anything evergreen, and it is safe as a winter fungus killer for trees and shrubs, if necessary.

Bordeaux Mixture is, however, safer for rose mildew and any of the Powdery Mildews which attack a whole range of plants in dry summers, especially Michaelmas daisies and delphiniums. The Downy Mildews which are less a powder on the leaves than a felty coating are best attacked with Lime Sulphur. This like Bordeaux Mixture, is bought ready mixed for dilution in water, but some gooseberries are 'sulphur shy', notably 'Leveller', and Bordeaux should be used instead. Snipping off the tips of attacked shoots in August and burning them is a help because the fungus winters there as small black spots, and the shoot tips should be pruned away anyhow in winter when they may as well come off before spreading is possible.

Bordeaux, Burgundy and Lime Sulphur mixtures are good standard fungicides without the 'House-that-Jack-built' effect of so many modern chemicals, that kill the owl that ate the birds that ate the slugs that cleared up the dead pests that lived on the leaves they were sprayed on. Any that splash about are merely adding some useful trace elements to the soil, and with luck they are rarely needed.

Apple and pear scab are less common in gardens than orchards because gardeners usually sweep up the fallen leaves on which most of the spores winter. The easiest method of control, especially on old, neglected trees is to spray with Burgundy Mixture, as recommended for Peach Leaf Curl, in February or early March before there are any leaves to damage. This is slightly less effective than normal spraying, but entirely safe, cheap and easy, with an added advantage for those who inherit fruit trees without knowing their names and so have no idea which of them hate sulphur and risk causing leaf loss. Burgundy Mixture has the advantage of sparing the best predator for Red Spider and a number of other pests, *Anthocoris nemorum*, which is destroyed by Lime Sulphur and winter tar oil washes.

The normal routine spraying is 1 part of the lime-sulphur mixture to 100 of water (or however the bottle directs for a 1 per cent solution) which will not harm the sulphur-shy 'James Grieve' and 'Cox's Orange Pippin', 'Lord Derby', 'Beauty of Bath', 'Worcester Pearmain' and 'Bismarck', or 'William' or 'Louis Bonne' or 'Jersey' pears. The apple 'Stirling Castle' is so sulphur shy that it must have Bordeaux Mixture, which, of course, is based on copper sulphate. Spray before the buds burst ('pink bud') and after the petals have fallen.

A garden way round is to look carefully at pruning time for shoots that have bark cracked and blistered near the base, and to take these out with the spur from which they grow for burning. There will be none unless the tree has scab. It was possible for skilled gardeners in the past to prune away scab, but such men are rare today, though a gardener with perhaps three trees to prune can see the difference between smooth healthy bark and infected shoots.

Pears are all sulphur-shy so should be given Bordeaux Mixture at the weaker strength recommended for them, as their foliage is tougher, but 'Doyenne du Comice' is 'shy' for both copper and sulphur so should have only Burgundy Mixture before the leaves, as recommended earlier. This particular set of sprayings also largely controls apple mildew and canker but there is no need to buy Lime Sulphur with a host of other poisons added to it. The cost of spraying a commercial orchard is so great that one spray has to hit everything that *may* be there—the gardener need only cross his bridges when he comes to them for his few trees. There is nothing more expensive or destructive of predators (insects that prey on pests) than spraying for pests you may or may not have.

Silverleaf and Die-back are fungoid diseases of apricots, cherries, laburnums, nectarines, peaches and plums which can be controlled by pruning, and it is a pruning stone fruit in winter, with the apples and pears, that lets in the spores of both fungi if they are about. So look over all trees that are liable to attack in late May for any shoots that have dead brown tips. Take these off with secateurs below the dead bit, and if there is a brown stain in the shoot-middle cut again until the wood shows white and clean. Early May is right for plums and mid-June for the cherries.

This doesn't mean very much work, for the odds are that nothing will have died back, or only a few shoots at most that can be quickly done; but the safe time for sawing out broken, dead or crowded branches is at the snipping season for all stone fruit, for it is then that there is least risk of the trees weakening themselves by bleeding gum. Complete the stone-fruit pruning before 15th July, which the Ministry of Agriculture's Silverleaf Order of 1923 sets as the date by which all dead wood should be sawn from apples and plums. This is because the fungus (*Stereum purpureum*) has a fruiting stage on dead wood, including apples, and this appears on the bark as flat plates, that are dull brown when dry but purple or lilac when moist. The sawing-off and burning of dead wood before spore scattering starts has led to this disease becoming quite rare, and the necessary precautions cost little.

Black Spot on roses is an increasing curse and perhaps the best answer is to stick to the varieties mentioned in Chapter 12 which are immune or resistant. This fungus (*Diplocarpon rosae*) causes round black patches on the leaves and in some cases on the young shoots. Snip these out, gather up all fallen leaves in the autumn, and dig them in deep, for the spores of the disease are spread back on to the roses by rain splashing them upwards from the ground.

Some roses hang on to leaves till spring and these should be picked off in February. Then spread a coat of peat, leafmould or good compost (one that has heated well enough to avoid a crop of seedling weeds) about 1 in. thick. This prevents any further infection from the soil. It works also for Rose Rust which shows as yellow-orange patches under leaves and powder on shoots, which can be distorted. Spray with Bordeaux Mixture in late February after pruning as well, with a plain colloidal copper preparation rather more effective, and wet the soil well too, as a precaution against spores. Then if any Black Spot attacks later, spray again from June onwards, though these precautions will start every season with a clean bill of health.

Leaf Spot is a fungus disease of currants (*Gloeosporium ribis*) which starts with small dark brown spots, which in a wet season can fetch off all the leaves in June and July. Spray with Buisol after the fruit is picked, but the best control is to rake up the fallen leaves and burn or bury them. The fungus develops the spores that spread on these leaves, and if some fall early, look for brown spots. 'Baldwins' and 'Boskoop Giant' get it worst, and too much farmyard manure makes it more likely. Compost (or cut and wilted comfrey) under a lawn mowing mulch avoids it.

Perhaps the commonest garden disease is the clubroot of the cabbage tribe, with spores that can live on in the ground for nine years. It is worst in warm wet summers, on ground that has been heavily manured, or is poorly drained, for these conditions enliven most spores to the zoospore stage, when they can make do with substitute foods. Mustard and charlock are well-known weeds, but clubroot can attack docks and the grasses: cocksfoot (*Dactylis glomerata*), bent grass (*Agrostis alba*), ryegrass (*Lolium perenne*), and Yorkshire fog (*Holcus lanatus*). This is how clubroot can appear in a neglected allotment or garden, or one cleared from a field, building up on the cabbage tribe which grows most fungi.

Resting the ground so that each summer wakes up its zoospore crop and then starves them is still the traditional farm control, but in gardens this involves keeping down shepherd's purse, their favourite weed, not growing candytuft, nasturtiums, stocks or wallflowers in the vegetable garden, and missing out kohl-rabi, turnips, swedes and radish, as well as cauliflowers, broccoli, sprouts, cabbage and kale.

The farmer's remedies for clubroot are lime and a long rotation, which is not possible in a small garden or allotment with only three positions at most for planting cabbages. Lime, however, is possible, but gardeners rarely use enough to make a difference to the fungus, which like an acid soil.

A farm dressing is 4–5 tons of slaked lime an acre, which is 2 lb.–2 lb. 5 oz. a square yard, and any allotment holder who puts on even 1 lb. is frightened of getting scabby potatoes, for this fungus (*Streptomyces scabies*) likes lime. The farmer also knows that lime does not prevent clubroot attack for twelve to eighteen months after it goes on, so he takes two grain crops before his field of cabbages, which he may follow with potatoes well away from his heavy liming.

Gardeners can do likewise by following lime with peas, beans, a winter dug and empty, then carrots and onions and finally the cabbage tribe. The problem is the need to grow potatoes and cabbage, but except for those who show their produce potato scab is not a serious disease, and putting the first lawn mowings in the potato trenches is a traditional way of reducing its attack. Heavy liming every three or even five years is better against clubroot than 4 oz. a square yard every year.

A quite effective garden remedy is smashing up old-fashioned naphtha moth balls and dropping a fragment about as large as a pea down each dibber hole at planting time. Another is dropping sections of rhubarb stem down the holes, which has some effect but a variable one. But there is no sure way of keeping down clubroot so that cabbages can grow year after year on the same close packed garden or allotment. The most certain remedy is calomel powder used according to the directions, but this is mercuric chloride and highly poisonous. Plenty of humus in the form of compost—not fresh manure for this increases the risk by adding nitrogen in quantity—good drainage, lime, and as long a rotation as possible are the best answers to the clubroot problem. So far not even the chemical remedies are 100 per cent effective.

Gardeners no more need books on plant diseases than housewives need medical dictionaries, but Ministry of Agriculture Bulletin 123, 'Diseases of Vegetables' is comprehensive and real value at 50p. Before reading any highly technical work and deciding that your garden is so full of viruses that digging up and burning everything is the only possible course, order *The Diagnosis of Mineral Deficiencies in Plants* from your local library. Published by H.M.S.O., and long out of print, this is one of the most valuable of all government publications. It contains a comprehensive and accurate set of colour plates showing the effects of mineral deficiencies in vegetables and fruit trees, and it is likely that many of your garden troubles can be cured by better feeding.

Though ample humus, and sturdy growth from not forcing plants ahead soft and fast with chemical fertilizers, *may* reduce pest attacks, it is rare that even the most 'organic' gardener escapes them completely. He learns to tolerate a reasonable number of pests because to have his crops completely clean would be more work and worry than it is worth. Every garden contains a large number of predators —the gardener's friends which eat our pests.

The ladybird is well known, and so is its larvae like a tiny black kipper, eating its way through the greenfly. The hoverfly and the lacewing fly both have aphis-eating larvae, while the devil's-coach-horse and violet ground beetles destroy the chrysalids of such pests as carrot-and-cabbage-root flies even in winter.

This balance, however, will always involve some scabby or maggoty apples, and though a few predators will gradually 'work themselves out of a job' most are concerned to keep on earning a living without exterminating their prey. The gardener will always need to compromise, and though the damage to his three trees may be part of the balance of Nature, it is after all *his* fruit crop, and he needs the best and safest answer. The remedies that follow are safe for birds, bees and men, even though many are less effective than the latest chemicals, and some are considerably cheaper. Those which depend on evasion, pruning, or some trick that does not involve even a non-persistent vegetable poison are the most desirable, because they spare the predators which are controlling other pests.

Ants

Apart from the borax remedy in Chapter 13, Pidero, Py-De, or any other mixture of pyrethum and derris, 2 fluid ounces to a 2-gallon can of water poured down a hole thrust into the nest will kill them. Derris and pyrethrum are two safe vegetable pesticides that are easily obtainable, and a mixture of the two is stronger than either. Always read the label, however, for they may well be merely the 'front' for a substance, hiding behind initials, that may be a deadly poison. If you have to use these poisons, the manufacturer who hides behind something of known safety is less worthy of trust than the one who honestly says what his product contains. The gardener's problem is that he (or she) is not a skilled chemist, and until there is a compulsory marking to show relative dangers, it is not possible to tell which new substances are cumulative poisons adding up to danger doses. Stick to derris and pyrethrum for 'Silent Springless Safety'.

Apple Blossom Weevil

The Apple Blossom Weevil (*Anthonomus pomorum*) is a small grey beetle, with a 'V'-shaped white mark on the wingcases, which lays eggs in apple and pear buds. The grubs feeding inside make the buds turn to a small brown button and die. They pupate, change to small weevils, and come out to feed on the foliage before walking down the tree to hibernate until the following spring. If these 'capped' buds are seen, tie sacking strips 6 in. wide round the trunks of standard trees, or on the main branches of bush trees in June, and leave them on till October when they should be removed and burnt, complete with weevils who have found unsafe winter quarters. Corrugated paper can be used instead, but sacking lasts best.

Apple and Green Capsid Bugs

Renewing the bands in spring is a useful practice when the Apple

Capsid Bug is observed. This is a wingless, tubby, light yellow bug about $\frac{1}{4}$ in. long, which runs rapidly about on the leaves on sunny days in May and June. They suck the leaves surrounding flower trusses, and the fruitlets later develop corky patches. Their instinct is to drop to the ground when the tree is disturbed, and spraying with plain water or hosing will bring them down, and a grease band prevents their return. The newspaper trick for weevils, with sticky-band material round the edge, is also usable for Apple Capsid (*Plesiocoris rugicollis*) and for the Green Capsid (*Lygus pabulinus*) which attacks gooseberries, currants, roses and flowering shrubs. This one is slender green and active in May and June, and capsids are easily distinguished from aphides because they move fast and are larger and greedier.

Apple and Pear Aphides

The introduction of summer pruning made it possible to control attacks of the Apple Aphides in small gardens. In May you shorten the leaders by a quarter of their length, which takes off the soft wood that the aphides attack. Then in June for pears, and July for apples, you choose side shoots that start thick as pencils, cutting them back to above the third leaf, not counting those round the base, leaving until later those that are too small for treatment.

This slows down trees that are growing too large for small gardens by reducing the food supply from the leaves and by setting them to ripening basal fruit buds instead of growing more wood. It also means that any aphides can go straight into the dustbin. The Pear Leaf Curl Midge with maggots, and the Pear Sucker which is a small mite, both curl leaves up so tightly that getting a spray inside is impossible, so it is well worth summer-pruning pears in the same way as apples if either pest occurs.

Though this pruning is extra work, pest control is a bonus on better fruit from smaller trees. Normal winter pruning is required as well, shortening main leaders to a third, and the spur to two buds, which means cutting away the late shoot that will have grown from the third bud. There is no need to summer-prune every year, and tip-bearing varieties mustn't be pruned in this way, so in their case one of the several safe aphis-killing sprays should be used after the blossom is over, thus missing the bees.

Apple Sawfly

The damage this creature does is often taken for that of codling moth, but the ends of sawfly tunnels in the fruit have a black mess round them. It is a fly (*Hoplocampa testudinea*), not a moth, which lays eggs in the blossom. The small caterpillars can be caught by spraying with quassia after the petals have fallen, and again fourteen to eighteen days later. Quassia is useless against codling moth caterpillars, but kills sawfly ones with something weak enough to be harmless to bees and relatively safe for predators. Derris dust is the alternative. Pick up your windfalls and always use the steps and pick the shrivelled little apple that hangs on after leaf fall; it has sawfly inside.

Quassia chips are still obtainable, because they are one of the district nurse's favourite remedies against lice in children's hair.

A standard recipe is to simmer 2 oz. of chips (the wood of a tree Picrasma) in a gallon of water for two hours. Strain through a jelly-bag, or use (as I did) a pyjama leg tied at the bottom and spread with strings to the clothes-horse, so that the liquid drips into a basin free from the spent chips that block syringes. Add a dessertspoonful of soft soap, or liquid washing-up soap if the first is hard to buy, to the liquid you will get from a gallon simmered that long, and bottle for future use.

A tablespoonful of this to a pint of water is the mixture for spraying, but it needs to be washed off vegetables before these are eaten because it tastes extremely bitter, though it is entirely harmless. A stronger mixture uses $\frac{1}{2}$ lb. of chips to the gallon, adding more water as it boils away, plus 1 oz. of soft or ordinary soap, to store and use at the rate of one part to five of water. This is effective against small caterpillars, especially those of the Gooseberry Sawfly. Liquid at this strength has been sprayed on gooseberry bushes and other fruit in spring, for the bitterness is reputed to be protection from birds. It lasts till it rains, and then needs renewal.

Apple Sucker

This (*Psylla mali*) is like an aphis, but the immature ones look like tiny crabs. You know you have it when the apple blossom petals are brown and withered as from frost, although there has not been a frost. The active adult insects which are winged are sucking the leaves from May to leaf fall, and rise in clouds when the foliage is disturbed. Their yellow eggs are laid on shoots and spurs in autumn, and a winter wash kills them completely, which is why the pest is now only found in neglected orchards. The other way to catch it is with derris or Pidero sprayed when the apple blossom buds are just showing pink; this serves to catch the newly-hatched young suckers as they settle. This means risk to bees, who will be the next arrivals, so the best way round is a winter wash. One good go kills the eggs and solves the problem before it gets out of hand, as it can if it is left to predators, which are fewer for this species than for aphides.

Apple Twig Cutter

This is a small blue weevil about $\frac{1}{6}$in. long (*Rhychites caeruleus*), which appears in May and feeds on foliage. It lays eggs about 6 in. from shoot tips and then severs the shoot so that it either falls or hangs till blown down. If tips are seen lying on the ground in June or July pick them up, and if any tips are hanging snip them off, burning both, for the grubs are inside feeding on the pith ready to come out and pupate in the soil. The attack from these weevils is serious, so the stooping and snipping for the first year pays dividends.

Asparagus Beetle

This creature (*Crioceris asparagi*), a beetle with a double black cross on its reddish-yellow back, lays eggs on developing shoots in June and on the 'fern', producing dirty-grey humpbacked grubs which feed on the foliage for about a fortnight, burrow in the soil, and pupate either to become more beetles or to last through the winter. Spray the grubs with liquid derris or Pidero.

Big Bud or Currant Gall Mite

This microscopic mite (*Phytoptus ribis*) attacks black, red and white currants, and sometimes gooseberries. It works its way into the buds of the new shoots, usually the tip ones in June, lays eggs, and the young mites feed and breed inside the buds; these swell, and the shoot goes blind. They migrate from the enlarged buds between late March and mid-April, not only crawling on the bush but carried by the wind, on the feet of birds, and even by bees.

Watch for enlarged buds after late July, at pruning time in the autumn, and even as late as early March, and pick them off to be burned. There can be as many as 500 mites in a bud, so picking the first few from chance can save a bad outbreak. The only way to get at these mites with a spray is when they are out on the branches. Their danger is that they carry Reversion virus, for which the only remedy is digging up the bushes and burning them; but because this is mite-carried and not from left-in roots, new currants can be planted in the same place.

The mites migrate between mid-March and mid-April and this is the only time a spray will catch them. Use derris, or a derris and pyrethrum mixture at the strength recommended for Red Spider, and do it when the leaves are the size of shillings, the most likely stage to catch the mites out without their 'big buds'. Lime-sulphur wash at 1–50 strength can be used instead, but not stronger, for some black-currants, like 'Davidson's Eight', are sulphur shy.

Blackfly

The Blackfly of broad beans (*Aphis fabae*) is responsible for more slaughtered bees than any other pest because it must be sprayed when the plant is in blossom. Sowing in November means early beans, and picking their tips out when they start blackfly colonies to dump in the dustbin or burn, leaves little soft growth for further attack, on the principle of Apple Aphis control by summer pruning.

This means only early beans and makes it impossible to grow the 'Windsors' and other spring-sown types; but it saves Blackfly trouble, and avoids broad beans clashing with the early peas. Pull up the beans when the crop is over, for they make good compost and they are only harbouring fly from late shoots.

Another sowing that dodges Blackfly is one of a 'Windsor' or other spring variety in early June for a crop from August to late autumn. The Blackfly (*Aphis fabae*) multiplies sexlessly and fast in summer on broad, french and runner beans, also attacking beet, rhubarb, spinach, turnips, dahlias, nasturtiums, poppies, a range of annuals, fat-hen and thistles. At the end of its season it produces winged males and females which migrate, so this late sowing gives a crop after they have gone.

They fly off to Euonymus, both wild and cultivated, and viburnums, where they lay small, shining, black eggs that spend winter safe in the joints of leaf and stem. These hatch to black wingless creatures that increase through spring while beans and other hosts are growing, then winged forms, all females, again are produced, flying off to start the cycle again.

Those who have a Euonymus hedge can spray their Blackfly before these start on the beans. A tar-oil winter wash in December will destroy the eggs, and the hibernating caterpillars of the Small Ermine Moth (also a fruit pest), which is the one that swarms with untidy webs and leaf stripping in these hedges in June and July. It is also possible to catch the first stage of Blackfly between March and April with any safe pesticide. Quassia and pyrethrum spare most predators for there can be large quantities of Anthocoris bugs at work with ladybird and other larvae.

The pesticide for the man who has a long hedge of Euonymus, a hedge which would cost about £20 to spray with aerosols of chemicals in spring, to catch the first Blackfly stage for gardens for miles, is nicotine. This is poisonous, but he is not going to eat the hedge. No bees are attracted to it and the hard work (or labour cost) of spraying is quite enough without expensive chemicals.

Boil 4 oz. of non-filtertip cigarette ends, or $\frac{1}{2}$ lb. of filters (less nicotine but purer) in 2 gallons of water for half an hour, strain like the quassia, and heat the clear brown liquid with 1 lb. of soft soap till this is dissolved. Mix one part to four of water when spraying. The merit of this mixture is cheapness, and it will knock out Small Ermine Moth caterpillars too, if they are starting. Bought nicotine washes are far more reliable, but they are worth using only for leaf-miners; and with only a few leaves on celery or chrysanthemums showing the pale zigzags from the maggot tunnelling within, it pays to pick off and destroy. Finding the first of a pest that has just arrived by keeping one's eyes open and destroying at once, saves many sprays.

Cabbage Aphis

This is also called 'Mealy Cabbage Aphis', and it winters on left-in brassica stumps. Destroying these is the best control, even stacking to dry before burning, for it is very hard to get heat on a compost heap in early spring to kill the small, black, over-wintering eggs. New plantings can be sprayed with pyrethrum, derris or Pidero, and so should 'spring cabbage' of all types, before the winged migrant stage in mid-May. With aphides of all kinds it is spraying of the first colonies that pays.

Cabbage Gall Weevil

The attacks of this are often taken for clubroot, but if the 'clubs' are round, or made up of a number of roughly round distortions, cut them open and see if there is a maggot inside. The first effect is of flagging on hot days, and a teaspoonful of dried blood will grow them past the trouble enough to heart and save something from the waste. This applies even if it is clubroot, or Cabbage Root Fly. Dig, do not pull your cabbage stumps, so that the galls stay on and the stumps can be stacked to dry for burning. A policy of drawing stumps early and cutting up for compost or burning pays with the whole cabbage tribe. The 'spring greens' that grow from the stumps are not worth the pests they harbour.

Cabbage Root Fly

This is a grey fly, rather like a house-fly, $\frac{1}{4}$ in. long; and in late April and May, late June to mid-July, and in August and September, it lays its eggs just below the soil near the roots of cabbages and cauliflowers, other brassicas less often, and the grubs burrow down and then up into the lower part of the stem. This shows in stunting, flagging and bluer-grey leaves, so any attacked cabbage should be dug up and replaced with a new one, for the one with the maggot will do no good and may well mean as many as twenty small chestnut-brown chrysalids in the soil, either hatching quickly to repeat the process, or waiting until the spring for the April attack.

The traditional defence is a 4-in. square of tarred roofing felt with a $\frac{3}{8}$ in. or $\frac{1}{4}$ in. punch hole in the middle. The best system is to poke the straight cabbage plant root through the hole, slide it up the stem and hold it with the leaves while planting normally with a dibber. As the stem grows it fits the hole tightly and can force the felt to make room. This is a fly-proof barrier that lasts all through the season and is effective if the soil is level enough for the square to sit flat, leaving no room for the fly to crawl underneath.

Cabbage White Caterpillars

Derris or derris and pyrethrum mixtures are the best caterpillar killers, and both are entirely non-poisonous to human beings, though derris kills fish—so keep it away from the goldfish pond. The nicotine spray from cigarette ends can be used while the plants are small, but it is too poisonous any time near to the eating stage, or when they are heartening. The Cabbage Moth caterpillars which vary in colour and can be black as well as green, are even worse and burrow right into the hearts of the cabbages, so it is best to catch them early with Pidero or Py-De. A cheaper spray is 2 oz. of soft soap dissolved in a gallon of water. Soft soap can still be bought from ironmongers or builders' merchants for it is used for cleaning paint.

A reputed repellent is $\frac{1}{2}$ pint of milk in a gallon of water sprayed on in May to keep the egg-laying butterflies off, repeating about every three weeks. It is extremely difficult to be sure that a repellent is responsible for the ending of an attack, but this might keep a few off cheaply.

Cabbage White Fly

This is a relation of the greenhouse pest of tomatoes and now rare, for the winter of 1962–3 seems to have killed all but a few.

Spray the undersides of the leaves with nicotine if the brassicas are a long way from eating stage. Otherwise mix $\frac{1}{4}$ lb. of soft soap in a 2-gallon can and syringe under the leaves with it at weekly intervals for three weeks. This pest has immobile larvae-like 'eggs', flat, oval and brown, which produce sooty droppings in quantity and clouds of small flies, as its greenhouse relation does. Removing and burning lower leaves is the best control when the first larvae are seen on brussels sprouts, cabbage, cauliflower, broccoli, kale and kohl-rabi, always under the leaves. There are four to five generations a season, and picking for the first stops the rest.

Capsid Bugs

The Green Capsid (*Lygus pabulinus*) is rather like the apple one, a small active six-legged creature like a more nimble aphis, which lays eggs on currants and gooseberries in November, to hatch in April and feed on the buds. The second brood attacks herbaceous plants, strawberries and potatoes. These can be sprayed with derris or Pidero as a direct killer. The Bishop Bug (*Lygus pratensis*), or Tarnished Plant Bug which attacks the buds of chrysanthemums, arctotis, dahlias and zinnias, can also be killed by this direct spraying, but it is far better to keep down docks, groundsel and sorrel, the weeds it lives on in the spring when it has come out of hibernation. Derris dusting is also effective against this creature.

Carrot Fly

The Carrot Fly (*Psila rosea*) also attacks celery, parsley and parsnips. It is a small, greenish-black fly about $\frac{1}{4}$ in. long, which lays eggs near the young carrots in disturbed soil in May and June mainly, but later attacks are common in dry seasons; and the second in August and September is usually less severe. The legless maggots, white first then yellow, wriggle straight down and then work upwards into the roots, wriggling out into the soil and becoming small yellow chrysalids. These can become flies and repeat the process in a week, but most of them spend the winter in the soil. Any bed that has grown maggoty carrots should be dug over twice or even three times in winter to give the birds, especially the robins, a better chance at the chrysalids. The attack shows first in foliage turning rusty red from root damage, but there is no way of killing the maggots once they have started, for no pesticide however deadly will run *up* the tunnels. The two standard methods of protection involve preventing the fly from finding the carrot bed, which is why the dig-over system is always desirable, for chrysalids hatching at close range mean carrot flies can be too near for evasive action.

Planting spring onions ('White Lisbon') as plants, or onion sets round the carrot bed, is a traditional method of 'jamming' the scent that can draw Carrot Flies across more than a mile of gardens. The advantage of the spring onions is that they are cheaper than bought onion plants and have plenty of scent going for the first attack in May. Those who like onion flavour in salads can snip off the leaves, which will grow again. This increases the Carrot-Fly-baffling effect, while the bulbs are still fit for cooking as non-keeping onions that make the storing varieties go further.

Naphthalene flake at the rate of 2 oz. a square yard every ten days is costly, so the best remedy of this type is sand soaked in paraffin scattered thinly between the rows. Another is tarred string of the type sold for tree tying, cut into lengths to allow for tying round a peg at each end of the carrot row. Tie the ends to the pegs first, then soak the middle in creosote, and with careful carrying of the pegs the lasting and cheap creosote scent stays on the string instead of coming off on hands and clothing.

An easier method is to spread lawn-mowings in a $\frac{1}{2}$-in.-thick coat between the rows, scattering some more at every mowing to keep up a hay smell from the drying mowings which can be dug in for humus when the carrots are lifted. This is least effective, but costs nothing and will beat a small attack.

The best evasive action is to sow in late May or June to avoid the worst attack, and to grow 'Lock's Maincrop', or any other quick-maturing maincrop variety that will grow to keeping size by October. The scent of crushed carrot foliage fetches the furthest-off flies, so thin sowing to reduce thinning to a minimum is a great advantage. Firm the soil back by treading and water the rows so the soil settles hard again quickly, because the flies prefer to lay eggs in soil disturbed by thinning.

The Henry Doubleday Research Association is working on a new way round this problem and that of the Cabbage Root Fly. Both feed on pollen of flowers of the order Umbelliferae, notably cow-parsley and wild hemlock *Conicum maculatum* (in the roots of which they lived before gardeners grew carrots, and they still do), while they are in search of carrots or cabbages to lay eggs round. Oil of Coriander, suitably diluted, is added to water at the bottom of 1-lb. jam jars covered with suitable grids to exclude bees and wasps, and this appears most effective in trapping the creatures in sheltered places away from the vegetable area. Whether sufficient can be caught before they do the damage to make a difference remains to be seen, but May and June trapping prevents the later hatches and means few pests wintering as chrysalids and in peril from the predators. This may well be the method of the future.

Chafers

There are three of these, the Common Cockchafer or May Bug, a large red-brown beetle with a black thorax and reddish-brown wing-cases, about 1 in. long, the Garden Chafer which has a green thorax and is $\frac{1}{2}$ in. long, and the Rose Chafer which is vivid golden green with some white spots. Their larvae are much the same, ugly dirty white grubs shaped like a fat capital 'C', that spend up to three years underground eating the roots of fruit trees and shrubs, potatoes, dahlias, zinnias and a number of herbaceous and alpine plants, as well as grass roots, where they may be responsible for round dead patches on lawns.

The adult beetles feed on leaves, rose and strawberry flowers and gnaw the skins of young apples and pears. Their natural controllers are rooks and seagulls, and vast numbers are eaten by birds following the plough. If the larvae are found by digging where a tree or shrub appears to be suffering from root damage, or when forking between herbaceous plants, apply 3–4 oz. a square yard of naphthalene flake, fork it under and water well to soak it down.

The only way to cope with the adults is handpicking and dropping in strong nicotine wash, for though D.D.T. and other powerful killers are recommended, very large quantities are required, and the lead arsenate of the past is just as dangerous. An inverted umbrella held under an attacked bush which is shaken will collect them quickly, but this cannot be done with a large oak tree which the Common Chafer can attack. A beetle that eats flowers is impossible to poison with a bait, and naphthalene for the larvae is still the best answer, apart from the birds. Chickens are very fond of the beetles if any adults are collected.

Codling Moth

This small grey-brown moth (*Cydia pomonella*) is one of the worst apple pests, and one which sometimes attacks pears. Its egglaying is from mid-June until mid-August, with two and sometimes three batches of caterpillars a year. The only chance for effective spraying is between the time when the eggs are laid on the fruitlets, spurs, shoots and leaves, and the advent of the small caterpillars which bore inside the fruitlets.

The $\frac{1}{4}$–$\frac{1}{3}$-in.-long grubs—the familiar 'maggots in the apple'—are full-fed in three to four weeks, and they can either drop direct to the ground, or come down in windfalls. Though picking these up and dumping them or feeding them to chickens gives partial control, the grubs that drop direct escape. Most of them then search for a hibernation place, though some of the first to fall spend only a short time in their whitish or brown cocoons before becoming Codling Moths for a late attack.

Those that hide under leaves are in peril from many predators, and still more are caught crawling to safety, and their best bet is to go up the trees again and into bark crannies. Therefore the sacking strips used for weevils serve also as Codling Moth traps, and though there may be only twenty or so per tree, these had the best chance of wintering safely.

Collect all windfall apples and feed to pigs or chickens, or give them away. A great many caterpillars are not yet fully fed when the fruit falls and these can finish off and hibernate successfully. It also pays to collect the leaves, and a gardener's trees in a mown lawn where dead leaves are removed by sweeper for leafmould are more likely to escape Codling Moth than a neglected orchard, unless this has chickens and ducks in it.

The only time that Codling Moth can be caught by spraying is between mid-June and the end of August, and the best spray is Ryania, which is made from a tropical plant like derris, with the merit of missing the Anthocoris bug that preys on Red Spider. Derris and derris and pyrethrum mixtures are also good, but kill predators, though they spare the bees, for the Codling Moth is not about till the blossom is over. Two sprays should be enough—one in late June or early July and another 3–4 weeks later. The Red Plum Maggot Moth is a close relation and lays eggs on plum fruit stalks in late June and early July. The same control measures apply, so spray the Victoria when you spray apples against Codling Moth which can also attack pears, and the ornamental crop apples.

Currant Aphides

The three Aphides that attack black, red and white currants all spend a 'summer holiday' on dead-nettles and sow-thistles, so these weeds should be kept out of the garden. They return in the autumn to hibernate on currant bushes where a winter-wash will catch them, but spraying the underside of the leaves in mid-April using the nicotine wash recommended for Euonymus against Blackfly will catch them when they have just started and before they curl the leaves and make spraying difficult.

Currant Clearwing Moth

The currant Clearwing Moth (*Aegeria tipuliformis*) lays eggs in June on young stems, and the caterpillars tunnel up the shoot causing sudden wilting of the foliage by late July and August. Watch for these and snip them off in August or September when you are sure. At pruning time bend any weak-looking shoot, and cut it out should it snap, for it may have a caterpillar still eating inside.

Currant Moth

This is also known as Magpie Moth (*Abraxas grossulariata*) and has 'looper' type caterpillars, black and white with yellow stripes down the sides. The moth, which is black, white and yellow, lays on the leaves in July and August, the eggs hatch and feed for a short time before hiding in dead leaves and rubbish to hibernate as caterpillars. They wake in spring and can strip the foliage completely from currants, gooseberries, apricots, plums, hazel-nuts, laurels and Euonymus. On the non-edible bushes use the nicotine and soap wash, otherwise derris which is safe and easy.

Currant Shoot Borer

The Currant Shoot Borer (*Lampronia capitella*) is related to the Raspberry Moth but it is larger, about $\frac{1}{2}$-in. wing span; it lays its eggs in the fruit, where the grubs feed on the seeds and after a time spin cocoons under the rough bark of the older branches. In spring they wake up, tunnel into buds and branches, and become moths in April and May. If buds and shoots are seen shrivelling and dying, cut them off and burn them.

The other answer is a winter wash in December, which kills the cocoons under the bark if squirted on strongly, and stops the outbreak with only one lot of damage.

Cutworms

These are also called 'Surface Caterpillars' and they are plump and leathery brownish-green caterpillars which hide in the daytime and appear at night, eating through the stems of newly planted cabbages, attacking turnips and also chrysanthemums, dahlias, asters, marigolds and zinnias. They are the caterpillars of the Turnip Moth, the Heart and Dart Moth and the Yellow Underwing.

The usual control method is to hunt for them at night with a torch, as with slugs, but a hedgehog in your garden will clear them completely. An alternative is to mix 2 oz. of the borax and icing sugar mixture for ants with 3 lb. of bran and add water to make a moist but not sloppy mash. Scatter this under pieces of slate to prevent birds taking it, and it will destroy the caterpillars much more safely than the old Paris Green, which was arsenic, good enough for Crippen.

Earwigs

There are of course many trapping methods; a neat one is a shotgun cartridge case on the top of each chrysanthemum cane (16 bore or ·410 for choice), but where they are really swarming up a tree, cloth ties round the branches make an effective trap. Pidero is the killer, for they are tough creatures, though not all that harmful. The earwig (*Forficula auricularia*) is in fact a part-time pest eater.

Flea-Beetles

These tiny skipping black beetles eat holes in seedling radish, turnip and cabbage tribe leaves. Dusting with derris is the best answer, but it is important to keep up the humus supply so that moisture is retained and the plants do not suffer from drought in May and June when the beetles are active. These creatures over-winter on left-in brussels sprouts and other brassica stems, so the same tidiness that removes these to prevent Mealy Cabbage Aphis and Cabbage White Fly serves also to keep down Flea-Beetle.

Gooseberry Sawfly

The Gooseberry Sawfly (*Pteronidea ribesii*) lays first in April and May, twenty to thirty eggs a leaf, white and in rows by the midrib underneath, on gooseberries and black, red or white currants, also ornamental Ribes. The caterpillars have black heads, green-and-black spotted bodies, and three orange-yellow marks, and they can swarm and strip the bushes. There are three generations, the first are ready to lay in June and their offspring can lay in September.

The answer is to spray with quassia, 2–3 fluid ounces to the gallon, which is a killing spray for all small caterpillars, and this will beat the apple and plum sawfly caterpillars too. Quassia of course leaves lasting bitterness on fruit, so use derris if anything is near harvest. Both are completely non-poisonous to human beings or birds and pets, but quassia is by far the cheaper.

Greenfly

The common Greenfly of roses is easily killed with the home-made nicotine wash, but another 'do-it-yourself' insecticide is even cheaper, for it is free for the trouble of making for those with rhubarb at the bottom of the garden. Cut up 3 lb. of the leaves and boil in 3 quarts of water for 30 minutes before straining and bottling. It keeps best without the soft soap which is a wetting agent, not a pesticide, in all these recipes. Dissolve 4 oz. of soft soap, which costs 20p a jar from a chemist, for the only grade now available is used for enemas, in 4 pints of hot water, and mix the two liquids when cool.

The large Rose Aphis (*Macrosiphum rosae*) spends the winter at egg stage hidden in the gnarled bark of the root stock of the rose. Syringe this with a tar-oil winter-wash in December or January, to kill the eggs before they hatch and start multiplying at slide-rule speed. This policy for standard rose stems, the stocks of ramblers and all established roses, pays in terms of saving hard work and predators. The sprays against greenfly kill the larvae of ladybirds, hoverflies and lacewing flies, but none of these hibernate on rose rootstocks.

Lackey Moth

At apple and pear pruning time look for neat bracelets of eggs round the thicker young shoots or spurs. If these are not pruned away and burnt with the other prunings, smash them with the secateurs while there are only a few. They are the eggs of the Lackey Moth which will hatch in April and become blue-grey hairy caterpillars, with reddish and white stripes, that live on leaves, making silk 'tents' in which they hide. Dusting with nicotine or derris is a killer best used in May before much damage is caused. The eggs are immune to winter washes, and as two hundred of them in one bracelet can easily be destroyed this is well worth doing. The pest is on the increase and appears suddenly in orchards, so watch for the egg bands on cherries and plums too.

Leaf-miners

These are maggots inside tunnels in the leaves, but a nicotine wash will get inside and kill; then the best policy is to pick off the attacked leaves and destroy them. Chrysanthemum Leaf-miner also attacks sow-thistle which should be kept out of the garden as a 'never-well weed' which is strong enough to harbour many pests and pass them on. Fen farmers do not bother about Leaf-miner (*Acidia heraclei*) on celery; the stripped leaves after harvest are ploughed in deep, which puts the leaves with pupae so far down they cannot emerge as adults. Deep digging, where there have been badly attacked celery or parsnips, is a garden application of the measure. Use a spade and tuck the rubbish well down in the trench bottom. Burning or composting foliage has the same effect, but it is rare that a winter heap heats to pupae-killing temperature.

Leather Jackets

These are the larvae of the Daddy-long-legs or Cranefly (*Tipula olearacea, T. paludosa* and *Pachyrrhina maculata*) and they can be troublesome in lawns, causing sudden and inexplicable bare patches from eaten roots. They are 1–1½ in. long, brown or grey caterpillar-like creatures with leathery skins, from eggs in August-September, feeding through the winter to spring. In early summer they become pupae, and these must push up to release the Daddy-long-legs (or Cranefly) in August to start the cycle again. All three kinds need the same treatment.

Drought-baked soil is awkward to push through, so they take every chance when the ground is moist. Water the lawn well and spread black polythene over the bare patches, leaving it on for about four hours. Then remove the polythene and run the roller or motor-mower over the turf, crushing hundreds of pupae and giving the local birds a treat. When this was done with tarpaulin rick-sheets borrowed from the Home Farm the sheets lay flat, but polythene needs stakes to weigh it down. Late July and August are good times, but May and June are also possible. Then the larvae come to the surface on damp nights, and watering or soaking from a lawn sprinkler, combined with use of black polythene, produces an artificial 'damp night'. Then after a mowing there will be a kill much appreciated by thrushes, blackbirds and starlings.

Lettuce Root Aphides

Lettuce plants that wilt in warm weather and suddenly decay and die, suffer from this creature (*Pemphigus bursarius*) in July and August, when its winged forms migrate from poplar trees to spend a summer honeymoon on lettuce, sow thistle and fat-hen. Their offspring live on the roots of these plants, and if the lettuces are dug up they can be seen as pale yellow aphides covered with white wool. If any lettuces suddenly flag, water the row with liquid derris or Pidero, aiming at a 6-in.-wide strip, and not soaking the plot, for there is no point in killing worms, and there is need only to soak lettuce to root depth.

Lettuce Root Maggot

Attacked lettuces wilt in the same way, but roots either break off completely or show slender, creamy maggots up to ¼ in. long burrow-ing in them. This creature is *Psila nigrocoris*, a close relation of the Carrot Fly, and all the repellent methods and even the trapping can be used against it. It is rather easier to control because its maggots bore downwards instead of up so there is a good chance that watering with derris will kill them. It is also the Chrysanthemum Root Maggot, and here it has not a thick carrot root to hide in, so watering with nicotine or even rhubarb insecticide will catch it.

Millipedes

The Centipede is flattened and light chestnut brown, with one pair of legs to a segment (Lithrobius); or it is slender and yellow (Geophilus) and the two groups are friends, eating large quantities of small slugs, eggs, and a range of pests. They may be the creepiest of crawlies but they do a great deal of good in a quiet way.

The Black Millipede (*Tachypodjulus niger*) looks like a short black length of metalled gas pipe, coils stiffly when disturbed, and has two pairs of legs to a section. Some gardeners call it the 'Black Wireworm' but this it is not; for unlike Wireworms, it does not change to something else (Click Beetle) but stays a greedy brute for several years. The Spotted Millipede (*Blanjulus guttulatus*) has a row of red spots along the sides of its body: it is rarer but greedier, and a curse to daffodil growers in Lincolnshire.

Both eat bulbs, especially lilies, potatoes, carrots and the roots of many plants, also boring into germinating peas and beans. Because their increase rate is relatively slow, they are worth trapping.

Punch holes in the sides of tins with an old-fashioned pointed tin-opener, or make cylinders of 1 in. or, better $\frac{1}{2}$-in.-mesh wire-netting roughly 3 in. wide and 8 in. deep, with the sides and bottoms laced together with wire. Fill these with potato peelings, cut-up potato or carrot, and bury them in the bed where Millipedes are; a wire handle on each helps when pulling them out at weekly intervals and fitting them back in the holes. Tip the contents into the dustbin, or a central-heating furnace or other fire; refill traps with peelings and start again.

Strong Pidero, 2 fluid ounces to a pint (a measure is provided with the tin of nicotine), will kill Millipedes for those who wish to tip them in a bucket and count the catch in the morning. No one who is cursed with Millipedes has any pity for them. There is no evidence that they do not attack healthy, compost-grown plants, but quite a bit of evidence that they prefer the more expensive lily bulbs and daffodils. A 'trapline', regularly attended to, will make a real difference to their numbers. They also eat decaying vegetable matter and a garden soil rich in humus can have more than a poor one. They are worst on damp and poorly drained soils that lack lime, and dislike surface soil that is often disturbed. This is why they are common in neglected gardens and with 'no-diggers'.

Onion Fly

Like the Carrot Fly this is small and grey, usually laying eggs just under the bulb in spring or early summer, and it also hunts by scent; but onions have a scent too strong to jam. The eggs are small, oval and white and can also be laid on the neck of the bulb or the leaves, and on leeks too.

They hatch and burrow in, and in about three weeks they leave the bulb to become chestnut-brown pupae in the soil, which hatch to flies quite thickly in the case of the first two broods; the last brood winters in the soil as pupae. The foliage of infested bulbs turns first yellow then white and the bulbs can become pulpy messes with as many as thirty maggots in each. Once a bulb is attacked it cannot keep, and digging up and burning saves attack by still more flies.

The garden answer is given at the beginning of this chapter. Grow onions from sets, either the flattened mild 'Stuttgarter Reisening', or the rounder Spanish types 'Invincible' and 'Marshall's Giant Fen'. The saving of thinning, replacing hand weeding by hoeing, and above all the start that these small bulbs have on the weather for ripening in wet summers makes onions an easy crop, not a trial of garden skill.

Pear and Cherry Slugworm

This is more like a slug than a caterpillar for it is the larvae of a sawfly (*Eriocampa limacina*), at first pale yellow but ageing to dark green or black. It is scarce for years then suddenly appears, from mid-June to September, feeding on the upper surfaces of the leaves of pears and cherries, but also apples, plums and Chaenomeles ('Japonica'). It can manage three generations in a season, the last over-wintering in cocoons, in the soil. Derris dust or spray in June will stop it easily, and because it is a sawfly, quassia has a chance.

Pear Midge

This tiny fly lays eggs in pear blossom, and its maggots bore into the developing fruitlets. So look for fruit in May which is either extra large and round or unnaturally long. Picking and cutting them open will disclose a mass of decay with ten to thirty maggots inside a single fruit, so these should be dumped in the dustbin or fed to chickens. Leaving them ungathered risks their falling off early and the maggots escaping and pupating in the ground. Chickens and pigs in old-fashioned orchards got rid of them, but any modern contact spray lasting long enough to kill the quite rare Pear Midge is going to destroy bees visiting blossom on their lawful occasions.

Pith Moth

The Pith Moth (*Blastodacna atra*) is quite common, but its damage is usually blamed on others. In May and June apple leaves and blossom on young spurs and growing shoots wilt, and their terminal buds die from no apparent cause. The tiny moths are about in late July and August, laying eggs in the leaf axils of young shoots which hatch to caterpillars that burrow into the stems, and continue to feed right through the winter. Normal pruning removes most of them, but tip-bearers like 'Blenheim Orange', can suffer badly. When the wilting shows, cut off the spur and burn it, for, like the damage done by the Twig Cutter, once it starts in an orchard it can be a real problem.

Raspberry Beetle

The Raspberry Beetle (*Byturus tormentosus*) is entirely different; it is yellowish or greyish-brown and lays eggs in the fertilized blossoms in June and July. The grub feeds on the fruit, becoming the familiar maggot in the raspberry. When full-fed they drop out and pupate in the soil, going down at least 3 in. (unlike the hibernating caterpillars of the Raspberry Moth), out of reach of a spray of winter-wash in December. The custom of digging in the summer mulch of mowings between the rows in October helps control the beetle, because it gives the birds, especially robins, a chance to get at the pupae which are small and hard to find.

A second dig in December or January, as suggested for Carrot Fly-attacked beds, increases this effect, and the writer has had no trouble from this pest after three years of this policy. The alternative is spraying with derris or quassia ten days after the raspberries start flowering, and again fifteen days later to catch the caterpillars at the tiny stage inside the blossom and crawling from the petals into the developing fruit. Always spray on a dull day with few bees about, or in late evening, for whole hives have been wiped out by raspberry growers using even derris. Quassia at Sawfly strength is rather safer for bees—they may recover—but pyrethrum is not strong enough.

Raspberry Moth

The Raspberry Moth (*Lampronia rubiella*) has about a $\frac{1}{4}$-in. wingspan and flies in daytime, laying eggs in the blossom in May and June. Its small red caterpillars bore through the fruit, up the stalks and down the cane, to hibernate in crevices, support stakes and round the cane bases. In April they attack the shoots again. At this time they are noticed when the shoots wilt, and cutting away any shoots that flag suddenly and burning them prevents a build-up of this pest before they turn to moths and repeat the process.

Red Spider Mite

The rise of the Red Spider Mite (*Bryobia praetiosa*) as a pest of apples is an example of the danger of winter-washes in orchards. These do not kill its eggs but destroy its most important predator, leaving the Black-Kneed Capsid Bug (*Blepharidopterus angulatus*) to struggle on alone with the help of such hover flies, lacewing flies and ladybirds as arrive during the summer.

The Black-kneed Capsid did its best, but when B.H.C. was used with petroleum sprays later in the year, even this hard-working creature was slaughtered. This is why Red Spider, though winter-washes began in the 1920's, did not become a major problem until the late 1940's. Before the 1920's, the Red Spider Mite had fed on the algae and lichens on the trunks, but when winter-washes wiped out their food supply they began to attack the leaves, and became the classic example of a serious pest caused by a pesticide.

The creature which had controlled Red Spider through the long history of England's orchards was *Anthocoris nemorum* and we only learnt how useful it was when modern chemicals destroyed it. The Ministry of Agriculture Bulletin No. 10, 'Beneficial Insects', by B. D. Morton (85p) tells the story of all these tiny helpers, of which only the ladybird is well known.

Anthocoris is like a small flat black-and-brown beetle about $\frac{1}{6}$-in. long, and it eats an average of fifty Red Spiders a day. Unlike its Capsid colleague it breeds twice a year, and the large numbers that can build up by autumn merely doze in winter; they not only eat Red

Spider and other pest eggs through the autumn but on mild winter days, and through the spring.

Luckily it does not only live on apple trees, or winter-wash might have exterminated it, but we have plenty left to increase again in gardens without sprays, for it can be killed quickly by even derris.

Red Spider Mite is a serious pest of many crops under glass where it can be destroyed by a number of fumigation preparations, but is best controlled by avoiding the hot, dry, conditions under glass that favour the pest, with higher humidity. On apples and other ornamentals it is best controlled by spraying with S.M. 133, which is a kind of liquid polythene that blocks the pores through which it breathes, which will spare the larger predators. It is far better to avoid it by winter washing only if it is essential and with a plain tar oil wash without B.H.C., to leave the Black-Kneed Capsid. This creature has only one generation a year so cannot increase fast enough to overtake the Red Spider as Anthocoris will, but they average 60–70 a day, and adult females studied by East Malling Research Station have eaten over 4,000 a season.

It is spraying in summer that kills the predators, and this is why Ryania is worth using against Codling Moth, and Burgundy Mixture before the leaves open for Scab, instead of the normal summer spraying programme, to spare as many predators as possible. The more of these there are, the less of their job remains for the gardener.

Scale Insects

The commonest of these is Mussel Scale (*Lepidosaphes almi*) which looks like a tiny mussel shell, sitting on all fruit trees and bushes, and also attacking ceanothus, cotoneaster and pyrus in the flower garden. In a bad attack the stems may be thickly encrusted with the creatures, which can even kill trees by sucking the sap like Tomato Whitefly larvae. A bad outbreak can be cleaned off with a winter tar-oil wash, but in the spring the eggs under each of the scales (which are female, the male is a tiny and quite rare winged insect who flies from 'door to door') hatch; then minute and active creatures like slender aphides will run about, find new homes and settle down to put on weight by stationary sucking, while the few males fly off on their own affairs. At this stage lime-sulphur for scab will kill them, but if the colonies of scales are within reach, apply the modern synthetic turpentine ('white oils') to them with a paint brush, and you can kill without using a winter-wash, and only where you want it.

Slugs and Snails

The traditional slug trap is a basin sunk level with the soil surface and filled with sweetened beer or milk, which attracts the slugs that fall in and drown. Beer was cheaper when the trap was invented and a 50–50 mixture of milk and water is a modern economy mixture; but tipping away several basinfuls of drowned slugs every morning is a less attractive job for housewives than it was to the garden boys who are now park superintendents.

One part powdered alum to seven of slaked lime scattered on warm summer evenings produces a kill by contact, rather more effective than surrounding the lettuces with soot.

The Metaldehyde baits have the disadvantage of allowing many slugs to recover in wet summers, when infestation is worst. Very large quantities of small slugs are eaten by centipedes, Devil's-Coach-Horse beetles, and Violet Ground beetles and their larvae, and the cumulative effect of poisonous metaldehyde (see *Chemicals in Food* by Dr. Franklin Bicknell, Faber and Faber, for notes on a British poisoning case) kills predators. In their official capacity as garden scavengers slugs eat a great many creatures killed by chemicals, and their high resistance to chlorinated hydrocarbons means that anything eating them, especially birds, has an accumulating dose.

Digging in a pound of fine-ground copper sulphate mixed with 7 lb. lime is an old remedy for the Keeled Slug that attacks potatoes underground; and if this is done in the spring at the rate of 4 oz. a square yard it can be effective.

A herbal preparation, Fertosan Slug Destroyer, can be watered on the soil and appears to be quite effective, though unpopular, because it does not leave large ones lying dead, for it seems to hit the small ones hardest. Baiting with bran and borax with icing sugar as for Cutworms is also possible and safe, for soils are more likely to suffer from shortage of copper and boron than excess, though both should be used with caution.

The Carnivorous Slug (*Testacella haliotidea*) deserves our moral support. It can be distinguished as it wears its 'mantle' or vestigial shell, which other slugs have round their shoulders, about where its hips would be if it had any. Though it eats earthworms also, it does account for a great many slugs.

The Slow-worm (*Anquis fragilis*) is a small 'snake' or rather legless lizard, and a far more attractive creature which feeds largely on slugs. They are usually chestnut brown, all one colour as distinct from the adder with its zigzag markings, and their main enemy is man for many are killed every summer as 'dangerous'. Usually they are 1 ft. long, though they can be 18 in., and are mostly about at night but can be seen in the open sunning themselves sometimes. If picked up they lie still and stiff on your hand, and if frightened will break off their tails like the lizards they are, which reduces their length by about half. They move slowly because they eat slugs and earthworms; anything thick, like a hose 2–3 ft. long, and moving like a whiplash when alarmed in a damp place, is a Grass-snake. It is *never* something escaped from the zoo; they get hundreds of telephone calls every summer and it always *is* a grass snake, and harmless.

Slow-worms are poor slug controllers because they cannot increase fast enough to keep pace with a bad slug year. Their young are born alive in June and July, one batch a year, and the litter is from 8 to 26 (which is the record) with 10–12 usual. They hibernate in winter and if anyone finds them they should be covered with dead leaves and left if the hiding place has been destroyed. I have found them under pot stacks on nurseries in my youth, but have never found the burrow they are supposed to make for mass hibernation, up to two dozen together. Those who find slow-worms should let them alone to get on with the good work.

Thrips

These small, brownish-yellow, active insects cause leaf mottling by their attacks, and carry some of the viruses, as they attack a large number of plants both outdoors and under glass. The Apple and Pear Thrip (*Taeniothrips inconsequens*) can attack the blossoms of these and of plums, causing the petals to distort and russetting the fruit. They lay eggs in the blossom, so pyrethrum in the evening is the best, for it can have lost its effect by the time the bees arrive again. A thunder-shower will clear the trees (hence the name 'thunder flies') and an artificial one from a hosepipe is worth trying.

Pidero and derris are also killers, especially for Onion Thrips which are much worse in greenhouses on a range of flowers than on onions in open. They carry Spotted Wilt Virus of tomatoes.

Wasps

Derris or Pidero will kill wasps, but though trapping relieves one's feelings when pears and plums are gnawed, wasps are quite useful creatures for controlling flies. A good poison bait for them is derris dust mixed with jam, put where they gather, because this will be taken home. Another is liquid derris, one tablespoonful to a quart or whatever strength is recommended for killing ants or beetles, with as much brown sugar added as will dissolve easily in it. This painted on a fence, near the nest if possible, will bait plenty to their doom. It will of course draw an assortment of moths, but these do not scrape up wood and take it home.

Weevils

A stone-fruit pest which can appear suddenly is the Red-Legged Weevil (*Otiorrhynchus clavipes*) attacking cherries, trees of the peach family, and plums, but also raspberries and gooseberries. It is an oval black beetle about $\frac{1}{2}$ in. long, with red legs, and it makes its appearance towards the end of April or in May, feeding at night on the blossoms and developing fruit, and eating holes in leaves and gnawing shoot bases. The damage is easy to see but there is no apparent cause, for at first light the Weevils let go and drop to the ground, hiding until they crawl back again when darkness comes.

The best answer is a grease band—not sacking, because the Weevils are not looking for a hibernation place but making a regular journey to work and back, and they would simply go over or under it. A greaseband, with the grease renewed if it becomes congested with rush-hour traffic, is the answer also to the smaller $\frac{1}{4}$-in. Clay-Coloured Weevil (*Otiorrhynchus singularis*), which is brown-speckled and about somewhat earlier, starting in March with a taste for bark as this comes alive again in spring. It is also known as the 'Raspberry Weevil', because it is most commonly found on raspberry canes.

Banding, however, merely leaves a full supply of both to eat where there are no easy trunks to tie round. They lay eggs in the soil, and the legless grubs feed on the roots of a wide range of plants from June until the following February. The grubs are less destructive than the Weevils which attack roses (especially ramblers), rhododendrons, and all tree and bush fruit. Because Weevils are tough the old remedy was to spray with lead arsenate, and modern poisons are still stronger: but they all have to be stomach and not contact ones like pyrethrum, for midnight spraying is rarely possible.

The best method of control is to spread sheets of newspaper, which have been given belts of grease-band mixture round the edges, under the trees after dark, and then to shine a powerful torch up into the branches (acetylene motor-car headlights were once used), and this will produce 'instant daylight', bringing the creatures down in showers. The grease trap round the edge will stop them running off, and gathering the sheets up and burning them is a quick-killing method. Tipping into strong nicotine or Pidero, 2 fluid ounces to 1 pint of water, will produce a kill by morning. Anyone who has coped with even a hundred active Weevils will have no pity.

Grease-coated boards to slide under gooseberry bushes or bush fruit are also useful, and shaking the bushes is another idea, and shining the torch down means fewer pricks. No light must be shown in placing the traps, for the creatures can drop in a flash. Putting down paper and shining a light up into one's trees is a sure test of whether you have either Weevil, for anything that drops is up to no good.

Winter Moth

Grease bands to stop upward traffic are extremely useful pest controllers—harmless to birds, bees and predators, for ladybirds 'fly away home' to hibernate, and nothing useful has a regular seasonal migration up and down the trunks. Modern materials of vegetable origin can be spread direct on to the bark which is the best way of dealing with old trees that have hollows in the bark that leave gaps under ordinary bands. A small band even 1 in. wide round a rose bush will stop the ants pasturing aphides and moving these from one to another, and there are aerosols which will spray stickiness on the lower branches of even a gooseberry.

Grease bands that are ready spread with sticky material, needing only removal of protective paper, are now available from most garden shops. The best positions for them are 18 in. above ground level on standards or round every branch of a bush tree that forks lower than this, for rain can splash soil, and leaves can blow on bands set too low. Inspect the bands to see that nothing has blown against them to make bridges. The bands should go on in October and be removed and burnt in April, but renewed if there are summer crawling pests about, or replaced with sacking to catch the down traffic.

The most important pest they stop is the Winter Moth (*Cheimatobia brumata*) whose wingless females crawl up the trees during the grease band period. Their caterpillars are at first grey with darker heads then green with a white stripe; they feed on buds, foliage and fruitlets. The March Moth (*Erannis ascularia*) climbs in February and March, which is why bands should stay on till April, and its cater-pillars are much the same, but they are 'loopers' not straight crawlers, and attack pears, plums and hazel-nuts as well as apples. The Mottled Umber Moth (*Hybernia defoliaria*) has 'looper' caterpillars but these are chestnut brown with yellow sides. They attack all fruit trees, in-cluding currant and gooseberry bushes. All three are beaten by grease bands because their wingless females must go up the trees to lay their eggs, and prevention is better than cure, especially if the prevention is simple and harmless.

Winter-washing

Thousands of gardeners escape most pests by spraying with an old-fashioned winter tar-oil wash like Mortegg in December or January at apple pruning time. The bees are safely asleep, and the ladybirds rarely at home for they hibernate under dead bark or posts, under the eaves of sheds and in many other places which small gardens provide and orchards rarely do.

The disadvantage of winter-washes is that though they kill a large range of pests as eggs or when hibernating, including Red Plum Maggot Moth, Apple Clearwing Moth (*Conopia myopidormis*), Cherry Fruit Moth, Codling Moth (missing ground hibernators) and Small Ermine Moth (*Yponomeuta malinella*), they also destroy useful predators.

Until we can find a way round by trapping they are useful, and they also destroy all members of the Aphis family. Never winter wash as a preventative, only if you have already had an attack of a pest they kill. These are listed on the label on the tin.

Wireworm

The Wireworm is the larva of the Click Beetle; our three species of Click Beetle have much the same habits and appearance, and *Agiotes lineatus* is commonest in gardens. They are slender, light brown and smooth, with a bunch of legs and jaws at one end, usually from $\frac{1}{2}$–$\frac{3}{4}$ in. long, mainly pests of gardens new-cleared from pastures; though they can be a problem in old and neglected beds and allotments, for they like undisturbed soil.

Click Beetles prefer to lay their eggs (average 100 each) between May and July in grass roots; and the larvae take from three to five years to become beetles, according to the availability of food. At first they are small and white, eating only decaying vegetation, and are preyed on by many predators, so only about 15 per cent ever reach destructive stage; that is to say from $1-2\frac{1}{2}$ million an acre, with a full count reaching something like 8 millions in pastureland on many farms.

They moult their leathery skins as they grow, usually nine times in the course of their long lives, and are 'off their feed' until this is achieved. Their routine is to feed from early March to the end of May, rest and moult in June, eat again from July to October, then rest and moult ready for a start in spring. They move up and down in the soil with 80 per cent in the top 3 in. in March and April, and only 50 per cent in June, and in winter they go lower still, with 100,000 an acre counted between 18 in. and 3 ft. down.

Their first choice of food is potatoes, which are the usual clearing crop for new gardens and allotments, but they eat the roots of a wide range of vegetables and ornamental crops. Trenching and putting the turf grass downwards in the trench bottoms keeps them down, feeding on the grass roots, if broad, french, haricot or runner beans, peas, parsnips, kale and spinach are sown. These are the least attractive to Wireworm, but for carrots or potatoes they will leave the buried turf and attack.

Another method is to take up the turf 1–2 in. thick, in spade-wide strips about 1 ft. long. Scatter naphthalene flakes at the rate of 3 oz. a squard yard on an area at the bottom of the garden convenient for a stack, and start building grass side downwards with another dose of naphthalene for every three layers of turf. The heap will decay in good usable loam to spread back in three years, including the decayed couch grass roots.

An alternative is to burn the turves, killing Wireworms and couch, on slow bonfires smouldering in hundreds across the fields. These make burnt red earth, and the lumps that were merely cooked enough for a kill produce the quickly spent nitrogen from partial sterilization, of which gardeners see evidence wherever bonfires have been.

Modern gardeners on heavy clay full of couch grass, where a trial dig has shown plentiful Wireworms, can use this method. It calls for enough dry wood to start and keep the fires going. Later, they can spread the part-baked clay as a valuable lightener for their soil. Humus and some fertility are lost but there is plenty more in clay for those who dig for it. March and April are the best times, for then the Wireworms are caught in the top 3 in.; August and September are not so good, and between November and February hopeless because the Wireworms have mostly gone down for winter.

Wireworm traps are rather easier than those for Millipedes for they can be made from perforated zinc since the larvae are thin enough to get in through the holes. Millipede traps serve for them, and in an unfortunate garden can catch both. Make tubes of the zinc about 8 in. long and 2–3 in. in diameter, 'sewing' sides and flattened bottom together with wire threaded through the holes, and adding a wire handle.

Fill with carrot fragments or potato peelings and pieces and bury with the handles out, and pull up once a week, dumping the contents in dustbin, chicken run or strong Pidero. Those who do not keep chickens will find this the cheapest and easiest way of getting rid of the results of trapping.

Woolly Aphis or American Blight

Woolly Aphis is the pest that makes cotton-wool-like masses on apples and can cripple whole branches with its sucking. It also attacks pears, quinces, crab-apples, hawthorn, cotoneasters and very rarely roses. It does not winter as eggs but hibernates in bark cracks, and in the autumn it migrates down the tree and can spend winter just under the soil surface on the underground part of the trunk. So if you winter-wash against it, twist off any suckers, scrape away the soil and squirt the immediate ground area to catch them, where you will do little harm to sleeping predators.

The best way of getting rid of a small outbreak is by spraying or painting the woolly patches with a mixture of two-thirds paraffin and one-third creosote. Methylated spirits and petrol are also effective and rather less messy and awkward to get off the hands.

The petrol mixed with oil now sold for two-stroke mopeds is excellent, and there is no need to buy a Premium Grade, in fact, low-octane petrols seem best. Get it well into the bark. Though winter tar-oil wash is recommended against eggs laid by the winged forms, attacking with paraffin or petrol when you first see the wool is better than spraying the whole tree for eggs that may not be there.

16

Last Come the Lists

The only way to cover even a useful fraction of the plants, trees and shrubs that will grow easily in every garden in Britain is in a chapter of lists. Some outstanding species and hybrids have been described in the separate chapters, but here the selection must be wider and more concentrated. There are only about fifty vegetables and seventeen bush and tree fruits counting strawberries but not rhubarb, but a 'book about flowers' is almost like a book about human beings—there are so many more than you think if you only know the ordinary yellow, the black and the pinky-white kinds.

The first list is of hardy annuals, which are sown in the open, where they are to flower in March. Those which can also be sown in September to grow outside through the winter are marked with a † and these have two seasons in the column headed 'Time'. As an example, clarkias sown in September start flowering as early as May, but by August they are finished, while the March sowing should be flowering in July and finish with September in nice time for bulb planting. The 'Space' column says how far apart each way they should be thinned to, or sown in the case of large seeded species, while a * indicates flowers that last well cut in water for the house.

Hybrids are excluded because they would make the list impossibly long. Where a species, as an example *Centaurea Cyanus*, has 'Blue, rose, white, mauve' under 'Colours', it means that named varieties can be bought in all these colours and their different shades. When, like *Collinsia bicolor*, there is 'lilac and white' in the column, this indicates that the flower itself is in *two* colours, 'and' is used to show the difference. The heights are averages and on good soil some grow higher, while poor soil or drought keeps them smaller. Where two heights are given, this shows that there are tall and dwarf varieties of the species, and two figures under 'Space' show that these smaller kinds go closer together.

Hardy Annuals

	HEIGHT	SPACE	TIME	COLOURS
Agrostemma Githago	2½ ft.	6 in.	June–Sept.	White, lilac, purple
Alyssum maritimum	3 in.	6 in.	June–Oct.	White, pink, violet, rose
Argemone grandiflora	2½ ft.	12 in.	July–Sept.	White
*Asperula azurea**	1 ft.	6 in.	April–June	Blue
Aster tanacetifolius	1½ ft.	6 in.	July–Oct.	Blue
Bartonia aurea	1½ ft.	8 in.	June–Oct.	Yellow
*Calendula officinalis** (Pot Marigold)	2 ft.	8 in.	June–Oct.	Yellow, orange
*Centaurea Cyanus**† Cornflower)	2½ ft.	6 in.	June–Aug. July–Sept.	Blue, rose, white, mauve
*Centaurea moschata**† (Sweet Sultan)	1½ ft.	9 in.	July–Aug. Aug.–Sept.	Blue, white, pink, yellow
*Chrysanthemum carinatum**	2 ft.	9 in.	June–Oct.	Yellow, copper, bronze, white
,, *coronarium**	2½ ft.	9 in.	June–Oct.	Yellow, white
,, *segetum**	1½ ft.	8 in.	June–Oct.	Yellow
Cladanthus arabicus	3 ft.	12 in.	June–Sept.	Yellow
Clarkia elegans†	2 ft.	9 in.	May–Aug. July–Sept.	Pink, crimson, orange, scarlet, white
Collinsia bicolor	1 ft.	6 in.	July–Sept.	Lilac and white salmon pink
Collomia biflora	2 ft.	6 in.	July–Sept.	Scarlet
Convolvulus tricolor†	1 ft.	6 in.	June–Aug. July–Oct.	Blue, crimson
Cotula barbara	6 in.	4 in.	June–Sept.	Yellow
Crepis rubra	2 ft.	6 in.	June–July	Rose pink
*Delphinium Ajacis**† (Larkspur)	2½ ft.	9 in.	June–Aug. July–Sept.	Blue, pink, white
Dianthus sinensis	6 in.	6 in.	July–Oct.	Red, pink, white
,, *Heddewigii*	9 in.	8 in.	July–Oct.	Scarlet, crimson, pink, white
Echium plantagineum	2 ft.	12 in.	July–Aug.	Blue
Eschscholtzia californica	1 ft.	6 in.	June–Oct.	Orange, yellow, pink
*Gilia achilleifolia**†	2 ft.	9 in.	May–July July–Sept.	Blue
,, *capitata**†	2 ft.	9 in.	May–July July–Sept.	Pale blue
,, *hybrida* (*Leptosiphon Hybridus*)	6 in.	4 in.	July–Sept.	Yellow, cream, red, pink
,, *tricolor*	2 ft.	6 in.	July–Sept.	Violet and white

R

	HEIGHT	SPACE	TIME	COLOURS
Godetia grandiflora	9 in.– 2 ft.	6 in.	May–July July–Oct.	Reds, pinks, white, lavender
Gypsophila elegans*†	1½ ft.	9 in.	May–July Aug.–Oct.	White, pink, crimson
Helianthus 'Autumn Beauty*	4 ft.	18 in.	Aug.–Oct.	Yellow, bronze, maroon
,, 'Excelsior'	3 ft.	15 in.	Aug.–Oct.	Yellow, bronze
Iberis umbellata†	1 ft.	8 in.	May–July June–Aug.	White, pink, crimson, lilac
Kaulfussia amelloides	9 in.	6 in.	July–Aug.	Blue
Limnanthes Douglasii†	9 in.	4 in.	June–Aug. July–Sept.	White and yellow
Lavatera trimestris	3 ft.	12 in.	June–Oct.	Rose, white
Linaria maroccana*†	1 ft.	6 in.	April–June June–Sept.	Crimson, pink, purple, yellow
Linum grandiflorus†	2½ ft.	4 in.	April–June June–Sept.	Crimson, pink, blue
Lupinus Hartwegii†	3 ft.	8 in.	May–June July–Sept.	Blue and white
Malcolmia maritima*† (*Virginia Stock*)	1 ft.	4 in.	April–May June–Aug.	Crimson, pink, white, yellow
Malope grandiflora	3 ft.	9 in.	June–Sept.	Rose-red, white
Nemophila Menziesii†	4 in.	6 in.	April–June July–Sept.	Blue
Nigella damascena*	1½ ft.	9 in.	July–Sept.	Blue, white, pink
Papaver Rhoeas (Shirley Poppy)†	2 ft.	12 in.	May–June July–Aug.	Scarlet, pink, white
,, *somniferum*† (Opium poppy)	2 ft.	12 in.	May–June July–Aug.	Red, pink, white, purple
Phacelia campanularia	8 in.	6 in.	June–Sept.	Blue
,, *Parryi*	15 in.	6 in.	June–Sept.	Purple-blue
,, *viscida*	2 ft.	9 in.	June–Oct.	Blue and white
Platystemon californicus	9 in.	4 in.	July–Sept.	Cream
Reseda odorata (Mignonette)*	1 ft.	8 in.	June–Oct.	Red, orange, white
Salvia Horminum	1½ ft.	6 in.	July–Oct.	Blue, pink, purple
Saponaria Calabrica†	9 in.	3 in.	April–June July–Sept.	Red, pink, white
,, *Vaccaria**†	2 ft.	9 in.	April–June July–Sept.	Pink, white
Scabiosa atropurpurea*†	3 ft.	9 in.	April–June July–Sept.	Blue, pink, crimson, scarlet, purple, white
Silene pendula compacta†	9 in.	6 in.	May–June July–Sept.	Crimson, rose, pink, white
Specularia speculum *grandiflora*	1 ft.	4 in.	June–Oct.	Blue

	HEIGHT	SPACE	TIME	COLOURS
*Thelesperma Burridgeanum**	1½ ft.	6 in.	July–Sept.	Orange
Tropaeolum (Nasturtium)	Trlg.	6 in.	July–Oct.	Yellow, scarlet, crimson, salmon
„ *nanum* (Tom Thumb)	9 in.	6 in.	July–Oct.	Yellow, scarlet, crimson, salmon
„ *peregrinum* (Canary Creeper)	Trlg.	9 in.	July–Oct.	Yellow
*Viscaria coeli-rosa oculata**	1 ft.	6 in.	June–Sept.	Blue, pink, crimson, white
*Xanthisma texanum**	2½ ft.	6 in.	July–Sept.	Yellow
*Xeranthemum annuum**	2½ ft.	6 in.	July–Sept.	Purple, pink, white

Though a great many of these species will be unknown to gardeners who choose by the picture on packets for sale in chain stores, they are all in cultivation and available from first-class seedsmen. Many have been excluded because they do not flower long enough or make a good enough show for their space, and the unfamiliar ones are all good gambles, while those with a range of colours can be bought in mixtures from famous firms who take great pride in blending these like tea. It is possible to devote a whole bed to one favourite species, and there are as an example seventeen varieties of Scabiosa listed by one famous firm. Sowing in both spring *and* autumn extends the season, but not in the same bed, and September-sown hardy annuals can fit in before the dahlias in mild districts.

The list of half-hardy annuals which follows does not of course include any suitable for sowing in the open in September, and so here the sign † means 'an annual that needs extra heat to start it' either from soil-warming wires and tubular heaters in a cold frame, or in a heated greenhouse. Those that are without this sign could be sown in the open in late April, or early May and will flower far later than if frame-raised, but enough to show what they look like. The original * still indicates good cut bloom plants, and 'space' indicates how far apart each way they should be planted. 'C' indicates a climber.

Half-hardy Annuals

	HEIGHT	SPACE	TIME	COLOURS
Ageratum Houstonianum	6 in.	6 in.	June–Oct.	Blue, pink
Alonsoa acutifolia†	2 ft.	9 in.	June–Oct.	Scarlet
„ *Warscewiczii*†	1½ ft.	9 in.	July–Oct.	Scarlet

	HEIGHT	SPACE	TIME	COLOURS
Amaranthus caudatus (Love lies bleeding)	2 ft.	1½ ft.	July–Sept.	Crimson
Anagallis linifolia Parksii	6 in.	6 in.	July–Oct.	Bright red
„ „ *Phillipsii*	6 in.	6 in.	July–Oct.	Gentian-blue
Anchusu capensis 'Blue Bird'	1½ ft.	12 in.	July–Sept.	Blue
Anoda cristata	2½ ft.	12 in.	July–Sept.	Pink, white
Antirrhinum majus	2½ ft.	8 in.	May–Oct.	Yellow, pink, white, crimson, orange
„ *majus maximum*	3 ft.	8 in.	May–Oct.	Pink, crimson, white, yellow
„ *nanum*	1½ ft.	8 in.	May–Oct.	Crimson, pink, white, yellow, orange
„ *nanum compactum*	9 in.	6 in.	May–Oct.	Pink, white, yellow, crimson
Arctotis grandis†	1½ ft.	12 in.	July–Oct.	White and yellow
„ *hybrida*	1½ ft.	12 in.	July–Oct.	Yellow, orange, crimson, purple
Brachycome iberidifolia†	1 ft.	4 in.	July–Aug.	Purple, lavender
Calliopsis tinctoria	2½ ft.	12 in.	July–Oct.	Yellow, red, bronze
Callistephus (Annual Aster)	2 ft. 8 in.	12 in. 12 in.	June–Oct.	Pink, blue, red, white, violet
Celosia cristata†	1 ft.	12 in.	July–Sept.	Red, yellow
Cleome spinosa†	3 ft.	12 in.	July–Aug.	Pink, white
Cobaea scandens† (C)	Trlg.	12 in.	Aug.–Sept.	Pale violet
Cosmos bipinnatus	3 ft.	12 in.	July–Oct.	Crimson, pink, white
Dimorphotheca aurantiaca†	1½ ft.	8 in.	July–Sept.	Apricot, orange, yellow, white
Emilia flammea*†	1 ft.	6 in.	June–Sept.	Scarlet, yellow
Heliotropium peruvianum†	1½ ft.	12 in.	June–Oct.	Violet shades
Helipterum roseum (Everlasting flowers)	1 ft.	6 in.	July–Aug.	Red, pink, white
Impatiens balsamina	2 ft. 6 in.	12 in. 9 in.	June–Sept.	Scarlet, orange, salmon, pink, rose
Ipomaea purpurea (C)	Trlg.	9 in.	May–Sept.	Pink, red, purple
„ *rubro-caerulea* (C)	Trlg.	9 in.	July–Sept.	Blue, scarlet
Kochia scoparia trichophylla	3 ft.	9 in.	Foliage only	Dull red
Layia elegans*	1½ ft.	9 in.	July–Sept.	Yellow
Lobelia erinus†	3 in.	4 in.	July–Oct.	Blue, white, carmine
Matthiola (Ten Week Stocks)*	1½ ft.	12 in.	June–Sept.	Crimson, pink, white, blue

	HEIGHT	SPACE	TIME	COLOURS
Mesembryanthemum crinifolium	Trlg.	6 in.	June–Sept.	Pink, crimson, buff, orange
Microsperma bartonioides	9 in.	6 in.	July–Sept.	Yellow
Mirabilis Jalapa	2 ft.	12 in.	July–Sept.	Crimson, pink, white
,, *multiflora*	3 ft.	12 in.	July–Sept.	Purple
Molucella laevis (Bells of Ireland)	1½ ft.	9 in.	July–Aug.	White, scented
Nemesia strumosa	1 ft.	6 in.	June–Sept.	Blue, scarlet, yellow, orange, white
Nicotiana affinis†	3 ft. 1 ft.	15 in. 9 in.	July–Sept.	White, red, pink
Nolana atriplicifolia	6 in.	6 in.	July–Sept.	Lavender-blue
Othake Hookeriana	1½ ft.	12 in.	July–Oct.	Rose, pink
Pentstemon Hartwegii	2 ft.	9 in.	July–Oct.	Red, pink, purple
Petunia hybrida†	1 ft.	12 in.	July–Sept.	Crimson, pink, purple, blue, scarlet
Phlox Drummondii	1 ft.	9 in.	June–Sept.	Pink, crimson, violet, yellow
,, ,, *nana compacta*	8 in.	9 in.	June–Sept.	Pink, blue, salmon, scarlet, purple, orange, yellow
Quamoclit lobata (C)	Trlg.	12 in.	June–Sept.	Orange and yellow
Rudbeckia bicolor	2½ ft.	6 in.	July–Oct.	Yellow
Salpiglossis sinuata†	2 ft.	12 in.	June–Sept.	Crimson, yellow, scarlet, purple
Salvia splendens†	1 ft.	12 in.	June–Oct.	Scarlet, pink, red-purple, salmon
Senecio elegans	1½ ft.	6 in.	June–Sept.	Purple
Statice sinuatum (Everlasting for drying)	15 in.	9 in.	July–Oct.	Blue, purple, lavender, rose, pink
Tagetes erecta (African Marigold)	3 ft. 2 ft.	12 in. 9 in.	June–Oct.	Yellow, orange
,, *patula* (French Marigold)	15 in. 6 in.	9 in. 6 in.	June–Oct.	Yellow, orange, brown
,, *signata*†	5 in.	6 in.	June–Oct.	Yellow, orange
Thunbergia alata† (C)	Trlg.	9 in.	July–Oct.	Cream, yellow, purple
,, *Gibsonii* (C)	Trlg.	9 in.	July–Oct.	Apricot-orange
Tithonia rotundifolia†	4 ft.	18 in.	July–Oct.	Orange-red
,, *speciosa* 'Torch'	3 ft.	12 in.	July–Oct.	Orange-scarlet
*Tripteris hyseroides**	1½ ft.	6 in.	June–Sept.	Orange
Ursinia anethoides	1½ ft.	6 in.	June–Sept.	Yellow, orange, scarlet
*Venidium fastuosum***†	2½ ft.	12 in.	June–Oct.	Orange

	HEIGHT	SPACE	TIME	COLOURS
Verbena hybrida	1 ft.	12 in.	June–Oct.	Blue, rose, pink, scarlet, white
Zinnia elegans	2½ ft.	12 in.	June–Sept.	Scarlet, yellow, pink, rose, white, violet

There are many very lovely climbers among half-hardy annuals which today are rarely seen, with the decline of the Victorian conservatory to a few houseplants in the flats of the fashion-conscious. Those whose gardens are reduced to paved courtyards or slots between houses can use their shut-in shelter, if it has sunshine for some part of the day, as an 'upright garden'.

Secure a 12-ft. length of 3–4 ft.-wide 2-in. mesh wire-netting to the wall with vine eyes as for wall shrubs or other climbers, and grow the half-hardy ones like the impomaeas, with their glorious small-saucer-size flowers, in large pots, or a long box with drainage holes in the bottom. With John Innes potting soil available easily in all towns this kind of enterprise is easy, and these annual climbers have the advantage that they are not growing when smoke and smog are worst in winter, and the netting can be unwired from the vine-eyes and rolled up to be put out in June when the climbers are nearly ready to need it. In sheltered west coast or southern gardens they can be grown as screens or in positions where the hardy climbers were recommended earlier.

The perennials in the list that follows can all be raised from seed in a cold frame in spring or summer, also in the open ground for those recommended in the earlier chapter, but this is a risk. None need extra heat so this releases the † sign, which now means a race of hybrids. After these is a 'C' for cuttings or a 'D' for division, whichever is the usual way of increasing named varieties of the species in question. It is possible to raise a great many attractive plants from seed 'saved from named varieties' but never expect them to be as good as their parents. Most of those listed are *species* and these are usually true from seed.

The * sign shows that a plant will last well in water as a cut flower for the house, as it indicates in all these lists, and the distances apart are for planting in threes in new borders as in the plans in Chapter 11. This list is mainly of additional plants to those in the specimen borders, so that variations can be planned, therefore (S) has been added to those which are suitable for shade provided that they do not get too dry.

Further named varieties of the perennials recommended in the lists in Chapter 11 can be found in the catalogues of first-class firms. The list that follows is selected as a hunting ground for surprises, including old and forgotten species and very new ones, with the common qualities that all are good garden plants that deserve to be better known, all are obtainable as seed from specialist seedsmen (not chain stores), and all are quite easily raised in a cold frame.

Hardy Perennials

	HEIGHT	SPACE	TIME	COLOURS
Acanthus spinosissimus	4 ft.	12 in.	June–Aug.	Purple and white
Achillea filipendulina*	4 ft.	15 in.	June–Aug.	Yellow
,, *ptarmica* 'The Pearl'*	2 ft.	12 in.	June–July	White
Aconitum napellus bicolor*	3 ft.	9 in.	June–July	Blve and white
,, ,, 'Bressingham Spire'* (C)	3 ft.	9 in.	July–Aug.	Violet-blue
,, *Wilsonii* 'Barker's Var.'	5 ft.	12 in.	Aug.–Sept.	Violet-blue
Adenophora Potaninii	1½ ft.	9 in.	June–Aug.	Pale blue
Adonis vernalis	1 ft.	6 in.	April–May	Yellow
Ajuga pyramidalis (S) (also called *A. genevensis*)	8 in.	6 in.	May–June	Blue
Anchusa italica	3 ft.	12 in.	May–Aug.	Blue
Anemone hupehensis (S)	2 ft.	9 in.	Aug.–Sept.	Pink, red, white
Anthemis sancti-johannis*	1½ ft.	12 in.	June–Sept.	Yellow
Aquilegia caerulea	2½ ft. 1½ ft.	6 in.	May–June	Blue, crimson, yellow, pink, purple
Armeria formosa	1½ ft.	9 in.	June–Aug.	Pink, red, white
,, *maritima* (Thrift) (D)	6 in.	6 in.	May–July	Pink, white
Artemisia lactiflora	4 ft.	15 in.	Aug.–Oct.	White
Aster amellus*† (D)	2 ft.	9 in.	Aug.–Oct.	Blue, pink, rose, lavender
,, *novae-angliae* 'September Ruby'*	4 ft.	12 in.	Sept.–Oct.	Red
,, *novae-belgiae** (D)	4 ft.	12 in.	Sept.–Oct.	Blue, red, pink, white
Astrantia carniolica* (D) (S)	1½ ft.	12 in.	July–Aug.	White
Baptisia australis	3 ft.	12 in.	July–Aug.	Dark-blue
Boltonia latisquamata	4 ft.	12 in.	Sept.–Oct.	Mauve
Borago laxiflora	9 in.	9 in.	June–Sept.	Blue
Brunnera macrophylla (S) (*Anchusa myosotidiflora*)	1½ ft.	9 in.	April–June	Blue

	HEIGHT	SPACE	TIME	COLOURS
*Buphthalmum salicifolium**	2 ft.	12 in.	June–Aug.	Yellow
Campanula Burghalti	2 ft.	9 in.	June–July	Grey-blue
„ *glomerata*	1½ ft.	9 in.	June–July	Violet-blue
„ *lactiflora*† (D)	3 ft.	9 in.	June–Aug.	Blue, white
„ *persicifolia* (D)	2½ ft.	9 in.	June–July	Blue-white
*Catanache caerulea major**	2 ft.	12 in.	June–Aug.	Blue
*Centaurea ruthenica**	4 ft.	12 in.	July–Sept.	Yellow
Chelone barbata	2½ ft.	12 in.	June–Sept.	Red, pink, salmon
„ *obliqua*	2 ft.	9 in.	June–Sept.	Rose-purple
Coreopsis lanceolata 'Mayfield Giant'	3 ft.	12 in.	June–Sept.	Yellow
Cynoglossum nervosum (S)	1½ ft.	9 in.	June–Aug.	Blue
*Delphinium elatum** (C)	5 ft. 4 ft.	15 in.	June–July	Blue, mauve, white
„ *Belladonna*	3 ft.	12 in.	June–Aug.	Blue, white
Dianthus caryophyllus† (C) (Border carnation)	1½ ft.	9 in.	June–Aug.	Red, pink, white, crimson, yellow
„ *plumarius*† (C) (Garden pink)	1 ft.	6 in.	June–July	Pink, white, crimson
*Digitalis purpurea** (Foxglove)	2½ ft.	9 in.	June–Aug.	Pink, brown, white, red, orange, yellow
*Doronicum caucasicum** (S)	1½ ft.	9 in.	May–June	Yellow
Dracocephalum Ruyschianum	1½ ft.	9 in.	June–July	Dark blue
*Echinops rito**	3 ft.	12 in.	July–Aug.	Blue
Erigeron hybridus 'Azure Beauty'	2 ft.	9 in.	July–Sept.	Blue
*Eryngium alpinum**	2 ft.	9 in.	July–Sept.	Blue
„ *tripartitum**	3 ft.	12 in.	July–Sept.	Blue
Euphorbia polychroma (E. epithymoides)	2 ft.	12 in.	April–May	Yellow
*Gaillardia aristata**	2 ft.	12 in.	July–Aug.	Yellow, red
Gallega officinalis 'Lady Wilson'	3 ft.	12 in.	June–July	Blue and white
Gaura Lindheimeri	3 ft.	12 in.	July–Oct.	White
Geranium Endressii 'Wargrave Pink' (S)	1 ft.	15 in.	June–Sept.	Pink
„ *ibericum* (S)	1½ ft.	12 in.	June–July	Blue-violet
*Geum Borisii**	9 in.	9 in.	May–July	Orange-red
„ *chiloensis** (Border Geum)	2 ft.	9 in.	June–Aug.	Red, yellow
*Gypsophila paniculata** 'Snow White' (double)	3 ft.	12 in.	June–Sept.	White
Helenium Bigelovii	2 ft.	12 in.	June–July	Yellow
„ *Hoopesii**	2 ft.	12 in.	May–June	Yellow
*Heliopsis scabra vitellina**	4 ft.	12 in.	July–Sept.	Yellow

	HEIGHT	SPACE	TIME	COLOURS
*Heuchera sanguinea** Bressingham Hybrids†	1½ ft.	12 in.	May–July	Scarlet, red, pink, white
Hyssopus aristatus	15 in.	9 in.	July–Aug.	Blue, pink
Incarvillea delavayi	1½ ft.	9 in.	May–July	Rose-red
Inula ensifolia 'Golden Beauty'*	2 ft.	9 in.	July–Aug.	Yellow
*Kniphofia uvaria (Tritoma)** (Red hot poker)	4 ft.	12 in.	Aug.–Sept.	Yellow, orange
Lavatera cashmiriana	5 ft.	18 in.	June–Sept.	Pink
*Liatris callilepis**	2½ ft.	9 in.	July–Sept.	Purple
,, ,, 'Kobold'*	2 ft.	9 in.	July–Sept.	Deep purple
,, *scariosa* 'Snow White'*	2 ft.	9 in.	July–Sept.	White
*Ligularia clivorum**	4 ft.	15 in.	Aug.–Sept.	Yellow, orange
Lindelofia spectabilis (S)	1 ft.	9 in.	May–Aug.	Blue
Linum perenne	2 ft.	6 in.	June–Aug.	Blue
Lirope graminifolia (S)	15 in.	9 in.	Sept.–Oct.	Lilac
Lupinus polyphyllus† (C)	3 ft.	12 in.	June–July	Blue, red, yellow, pink, purple
*Lychnis chalcedonica**	1½ ft.	9 in.	June–July	Scarlet, salmon- pink
Lysimachia clethroides (S)	2½ ft.	12 in.	Aug.–Sept.	White
,, *euphemerum* (S)	3½ ft.	15 in.	July–Aug.	White
,, *punctata* (S)	1½ ft.	9 in.	June–Aug.	Yellow
Lythrum salicaria† (C)	3 ft.	12 in.	July–Aug.	Reds, pinks
Malva alcea fastigata	4 ft.	12 in.	June–Oct.	Pink
,, *setosa hybrida*	6 ft.	18 in.	June–Sept.	Pinks
Mertensia virginica (S)	1½ ft.	9 in.	April–May	Blue-purple
*Monarda didyma**† (D)	2 ft.	12 in.	June–Sept.	Scarlet, white, pink
Morina longiflora	2½ ft.	12 in.	June–July	Pink
Nepeta Cataria (True Catmint)	2 ft.	12 in.	June–Sept.	Lilac
,, 'Souv. d'André Chaudron'*	1 ft.	9 in.	June–Aug.	Blue
Oenothera fruticosa	1½ ft.	9 in.	June–Aug.	Yellow
,, *tetragona*	1½ ft.	9 in.	July–Sept.	Yellow
Phlomis samia	2 ft.	12 in.	June–Aug.	Yellow
Phlox paniculata†* (C)	2½ ft.	9 in.	July–Sept.	Red, pink, white, violet
Phygelius aequalis	2½ ft.	12 in.	July–Oct.	Crimson and purple
,, *capensis*	2½ ft.	12 in.	July–Oct.	Scarlet
*Physostegia virginiana**	2 ft.	12 in.	July–Aug.	Lilac, pink, white
Platycodon grandiflorus	1 ft.	9 in.	July–Sept.	Violet-blue
Polemonium foliosissimum	1½ ft.	9 in.	June–Aug.	Blue-violet
,, *Richardsonii*	2½ ft.	12 in.	June–July	Blue
Potentilla recta	1½ ft.	9 in.	June–Aug.	Yellow

	HEIGHT	SPACE	TIME	COLOURS
Pulsatilla vulgaris * (Anemone Pulsatilla)	1 ft.	9 in.	April–May	Violet, red, pink, white
Pyrethrum roseum *† (D)	2 ft.	9 in.	May–July	Red, pink, white
Rudbeckia nitida Herbstsonne	4 ft.	15 in.	Aug.–Sept.	Yellow
„ *purpurea* *	3 ft.	12 in.	Aug.–Sept.	Purple
„ *speciosa* *	2 ft.	12 in.	Aug.–Oct.	Yellow
„ *tetra gloriosa* * (Gloriosa Daisies)	3 ft.	12 in.	July–Oct.	Yellow, brown, red
Salvia superba (*S. virgata nemorosa*)	2½ ft.	12 in.	July–Aug.	Violet
Sanguisorba canadensis *	4 ft.	12 in.	Aug.–Oct.	Creamy-white
Scabiosa caucasica *	2½ ft.	12 in.	July–Oct.	Blue, white
Sedum telephium	15 in.	9 in.	Sept.–Oct.	Red-purple
Sidalcea malvaeflora† (C)	3 ft.	9 in.	July–Sept.	Rose, pink, lilac, salmon
Solidago canadensis 'Golden Baby' * (Golden Rod)	2 ft.	12 in.	Aug.–Oct.	Yellow
Stokesia cyanea *	1 ft.	9 in.	July–Sept.	Blue
Thalictrum aquilegifolium, * (S) 'Dwarf Purple'	2½ ft.	12 in.	May–June	Purple
„ *speciosissimum* * (S)	4 ft.	15 in.	June–July	Yellow
Thermopsis caroliniana	2 ft.	9 in.	June–July	Yellow
Tiarella Wherryii (S)	15 in.	6 in.	May–Aug.	Creamy-pink
Trollius hybridus† (D)	2½ ft.	12 in.	May–June	Yellow
Verbascum Chaixii	5 ft.	12 in.	June–Aug.	Yellow
„ *phoeniceum*†	3 ft.	12 in.	May–Aug.	Violet, pink, salmon, white
„ *Wiedemannianum*	3 ft.	12 in.	June–Sept.	Indigo blue
Veronica spicata†	1½ ft.	6 in.	June–Aug.	Blue, pink, white
„ *virginica*	4 ft.	12 in.	Aug.–Sept.	Pale blue, white

The list that follows is of plants for the Dry Wall Garden. Those which trail are marked with a 'T', and those that make domes or clumps sitting against the wall have a 'C', in the 'Height' column. This height for a trailing plant means how far they stick out from the wall, but it applies to the clump plants, which can also be used as extras in the alpine border, where they grow this high. The 'Space' figure relates to their each way apart planting distance in the border or from plant to plant horizontally on the wall. This figure should be doubled below a trailer, for the lovely *Aethionema grandiflorum*, as an example, will spread to a clump reaching down 1 ft. below its rootstock and 6 in. each side, but *Arabis albida* needs 2 ft. of space below the plant to trail down and will need cutting back like an aubrietia after flowering to keep it in bounds.

Most of these plants can be raised from seed in the cold frame and potted to plant in the spring, but where a plant like aubrietia can be raised as a mixture of seedlings, it has (D) for 'division as well as (S) for 'seed'. The (C) for cuttings is awarded only to those which cannot be raised easily from seeds or because they are hybrids, but soft cuttings of non-flowering wood can be taken if available. This is especially worth doing when something good has been raised from a packet of mixed seed.

All the plants on this list do really well on walls. The Androsaces, Callirhoes and Onosmas are cliff dwellers by nature and are hardier edgeways than flat. Where the wall is in shade, use Mossy saxifrages, Vincas and other low plants from the front of the herbaceous border for dry shade.

Wall Plants

	HEIGHT HABIT	SPACE APART	TIME	COLOURS
Achillea Clavenae (D)	4–6 in. (C)	6 in.	June–Aug.	White
,, *Lewisii* (C)	4–6 in. (C)	6 in.	June–Aug.	Yellow
,, *tomentosa* (S)	4–6 in. (C)	8 in.	June–Aug.	Deep yellow
Aethionema grandiflorum (S)	8–12 in. (C)	12 in.	May–Aug.	Pale pink
,, *pulchellum* (S)	6–8 in. (C)	8 in.	May–July	Pale lilac
Alyssum saxatile (S)	8–9 in. (T)	12 in.	May	Yellow
Androsace lanuginosa (C)	3–4 in. (T)	8 in.	June–Sept.	Pale lilac
,, *sarmentosa Watkinsii* (D)	3–4 in. (C)	6 in.	May–June	Deep pink
Anthyllis montana rubra (S)	3–4 in. (T)	6 in.	June–July	Crimson
Antirrhinum Asarina (S)	4–6 in. (T)	6 in.	June–Sept.	Pale yellow
Arabis albida (D)	8–9 in. (T)	12 in.	April–June	White
,, *aubrietioides* (S) (D)	8–9 in. (T)	12 in.	April–June	Pale pink
,, *blepharophylla* (S)	4–6 in. (C)	6 in.	April–June	Deep pink
Arenaria montana (S) (C)	6–8 in. (T)	12 in.	May–June	White
Armeria corsica (D)	8–9 in. (C)	8 in.	June–July	Red
,, *maritima* 'Blood-stone' (D)	8–9 in. (C)	8 in.	June–July	Deeper red
Aubrietia (S) (D)	4–6 in. (T)	6 in.	April–June	Red, blue, pink, violet
Calamintha alpina (S)	3–4 in. (T)	6 in.	June–Sept.	Violet
Callirhoe involucrata (S)	2–3 in. (T)	15 in.	June–Oct.	Crimson
Campanula carpatica (S)	8–9 in. (C)	8 in.	June–Sept.	Blue, violet, white
,, *garganica* (S)	3–4 in. (C)	6 in.	June–Aug.	Blue, violet

	HEIGHT HABIT	SPACE APART	TIME	COLOURS
Campanula Porscharsky-ana (S)	9–12 in. (T)	15 in.	June–Sept.	Blue-grey
Convolvulus mauritanicus (S)	4–6 in. (T)	6 in.	June–Oct.	Deep lavender
Dianthus Allwoodii alpinus	4–6 in. (C)	8 in.	June–Sept.	Red, lilac, pink, white
,, *caesius* (S)	5–6 in. (C)	8 in.	June–July	Rose pink
,, *deltoides* (S)	4–6 in. (C)	8 in.	June–Aug.	Red, pink, white
Erodium chrysanthum (C)	3–4 in. (C)	6 in.	June–Sept.	Yellow
,, *macradenum roseum*	4–6 in. (C)	6 in.	May–Sept.	Pink
Geranium sanguineum (S)	6–8 in. (T)	8 in.	June–Sept.	Magenta to pink
,, *Wallichianum* (S)	4–6 in. (T)	8 in.	July–Sept.	Violet-blue
Gypsophila fratensis (C)	2–3 in. (T)	8 in.	June–Aug.	Pale pink
,, *repens* (S)	4–6 in. (T)	8 in.	June–Aug.	White
,, *repens rosea* (S)	4–6 in. (T)	8 in.	June–Aug.	Pale pink
Helianthemum nummu-larium (S)	6–9 in. (C)	8 in.	June–Aug.	Red, pink, white, yellow, mixed
,, 'Amy Baring' (C)	6–9 in. (C)	8 in.	June–Aug.	Orange
,, 'Ben Nevis' (C)	4–6 in. (C)	6 in.	June–Aug.	Yellow and Orange
,, 'Golden Queen' (C)	4–6 in. (C)	12 in.	June–Aug.	Yellow
,, 'Rose Queen' (C)	4–6 in. (C)	12 in.	June–Aug.	Pink
,, 'Watergate Rose' (C)	6–9 in. (C)	8 in.	June–Aug.	Crimson
Hippocrepis comosa (S)	3–4 in. (T)	6 in.	June–Aug.	Yellow
Hypericum olympicum (S)	6–8 in. (T)	8 in.	June–July	Yellow
Iberis gibraltarica (S)	8–9 in. (C)	8 in.	May–July	White
Leontopodium alpinum (S) (Edelweiss)	4–6 in. (C)	8 in.	June–Aug.	Dirty white
Lithospermum gramini-folium (S)	8–9 in. (C)	6 in.	June–July	Pale blue
,, *intermedium* (S)	8–9 in. (C)	6 in.	June–July	Deep blue
Oenothera riparia (S)	4–6 in. (T)	6 in.	June–Sept.	Yellow
missourensis (S)	8–9 in. (C)	15 in.	June–Oct.	Yellow
Onosma echioides (S)	6–8 in. (C)	8 in.	May–June	Yellow
Phlox subulata (C)	3–6 in. (T)	8 in.	April–June	Red, pink, white, lilac
Polygonum vaccinifolium (S) (C)	2–3 in. (T)	12 in.	July–Oct.	Pink
Potentilla fragiformis (S)	6–9 in. (T)	8 in.	May–June	Yellow

	HEIGHT HABIT	SPACE APART	TIME	COLOURS
Potentilla nepalensis 'Miss Wilmott (S)	8–12 jn. (T)	12 in.	July–Sept.	Deep pink
,, *nepalensis* 'Roxana' (S)	8–12 in. (T)	12 in.	July–Sept.	Orange-scarlet
,, *rupestris* (S)	8–12 in. (C)	8 in.	July–Sept.	White
Pterocephalus parnassi (S)	3–4 in. (C)	6 in.	July–Aug.	Lilac
Saponaria ocymoides (S)	3–6 in. (T)	12 in.	May–Sept.	Pink
Saxifraga Aizoon (S) (D)	4–8 in. (C)	6 in.	May–June	Creamy white
,, *cotyledon Caterhamensis* (D)	8–12 in.	8 in.	May–June	White
Sedum cauticolum (D)	4–6 in. (T)	8 in.	June–Oct.	Pink
,, *Middendorffianum* (D)	4–6 in. (T)	6 in.	June–July	Yellow
,, *spurium coccineum* (D)	4–6 in. (T)	6 in.	Aug.–Sept.	Crimson
Solidago brachystachys (D)	8–9 in. (C)	8 in.	Sept.–Oct.	Yellow
Thymus Doefleri (D)	3–4 in. (T)	8 in.	July–Aug.	Pink
Veronica armena rosea (C)	2–3 in. (T)	8 in.	June–Sept.	Pink
,, *pectinata rosea* (C)	2–3 in. (T)	12 in.	May–June	Pink
,, *rupestris* (C) (D)	3–4 in. (T)	12 in.	May–June	Blue
,, 'Mauve Queen' (C)	3–4 in. (T)	12 in.	May–June	Mauve
Zauschneria californica (C)	9–12 in. (C)	8 in.	Sept.–Oct.	Scarlet

Though the plan for the long-flowering alpine border uses most of the best alpines today for this purpose, for convenience these are listed with a few additions and their methods of propagation. This is most often cuttings or division, marked with a (C) or (D) because the alpines are frequently outstanding hybrids chosen for this purpose. It is perfectly easy to raise Dianthus from seed, as an example, but not to raise the new miniature long-flowering double varieties which are long-odds chances that came off. The only way to keep these true is from cuttings, which should be sought for the frame from June to August and inserted whenever they are found. This race is rare because it flowers so well that there are few flowerless shoots for cuttings.

The campanulas are listed as cutting or division subjects, because this is the only way to get them true, and the cuttings should be taken from soft shoots in May, *before* they flower. They are easy from seed also and those who do not mind mixtures can raise quantities for planting large borders. A (C) *before* the plant name marks a carpeter to grow bulbs under.

The 'Space' column shows roughly how far they eventually grow, and is a guide to planting so they do not interfere with each other in the rock garden. As an example *Aethionema* Warley Rose has '12 in.' for space; this means a square 12 in. along each side, i.e. a square foot not 12 square inches, which would be a space 4 in. long and 3 wide. Plants do not grow in squares like chess-boards, but anyone who has seen a good 'Warley Rose' will know that one 1 ft. across each way is about the biggest it grows. Think of your plant as the centre of a circle as many inches across as the figure in the column.

Alpine Border and Rock Garden Plants

	HEIGHT	SPACE	TIME	COLOURS
C. *Acaena microphylla* (S)	2 in.	12 in.	July–Aug.	Red
Acantholimon glumaceum (S)	6 in.	6 in.	May–July	Pink
Achillea Lewisii (C)	6 in.	8 in.	May–Sept.	Yellow
„ *rupestris* (C)	6 in.	8 in.	May–June	White
Aethionema 'Warley Rose' (C)	4–6 in.	12 in.	May–Aug.	Pink
Alyssum serpyllifolium (S)	2 in.	8 in.	June–July	Yellow
Androsace sempervivoides (D) (S)	2 in.	6 in.	April–May	Pink
C. *Antennaria tormentosa* (D) (S)	1 in.	12 in.	May–June	Pink
Arabis bryoides (D)	2 in.	4 in.	May	White
C. *Arenaria purpurescens* (D)	2 in.	6 in.	May–June	Pink
Armeria caespitosa (D) (C) 'Bevan's variety'	2 in.	6 in.	May–June	Pink
Astilbe chinensis pumila (D)	6–9 in.	12 in.	July–Aug.	Pink
Campanula carpatica (C) (D) 'Blue Moonlight'	6–8 in.	15 in.	July–Sept.	Pale blue
„ *carpatica* 'Isabella' (C) (D)	6–8 in.	15 in.	July–Sept.	Violet blue
„ *carpatica* 'White Star' (C) (D)	6–8 in.	15 in.	July–Sept.	White
„ *glomerata acaulis* (S) (D)	2–3 in.	8 in.	June–Aug.	Violet
„ *pulloides* (S) (D)	6 in.	8 in.	July–Sept.	Violet
„ *pulla* (D)	4 in.	8 in.	July–Sept.	Violet
C. „ *pusilla alba* (D) (S)	3 in.	15 in.	June–Sept.	White
C. „ *pusilla* 'Miss Wilmott' (D)	3 in.	15 in.	June–Sept.	Medium blue
C. „ *pusilla* 'Miranda' (D)	3 in.	12 in.	June–Sept.	Pale blue

		HEIGHT	SPACE	TIME	COLOURS
'Blue Moonlight'					
,,	*Raineri* (S)	3–4 in.	12 in.	June–July	China-blue
,,	*turbinata* (D) (S)	6 in.		July–Sept.	Purple blue
,,	*Warleyensis* (D) (C)	6 in.	12 in.	July–Sept.	Pale blue
,,	*Chrysogonum virginianum* (S)	8 in.	12 in.	May–Sept.	Yellow
C. *Claytonia australasica* (D)		1 in.	12 in.	June–Sept.	White
Chiastophyllum oppositifolium (D) (C)		4–6 in.	12 in.	May–July	Yellow
Coronilla cappadocica (S)		6 in.	15 in.	July–Aug.	Yellow
Dianthus alpinus (S)		3 in.	8 in.	June–July	Rose-pink
,,	'Grace Mather' (double) (C)	6 in.	8 in.	July–Sept.	Salmon
,,	double (C) 'Bombardier'	6 in.	8 in.	July–Sept.	Crimson
,,	'Little Jock' (C)	4 in.	12 in.	July–Sept.	Pink
,,	double (C) 'Oakington hybrid'	6 in.	8 in.	July–Sept.	Deep rose
,,	*neglectus* (S)	4 in.	6 in.	June–July	Cherry-red
,,	double (C) 'Pike's Pink'	6 in,	8 in.	July–Sept.	Pale pink
Erinus alpinus (S)		3 in.	6 in.	May–June	Lilac purple
,,	'Dr. Hanele' (S)	3 in.	6 in.	May–June	Carmine red
Edraianthus dalmaticus (S)		6 in.	8 in.	July–Aug.	Purple
Frankenia thymifolia (D)		1 in.	12 in.	June–Aug.	Pink
Gentiana acaulis (D)		4–6 in.	12 in.	April–May	Blue
,,	*lagodechiana* (S) (C)	4–6 in.	12 in.	Aug.–Sept.	Blue
Gypsophila cerastoides (S) (C)		1 in.	8 in.	June–July	White
Horminium pyrenaicum (S)		6 in.	6 in.	July–Sept.	Blue purple
C. *Hutchinsia alpina* (S) (D)		1 in.	8 in.	May–July	White
Hypericum reptans (S)		4 in.	8 in.	May–June	Yellow
C. *Hypsella longiflora* (D)		1 in.	8 in.	June–Oct.	White
Iberis saxatilis (S) (C)		6–9 in.	12 in.	May–July	Lilac
,,	*sempervirens* 'Little Gem' (C)	3–4 in.	12 in.	May–July	White
Inula ensifolia (S) (C)		9 in.	12 in.	July–Aug.	Yellow
Iris cristata (D)		6 in.	8 in.	May	Mauve
,,	*lacustris* (D)	3 in.	6 in.	April–May	Blue gold crest
,,	*melitta* (D)	4 in.	8 in.	April–May	Smoky red
Linaria alpina (S)		3 in.	8 in.	June–Aug.	Violet and orange
Linum arboreum (C) 'Gemmell's hybrid'		6 in.	12 in.	May–July	Yellow
,,	*alpinum* (S)	6 in.	12 in.	July–Aug.	Blue
,,	*salsoides nanum* (C)	2 in.	10 in.	May–Sept.	White

	HEIGHT	SPACE	TIME	COLOURS
Lithospermum intermedium (S) (C)	6 in.	12 in.	May–June	Blue
„ *diffusum* (C) 'Heavenly Blue'	6 in.	15 in.	May–Sept.	Blue
Lychnis alpina (S)	4 in.	6 in.	April–June	Rose-pink
C. *Mazus reptans* (D)	1 in.	9 in.	May–Aug.	Mauve
Micromeria corsica (C)	3–4 in.	6 in.	July–Aug.	Lavender
Morisia hypogaea	1 in.	4 in.	May–July	Yellow
C. *Nierembergia rivularis* (D)	2 in.	10 in.	May–June	White
Patrina palmata (S)	6 in.	12 in.	July–Sept.	Yellow
Pentstemon Roezlii (C)	6 in.	12 in.	May–June	Red
„ *heterophyllus* (C)	9 in.	12 in.	June–July	Blue
„ *confertus* (C)	4–6 in.	12 in.	June–July	Yellow
Phlox Douglassii 'Eva' (C)	2 in.	9 in.	May–June	Mauve
„ „ 'May Snow' (C)	2 in.	12 in.	May–June	White
„ „ *rosea*	2 in.	12 in.	May–June	Pink
Polygala Chaebuxus purpureus	4–6 in.	9 in.	May–July	Purple
Potentilla ambigua (S)	2–3 in.	9 in.	May–Aug.	Golden yellow
„ *verna pygmea* (C)	1 in.	6 in.	May–Sept.	Golden yellow
Primula auricula (S)	6 in.	6 in.	April–May	Red, yellow, purple mixed
Prunella incisa rubra (D)	6–9 in.	15 in.	June–Sept.	Crimson
„ 'Loveliness'	6–9 in.	15 in.	June–Sept.	Mauve
„ *grandiflora*	6–9 in.	15 in.	June–Sept.	Violet purple
C. *Raoulia australis* (S) (D)	1 in.	8 in.	Foliage only	White
„ 'Oakington ruby'	8–9 in.	6 in.	May–Oct.	Double crimson
„ 'Pixie'	6 in.	6 in.	May–Oct.	Pale pink and white, dwarf
„ *pumila*	8–9 in.	6 in.	May–Oct.	Double pink
Rosa 'Baby Gold'	6–9 in.	6 in.	May–Oct.	Double crimson
Saxifraga Burseriana sulphurea (C)	2–3 in.	6 in.	March–April	Light yellow
„ *Jenkinsea* (D)	2 in.	6 in.	Feb.–March	Pink
C. „ *Elizabethae* (D)	2 in.	8 in.	Feb.–March	Yellow
„ *oppositifolia* (D)	1 in.	12 in.	Feb.–March	Large rosy crimson
„ *oppositifolia alba* (D)	1 in.	12 in.	Feb.–March	White
Scutellaria alpina (S)	8 in.	12 in.	June–Aug.	Purple and yellow
Sedum cauticolum (D) (C)	3 in.	12 in.	June–Sept.	Rose red
„ *brevifolium* (D)	2 in.	6 in.	June–July	White
C. „ *dasyphyllum* (D)	1 in.	6 in.	Foliage	Pink purple
„ *Ewersii* (S) (C)	6 in.	12 in.	June–July	Lilac
C. „ *lydium* (D)	2 in.		Foliage	Green foliage turns scarlet

	HEIGHT	SPACE	TIME	COLOURS
Serratula Shawii (D)	9 in.	15 in.	Oct.–Nov.	Pink
Silene schafta (S)	6 in.	9 in.	Aug.–Sept.	Rosy purple
Sisyrinchium bermudianum (S)	9 in.	12 in.	Nearly all year	Deep violet
„ *brachypus* (S)	6–8 in.	12 in.	June–Sept.	Golden yellow
Solidago brachystachys (D)	9 in.	12 in.	Sept.–Oct.	Deep yellow
C. Stachys corsica (D)	1 in.	12 in.	June–Aug.	Cream
Teucrium chamaedrys (C)	6 in.	8 in.	June–Sept.	Pink
„ *lithospermifolia* (C)	4–6 in.	9 in.	June–Sept.	Rosy crimson
„ *Polium* (C)	4 in.	8 in.	July–Aug.	Golden yellow
„ *pyrenaicum* (C)	3–4 in.	8 in.	June–Sept.	Lilac cream
Thlaspi rotundifolium (S)	2 in.	8 in.	May	Lilac
C. Thymus serpyllum (S)	1 in.	15 in.	June–July	Purple
C. „ 'Bressingham' (D)	1 in.	12 in.	May–June	Pink
„ *serpyllum major* (D)	2 in.	15 in.	May–June	Bright crimson
Veronica Coralli (D)	9 in.	12 in.	July–Aug.	Salmon-pink
„ *selleri* (S)	6 in.	8 in.	Aug.–Oct.	Lavender blue
Zauschneria californica (C)	12 in.	12 in.	Aug.–Oct.	Orange scarlet

Most of the plants with an (S) are those which can be bought in packets, but if any alpines set seed, save it in a dry drawer and sow it either in the spring, or after the bedding plants clear. With careful weeding it will be found also that some have seeded themselves, and these can be dug and potted in September to give them a better chance of coming through the winter and hardening off for spring planting.

The damp-loving perennials for the primula bed are usually listed with the alpines, though most are on the large side for the alpine border or rock garden. Here a number of damp-loving herbaceous plants have been included to extend the season. An (S) marks those easily raised from seed which is freely available, and once the damp-loving primulas are going really well in a wet place, they will seed themselves. 'Space' here means distance between plants, in groups of three as in perennial borders.

As in earlier lists, species which do not come true from seed are marked †, but this is no disadvantage for most of them are very attractive mixtures. Primula seed germinates very much better fresh so as the tall spires go over, gather them as soon as the seeds will rattle in the pods. Sow the following spring with a far better chance of a cress-like germination than from bought packets which may have been years in a seed drawer. The damp-loving iris are also well worth raising and it is not necessary for any of these plants to be grown under wet conditions when they are young. Grow them like other perennials and transfer to the bog garden in spring. There are a number of foliage only water-side plants, like *Rheum giganteum*, the giant wild rhubarb, but in small gardens there is little room for anything that is merely large and does not flower.

Plants for the Wet Corner

	HEIGHT	SPACE	TIME	COLOURS
Astilbe (*Spiraea*) 'Fire'	2 ft.	12 ft.	June–July	Salmon-red
„ 'Granat'	3 ft.	15 in.	June–July	Deep pink
„ 'Rheinland'	3 ft.	15 in.	June–July	Bright pink
„ 'Tamarix'	4 ft.	15 in.	July	Pink
„ 'Vesuvius'	2 ft.	12 in.	June–July	Bright red
Caltha palustris plena (Double Kingcup)	1 ft.	12 in.	April	Yellow
Gillenia trifoliata (S)	2 ft.	12 in.	June–Aug.	White
Helianthemum Tuberaria (S)	9 in.	6 in.	June–July	Yellow
Iris Kaempferi† (S) mixed named (D)	2½ ft.	9 in.	June–July	Violet, blue, purple
„ *laevigata* 'Rose Queen'	2 ft.	9 in.	June–July	Pink
„ *Siberica*† (S-mixed) (D)	3 ft.	12 in.	June–July	Blue, violet, purple
Ligularia clivorum (S)	4 ft.	18 in.	July–Aug.	Yellow
„ „ 'Othello'	4 ft.	18 in.	July–Aug.	Yellow, purple foliage
Lysimachia clethroides (S)	2½ ft.	15 in.	Aug.–Sept.	White
„ *euphemerum* (S)	2½ ft.	12 in.	July–Aug.	White
„ *punctata*	3 ft.	12 in.	June–Aug.	Yellow
Mimulus cupreus 'Monarch† (S)	1 ft.	8 in.	June–Sept.	Red, yellow, pink, orange
„ 'Whitcroft Scarlet' (S)	3 in.	4 in.	May–Sept.	Scarlet
„ *luteus* (S)	1½ in.	6 in.	June–Aug.	Yellow
Primula alpicola (S)	1½ in.	8 in.	May–June	Yellow, white, violet
„ *aurantiaca*† (S)	1 ft.	6 in.	July	Orange-red
„ *Beesiana*† (S)	2 ft.	8 in.	June	Mauve shades
„ *Bulleyana*† (S)	2 ft.	8 in.	June	Apricot orange
„ *burmanica*† (S)	2 ft.	8 in.	June	Purple
„ *chungensis*† (S)	2 ft.	8 in.	June	Orange
„ *Cockburniana*† (S)	1 ft.	6 in.	June	Orange-red
„ *denticulata*† (S-mixed)	1 ft.	8 in.	March–May	Purple, lilac, crimson
„ *Florindae* (S)	3 ft.	15 in.	June–July	Yellow
„ *helodoxa* (S)	2 ft.	12 in.	June	Yellow
„ *japonica* mixed† (S)	2 ft.	9 in.	May–June	Crimson, rose, white

			HEIGHT	SPACE	TIME	COLOURS
Primula	,,	'Millar's Crimson' (S)	2½ ft.	12 in.	May–June	Crimson
,,	,,	'Postford White' (S)	2½ ft.	12 in.	May–June	White
,,	,,	'Poissoni† (S)	1½ ft.	8 in.	June	Purple
,,	'pulverulenta' (S)		2 ft.	12 ft.	June	Crimson
,,		,, 'Bartley Strain' (S)	3 ft.	12 in.	June	Clear pink
,,	*sikkimensis* (S)		1½ ft.	8 in.	May–June	Yellow
,,	*Waltoni* (S)		2 ft.	12 in.	May–June	Wine-red
Trollius europaeus (S)			1½ ft.	9 in.	May–June	Yellow
,,	*ledebouri* 'Golden Queen' (S)		3 ft.	12 in.	May–June	Yellow

There are a number of shrubs that are fairly fast and easy from seed, and those who plan a hedge ahead can raise their plants in quantity, provided that they have the space, and reasonable luck with seedlings. Apart from the very easiest there are others which are a far more rewarding gamble than unknown annuals because those who have space and perseverance can win a shrub that will be all the more enjoyable because it was entirely home grown.

In the list that follows (E) marks an Evergreen, and though the majority can be sown after the bedding plants have moved out, a few, marked with † need spring sowings, while still fewer need heat as well to start them: and these are marked with ‡.

Shrubs from Seed

	EVENTUAL HEIGHT	FLOWERING SEASON	COLOURS
Amelanchier ovalis	4–6 ft.	May	White
Amorpha canescens	2–3 ft.	July–Sept.	Purple blue
Aristrolochia macrophylla	Climber	June	Yellow and purple, not exciting
Berberis Thunbergii (Hedge)	2–3 ft.	May	Yellow, spiny
Buddleia variabilis (mixed)†	6–8 ft.	July–Aug.	Mauve, purple, red, white
Caragana arborescens	5–8 ft.	June–July	Yellow
Chaenomeles Cathayensis (Hedge)	5–6 ft.	April	White
Cistus Cyprius	4–8 ft.	June–July	White
Cornus Mas†	15 ft.	Feb.–March	Yellow
Cotoneaster Simonsii (E) (Hedge)	6–8 ft.	June	White, berries
Coronilla Emerus (mixed)†	5–7 ft.	May–Oct.	Yellow, pink

	EVENTUAL HEIGHT	FLOWERING SEASON	COLOURS
Cytisus Battandieri (wall)	12–15 ft.	June	Yellow
Deutzia crenata (mixed)†	6–8 ft.	June–July	White, pink
Diervilla rosea (Hedge)	4–6 ft.	May–June	Pink
Enkianthus campanulatus†	5–6 ft.	May	Yellow
Escallonia montevidensis† (E) (Hedge)	6–8 ft.	June–July	White
Euonymus Japonicus (E) (Hedge)	6–10 ft.	Insignificant	
Exochordia racemosa†	8–10 ft.	April–May	White
Genista virgata	10–12 ft.	June–July	Yellow
Halesia carolina	10–15 ft.	April May	White
Hippophaea rhamnoides (Hedge)	7–12 ft.	Insignificant berries	
Hydrangea villosa‡	6–9 ft.	Aug.–Sept.	Blue
Hypericum calycinum (E)	1½–2 ft.	June–Aug.	Yellow
Indigofera Gerardiana	4–6 ft.	July–Aug.	Purple
Kerria japonica	4–5 ft.	April–May	Yellow
Koelreuteria paniculata‡	8–10 ft.	July	Yellow, pink seedpods
Kolkwitzia amabilis‡	6–8 ft.	May–June	Pink
Leycesteria formosa‡	6–8 ft.	July–Sept.	Pink, purple bracts
Lonicera periclymenum	Clg.	July–Sept.	(Scented honeysuckle)
,, *Tellmanniana*‡	Clg.	July–Sept.	Yellow
,, *tartarica*	5–6 ft.	May	Deep pink
Mahonia aquifolium (E) (Hedge) (Excellent under trees)	3–4 ft.	April–May	Yellow, purple berries, jelly
Ononis fruticosa	2–3 ft.	June–Aug.	Pink
Osmaronia cerasiformis	4–5 ft.	March–April	White, glorious scent. Purple fruit
Philadelphus coronarius	6–8 ft.	June–July	White
Phillyrea angustifolia (E) (Hedge)	5–8 ft.	May	White, scented
Phlomis fruticosa	2–3 ft.	June	Yellow, grey foliage
Photinia villosa	8–15 ft.	April–May	White, leaves autumn colour
Prunus Myrobalana (Hedge)	8–12 ft.	March–April	White
Potentilla fruticosa (Hedge)	3–4 ft.	July–Sept.	Yellow
Pyracantha coccinea Lalandi (E) (Hedge)	8–10 ft.	May–June	White, red berries
Raphilepsis Delacourii (E)	5–6 ft.	April–Aug.	Pink, intermittent. Sun and shelter
Rosmarinus officinalis (E) (Hedge)	4–6 ft.	April–May	Pale violet

	EVENTUAL HEIGHT	FLOWERING SEASON	COLOURS
Sorbaria Aitchisonii† (Hedge)	4–6 ft.	Aug.–Sept.	White. Striking.
Stranvaesia Davidiana† (E) (Hedge)	10–12 ft.	June	White. Fruits best
Syringa vulgaris hybrids (Hedge)	10–15 ft.	May	Mixed, mostly lilac
Tamarix gallica (Hedge)	5–7 ft.	June–Aug.	Pink
Viburnum Carlesii	5–6 ft.	April–May	White, scented
,, *lantana* (Hedge)	6–8 ft.	May	White
Vitis inconstans (*Ampelopsis Veitchii*)	Clg.	Insignificant	Self-clinging climber, autumn tints
Wisteria sinensis	Clg.	May–June	Mauve

The germination speed of bought shrub seed varies and always some will race ahead and others hang about until the autumn. It is suggested that buddleias should be spring sown because they are away fast and can be planted out with time not only to ripen their growth and come through the winter, but to flower and allow any washy colours to show, and be discarded. Anything that has reached 3-in. height and is growing well can be planted in the open in September to come through the winter, though a mild season will mean weeding in the spring so that the seedlings are not strangled when small.

The others will need potting, to winter in the cold frame and move out into the 'annex' to harden off in March for April planting, leaving room in the frame for spring sowings. (It will be realized that those who want to raise shrubs cannot winter geraniums.) The hedging shrubs are all fast growing, and if they go out small in the autumn 6 in. apart in the rows and 1 ft. between for hoeing they should be ready to plant permanently by the following autumn.

All the hedge species listed can be planted 1 ft. apart, which is closer than for large specimens bought from a nursery, but make a good hedge, and because the young small seedlings have not had a rail journey, and can be dug with plenty of root, they will thrive. If a nurseryman sold plants that size you would have every right to complain, but your own are value for time and space if you can spare these. Wisteria, Indigofera, and Caragana are all Leguminosae (Pea tribe), like the Cytisus for hedging. These put down tap roots early, and though they will look small when you first put them in they will get ahead far better than if you moved them larger, because they suffer if their main tap root is broken, which is why they are often grown commercially and sold expensively in pots. Soak their seeds, like the Hedge Broom seeds, and plant them small, for success.

Though small gardens have room for so few trees that those mentioned in the text are enough for most people, there are two Pea tribe species that are easy by this method. *Robinia pseudoacacia Decaisneana*, is the pink form of William Cobbett's 'Locust Tree' with flowers like pink laburnum chains 4–7 in. long. It could grow 40 ft. high, but 30 is its usual maximum, and it does well on poor soils and cast light shade, while *R. viscosa* has nearer rose-pink flowers and is rather smaller. Both send up thorny suckers from the roots which should be twisted off with gloves on. The other species for those who want to sow a tree and have it growing while they are sleeping, is *Sophora japonica*. This is also laburnum-like but with 10-in. creamy-white tassels in September after every hot summer. It can in the course of years grow 80 ft. high, like the splendid specimen in the Oxford Botanic Gardens which is over a hundred years old.

When we begin gardening in new gardens, all shrubs are just names to us. We think in terms of colour—we should like something a vivid crimson, to flower in deep dry shade under trees, and for as long as possible and ideally evergreen. This wonder shrub does not exist, but there are hundreds that are worth growing in large gardens. In small ones, however, length of flowering season is all important and colour relative to space. The first lists are sorted under 'Colours' with their flowering seasons. All are without soil fads and suitable for sun. Those for awkward soils and situations come in at end of lists. The colours are very approximate, because there are so many shades of each, but at least the lists avoid having three pinks together 'swearing at each other' with the same flowering season.

White and Cream-flowered Shrubs

	FLOWERING SEASON	EVENTUAL HEIGHT
Amelanchier Canadensis	April	15–18 ft.
,, *ovalis*	May	4–6 ft.
Buddleia davidii 'White Profusion'	July–Aug.	9–12 ft.
Cistus cyprius (E)	June–July	4–6 ft.
Chaenomeles speciosa nivalis	March–April	5–7 ft.
Cotoneaster lactea (red berries also) (E)	July	10–12 ft.
Crataegus prunifolia	June	10–15 ft.
Cytisus albus	May	8–10 ft.
Deutzia pulchra	May	6–8 ft.
Erica carnea 'Springwood White'	Jan.–March	6–8 in.

	FLOWERING SEASON	EVENTUAL HEIGHT
Erica mediterranea 'Silver Beads'	Feb.–March	9–12 in.
„ „ 'W. T. Rackliffe'	March–April	9–12 in.
Escallonia montevidensis (E)	June–July	6–8 ft.
Eucryphia glutinosa	July–Aug.	12–18 ft.
Exochordia racemosa	May	10–12 ft.
Hebe (*Veronica*) *Darwiniana* (E)	June–July	2–3 ft.
Hydrangea grandiflora	July–Sept.	6–7 ft.
„ *macrophylla* 'White Wave'	July–Aug.	5–6 ft.
„ 'Madame E. Moulliere'	July–Aug.	4–6 ft.
Lonicera purpusii	Jan.–Feb.	7–9 ft.
Magnolia soulangiana alba	April–May	12–15 ft.
„ *stellata*	March–April	10–12 ft.
Olearia haastii (E)	July–Aug.	6–9 ft.
Osmanthus delavayi (E)	April	7–10 ft.
Osmarea burkwoodii	April–May	9–12 ft.
Philadelphus, all species	June–July	7–12 ft.
Potentilla mandschurica	May–Oct.	1–1½ ft.
Pyracantha atalantioides	June	15–18 ft.
Romneya trichocalyx	July–Oct.	5–7 ft.
Rubus tridel 'Benenden'	May	6–8 ft.
Skimmia fragrans (E)	May–June	3–4 ft.
Sorbaria aitchisoni	Aug.–Sept.	4–6 ft.
Spiraea arguta	April–May	6–8 ft.
„ *thunbergii*	March–April	5–7 ft.
Stranvaesia Davidiana (E)	June	10–12 ft.
Syringa (Lilac) 'Maud Notcutt' single	May	10–12 ft.
„ 'Madame Lemoine' double	May	10–12 ft.
Viburnum Burkwoodii	Dec.–Feb.	8–10 ft.
„ *Carlesii*	April–May	5–6 ft.
„ *plicatum grandiflorum*	May–June	6–9 ft.

The pruning of the shrubs on this list has mainly been given in earlier chapters, but Romneya and Sorbaria both need cutting down to the base in spring, for they flower late on this year's wood. The others need little pruning, but if they grow too large follow two rough rules, first, that autumn- or late-flowering species should be pruned or shortened in spring, and spring species after flowering, and second that 'when in doubt—don't'.

Pink Flowering Shrubs, All Shades

	FLOWERING SEASON	EVENTUAL HEIGHT
Abelia grandiflora Pale	July–Sept.	6–8 ft.
Ceanothus 'Perle Rose' Deeper	May–June	6–8 ft.

	FLOWERING SEASON	EVENTUAL HEIGHT
Chaenomeles 'Cameo' Peach	March–May	4–6 ft.
,, 'Moerloesei' Pale	March–May	4–6 ft.
Cistus purpureus (E) Rose	May–June	5–6 ft.
,, ,, 'Silver Pink' (E) Medium	June–July	3–4 ft.
Crataegus Oxyacantha Maskei Pale	May	10–15 ft.
Cytisus 'Enchantress' Rose pink	May–June	5–6 ft.
Daphne Mezereum Rose	Jan.–March	3–4 ft.
Deutzia rosa carminea Pale rose	May–June	4–5 ft.
,, *scabra* 'Codsall Pink' Deep rose	June–July	8–10 ft.
Erica carnea Pale	Feb.–March	6–10 in.
,, ,, 'King George' Pale	Nov.–Feb.	9–12 in.
,, ,, 'Ruby Glow' Deeper pink	Jan.–Feb.	9–12 in.
,, ,, 'Springwood' Pink, pale	Jan.–March	6–9 in.
Escallonia edinensis (E) Medium	June	6–10 ft.
Hydrangea hortensis domotoi (double) Pale	July–Sept.	4–6 ft.
,, 'Hamburg' Deep pink	July–Sept.	4–6 ft.
,, 'Madame Riverain' Pale	July–Sept.	4–6 ft.
,, 'Vicomtess de Vibraye' Pale	July–Sept.	4–6 ft.
Kolkwitzia amabilis Pale	May–June	6–8 ft.
Leycesteria formosa, Pale, purple bracts.	July–Oct.	4–5 ft.
Lavatera olbia rosea Medium	July–Oct.	5–6 ft.
Magnolia soulangiana rubra	April–May	6–8 ft.
Prunus glandulosa sinensis Pale	April–May	4–5 ft.
,, *sargentii* Pale	March–April	10–15 ft.
,, *tenella* 'Firehill' Deep	March–April	3–6 ft.
Ribes sanguineum 'China Rose' Medium	March–April	6–10 ft.
Spiraea japonica alpina Deep	June–Aug.	3–4 ft.
Symphoricarpus chenaultii Pale	June–July	6–8 ft.
Syringa (lilac) 'Esther Staley', Nearest pink	May	6–8 ft.
Tamarix pentandra 'Pink Cascade' Rose	July–Aug.	10–12 ft.
,, ,, *rubra* Deep rose	July–Aug.	10–12 ft.
,, *gallica* Pale	June–Aug.	10–15 ft.
,, *parviflora* Pale	April–May	12–15 ft.
Viburnum bodnantense 'Dawn' Pale	Dec.–Feb.	9–12 ft.
Weigela rosea Medium	May–June	8–9 ft.
,, *styrica* Deep rose	May–June	8–9 ft.

Pinks, like all colours, are difficult to define for everyone, for though the R.H.S. Colour Chart draws clear distinction, this is too costly and awkward to handle to be used by nurserymen and gardeners. If the colour names and numbers were used here they would convey nothing to the reader. Of the shrubs in the list that are not in earlier chapters, Leycesteria demands the spring cut-down policy, and the others need little pruning.

Red, Crimson and Scarlet Shrubs

	FLOWERING SEASON	EVENTUAL HEIGHT
Chaenomeles 'Boule de Feu' Vermilion	March–April	5–7 ft.
„ *Hollandia* Scarlet	March–April	5–7 ft.
„ *japonica alpina* Brick red (fruits)	Mar.–May	2½–3½ ft.
„ 'Rowallane' Deep red	March–April	5–7 ft.
Crataegus oxyacantha 'Paul's Double Scarlet' Rose red	May	15–20 ft.
Cytisus 'Johnson's Crimson' Rose red	May–June	4–5 ft.
Erica carnea vivellii Deep carmine	Jan.–March	5–8 in.
Escallonia 'Donard Brilliance' Crimson (E)	June	5–6 ft.
„ *ingramii* Rose red (E)	June–July	6–8 ft.
Hydrangea hortensis 'Ami Pasquier' Crimson	July–Sept.	4–6 ft.
„ „ 'Parsival' Rosy red	July–Sept.	4–6 ft.
„ „ 'President Doumer' Deep crimson	July–Sept.	2–3 ft.
Ribes sanguineum 'King Edward VII' Crimson	March–April	6–7 ft.
„ „ 'Pulborough Scarlet' Brighter crimson	March–April	6–7 ft.
Spiraea japonica 'Anthony Waterer' Carmine	June–Aug.	3–4 ft.
Syringa 'Mrs. Edward Harding' Nearest crimson	May	8–10 ft.
Weigela 'Bristol Ruby'	May–June	6–8 ft.

The relatively small number of red shrubs compared with the other colours is accounted for by azaleas and rhododendrons coming in the list of lime-haters. There are plenty of red-purples, mauves, and lilacs merging into blue, but these have lists on their own. The blue-flowering shrubs in the list that follows are true blues, which is why they are so few, for blues like those of gentians and linums are such splendid contrasts with whites and yellows.

Light and Dark Blue Shrubs

	FLOWERING SEASON	EVENTUAL HEIGHT
Caryopteris clandonensis 'Kew Blue'	Sept.–Oct.	3–4 ft.
Ceanothus burkwoodii Deep blue	July–Oct.	8–9 ft.
„ *dentatus russellianus*	May–June	8–9 ft.
„ 'Gloire de Versailles' Soft blue	June–Oct.	10–12 ft.
„ 'Topaz', Deepest blue	June–Oct.	8–10 ft.
Ceratostigma willmottianum Mid–blue	Aug.–Oct.	15 in.
Hydrangea acuminata 'Blue Bird'	July–Aug.	3–4 ft.
„ *hortensis* (Blued)	July–Sept.	6–8 ft.

	FLOWERING SEASON	EVENTUAL HEIGHT
Perovskia atriplicifolia Pale blue, grey foliage	Aug.–Sept.	6–8 ft.
Rosmarinus officinalis Pale blue	April–May	5–6 ft.

Ceratostigma needs cutting down each spring, after mid-March, and both Caryopteris and Perovskia should be cut back almost to the base of the previous year's shoots, for all three flower on their young wood. The shrubs that follow are all on the blue side of purple.

Violet, Near-Blue and Lilac Shrubs

	FLOWERING SEASON	EVENTUAL HEIGHT
Amorpha canescens Purplish blue •	July–Sept.	2–3 ft.
Buddleia alternifolia Lilac purple	June	15–20 ft.
,,　　*Davidii* 'Fortune' Lilac	July–Aug.	9–12 ft.
,,　　　,,　　'Mayford Purple' Dark violet	July–Aug.	9–12 ft.
,,　　*fallowiana* 'Lochinch' Lavender	July–Sept.	4–6 ft.
Hebe (*Veronica*) 'Margery Fish' Lavender (E)	June–Sept.	2–2½ ft.
,,　'Midsummer Beauty' Deep lavender (E)	July–Sept.	3–3½ ft.
,,　*Vernicosa* Lavender (E)	June–Aug.	1–2 ft.
Hydrangea 'Parsival' (Blue to violet)		
Lavandula spica Lavender (E)	July–Aug.	3–4 ft.
,,　　'Felgate' Lavender (E)	July	1–1½ ft.
,,　　'Hidcote' Deepest purple blue (E)	July	2–2½ ft.
,,　　'Twickel Purple' Dark violet (E)	July	2–3 ft.
Salvia hispanica Purple (E) Grey leaves	June	2½–3 ft.
Syringa 'Congo' Single, Deep purple	May	10–15 ft.
,,　'Massena' Single, Purple	May	10–15 ft.
,,　'Charles Joly' Double, Deep purple	May	10–15 ft.
,,　'Souvenir de Louis Spath' Single, Deep purple	May	10–15 ft.

Mauve and Red-Purple Shrubs

	FLOWERING SEASON	EVENTUAL HEIGHT
Buddleia Davidii 'Black Knight' The darkest Red purple	July–Aug.	9–12 ft.
,,　　,,　　'Royal Red' Red purple	July–Aug.	9–12 ft.
Indigofera Gerardiana Rosy purple	June–Sept.	2–3 ft.
Lavandula 'Hidcote Pink' Lilac-pink (E)	July	2–2½ ft.

	FLOWERING SEASON	EVENTUAL HEIGHT
Magnolia liliflora migra Wine purple	April–June	10–15 ft.
„ *soulangiana nigra* Red purple	May	12–18 ft.
Syringa 'Sensation' Deep red purple	May	10–15 ft.

Yellow and Orange Shrubs

	FLOWERING SEASON	EVENTUAL HEIGHT
Berberis Darwinii Orange-yellow, purple berries (E)	April–May	6–8 ft.
„ *stenophylla* Orange-yellow (E)	April–May	10–12 ft.
Buddleia globosa	May–June	8–12 ft.
Caragana arborescens	May	10–15 ft.
Chimonanthus fragrans Primrose	Dec.–Jan.	8–10 ft.
Cornus Mas	Feb.–March	10–15 ft.
Coronilla Emerus	May–Oct.	5–7 ft.
Corylopsis spicata Primrose	March–April	5–7 ft.
Cytisus 'Goldfinch' Yellow and crimson	May–June	4–5 ft.
„ *nigricans* Bright yellow	June–Aug.	3–5 ft.
„ 'Diana' Primrose and gold	May–June .	6–7 ft.
Forsythia intermedia 'Lynwood'	March–April	8–10 ft.
„ „ *spectabilis*	March–April	8–10 ft.
„ „ *primulina* Paler yellow	March–April	8–10 ft.
Genista virgata	June–July	10–12 ft.
Halimum lasianthum concolor Bright yellow	May–July	2–3 ft.
Hamamelis mollis Bright yellow, scented	Dec.–Feb.	10–15 ft.
Hypericum androsaemum	June–Aug.	3–4 ft.
„ *calycinum*	June–Aug.	1–1½ ft.
„ *patulum* 'Gold Cup'	July–Aug.	4–5 ft.
Kerria japonica	April–May	4–6 ft.
„ *pleniflora* Orange yellow, double	April–June	8–10 ft.
Koelreuteria paniculata	July	10–15 ft.
Mahonia aquifolium (E) Purple berries also	Feb.–May	3–5 ft.
„ *japonica* (E) Lemon yellow	Feb.–March	5–7 ft.
Potentilla arbuscula Primrose yellow	June–Oct.	3–4 ft.
„ 'Jackman's Variety' Bright yellow	June–Sept.	4–5 ft.
„ *fruticosa* 'Katherine Dykes'	May–Oct.	4–5 ft.
„ „ 'Primrose Beauty', Cream yellow	June–Oct.	3–4 ft.
Senecio laxiflorus, Grey foliage also	June–July	3–4 ft.
Syringa 'Primrose' Nearest yet	May	8–10 ft.

All the shrubs in the foregoing list have been chosen to grow in full sun on any soil. This includes chalk, provided that they have leafmould, compost and other sources of humus and plant foods added, for thin soils over chalk are in the same class as poor and pebbly ones full of broken glass and soot in towns. Note, however, that the cherries, almonds, peaches and plums will all thrive there, just as their fruiting versions will.

The next class, however, are the lime-haters—the shrubs, including rhododendrons, that everyone on chalk wants to grow. Though it is possible to use the new iron compounds, or Epsom salts, to cancel out the lime, it is not possible to fight your soil successfully except at great expense of money and trouble. It is far better to stick to the shrubs (and plants) that enjoy your soil.

When a soil is a borderline one, and you have merely limestone, not chalk, it is worth taking a chance with plenty of humus and chemical aids if necessary in emergencies. There are a number of part-hardy lime-haters and these have been given a *, because so many gardens with lime-free soils are in Devon and Cornwall, the west coast of Scotland and other warm areas. Here, however, there are high winds, and shelter is desirable. Camellias can also be grown in lime-free soil but though they are hardier than was thought, they flower so early in the year, with frost-tender flowers, that they have been excluded as unsuitable for beginners with small gardens.

Shrubs for Lime-free Soils

	FLOWERING SEASON	EVENTUAL HEIGHT
Andromeda polyfolia nana Pink	April	9–15 in.
Azalea coccinea speciosa Orange flame	May–June	4–6 ft.
„ *pontica* Yellow (first two hardiest)	May–June	6–7 ft.
„ *mollis* (deciduous) 'Frans Hals' Deep red	May–June	5–6 ft.
„ „ 'J. C. Van Thol' Orange-red	May–June	5–6 ft.
„ „ *altaclarense* Orange-yellow	May–June	5–6 ft.
„ „ 'Dr. M. Oosthoek' Salmon-rose	May–June	5–6 ft.
„ *obtusa* (Evergreen or Japanese)		
„ „ 'Adonis' White (E)	April–May	2–2½ ft.
„ „ 'Helena' Double pink (E)	April–May	2–2½ ft.
„ „ 'Kiritsubo' Mauve (E)	April–May	2–3 ft.
„ „ *macrostemon* Salmon-red (E)	April–May	2–3 ft.
„ *pulchrum Maxwellii* Rose-red (E)	May–June	2½–3 ft.
Calluna vulgaris alportii Deep purple (E) (Scottish Ling Heather)	Aug.–Sept.	1½–2 ft.
„ 'County Wicklow' Pale pink double (E)	Aug.–Sept.	15–18 in.

	FLOWERING SEASON	EVENTUAL HEIGHT
(Scottish Ling Heather)		
„ 'Goldsworth Crimson' Red-purple (E)	Sept.–Oct.	2–3 ft.
„ 'H. E. Beale' Double mauve-pink (E)	Aug.–Sept.	2–3 ft.
„ 'J. H. Hamilton' Double deep pink (E)	Aug.–Sept.	12–15 in.
„ 'Tib' Soft purple (E)	June–July	1½–2 ft.
Corylopsis spicata Primrose yellow, scented	March–April	5–7 ft.
Daboecia cantabrica Purple (E)	June–Oct.	1½–2 ft.
„ „ *alba* White (E)	June–Oct.	2–2½ ft.
„ *atropurpurea* Deeper purple (E)	June–Oct.	2–2½ ft.
Enkianthus campanulatus Yellow	May	5–7 ft.
Erica cinerea 'Smith's Var.' Blood-red (E)	June–Aug.	9–10 in.
„ „ 'Colligan Bridge' Deep purple (E)	June–Aug.	12–15 in.
„ „ 'Honeymoon' White (E)	July–Aug.	1–1½ ft.
„ „ 'Rose Queen' Bright pink (E)	June–Aug.	1–1½ ft.
„ *tetralix* 'Con Underwood' Crimson, grey foliage (E)	June–Oct.	12–15 in.
„ „ mollis White, grey foliage (E)	June–Oct.	12–15 in.
„ *vagans grandiflora* Mauve (E) (Cornish Heath)	Sept.–Nov.	1–1½ ft.
„ „ 'Lyonesse' White (E)	July–Sept.	1–1½ ft.
„ „ 'Mrs. D. F. Maxwell' Deep pink (E)	July–Sept.	1–1½ ft.
„ „ 'St. Keverne', Pale pink (E)	July–Sept.	1–1½ ft.
*Eucryphia glutinosa** White	July–Aug.	10–12 ft.
„ *intermedia* 'Rostrevor'* (E)	July–Aug.	10–15 ft.
*Fothergilla monticola** Creamy flowers, autumn tints	April	5–7 ft
Gaultheria procumbens Yellow, scented, white berries (E)	July–Aug.	6–9 in.
Kalmia latifolia Shell pink (E)	June	6–8 ft.
Pieris forestii 'Wakehurst' Cream (E)	April	7–9 ft.
Rhododendron 'Britannia' Ruby red	May–June	4–8 ft.
„ 'Kluis Sensation' Scarlet	May–June	4–8 ft.
„ 'Lord Roberts' Deep red	May–June	4–8 ft.
„ 'Mrs. R. S. Holford' Deep salmon	May–June	4–8 ft.
„ 'Pink Pearl' Rose pink	May–June	4–8 ft.
„ 'Purple Splendour' Royal purple	May–June	4–8 ft.
Stewartia sinensis White, autumn colouring	July–Aug.	5–7 ft.
Vaccinium corymbosum 'Grover', White (American blueberry, fruit edible)	May	5–6 ft.

It is not possible to do more than list a few outstanding hybrids of azaleas and rhododendrons, which are now botanically identical. Those given here are outstanding, but anyone who has a lime-free soil will find plenty in the catalogues of any good nursery, while those who have not should try just one to see how it goes before spending another £2 or more a plant. Apart from the absence of lime, and the presence of ample humus, their main need is to have the flower heads removed by bending these sideways as they finish. Though the *Erica carnea* and *E. mediterranea* varieties are in the ordinary soil list because they do not mind lime, they need peat or leafmould also. Their attitude to lime is one of tolerance, and, like tolerant people who put up with noisy neighbours, they do very well with nothing to tolerate, in a heather bed with the lime haters where they complete the flowering cycle.

Many of the species listed are grown also on walls, and though both Chaenomeles and Ceanothus can be grown in shrub borders, they are at their best against house walls. The next list supplements and brings together the wall shrubs which stand up and need tying back to the wall, and the climbers that need tying for support, such as clematis—which can of course trail down.

Many climbers will also thrive on north walls, and these have been given an (N), while those that must face south for maximum sunshine have (S). Those which are not suitable for northern gardens have been awarded a * as on the list of lime haters. This list of course repeats varieties given earlier for easy reference when planning wall planting. As with the azaleas and rhododendrons, there is only room for a very few of the many hybrid clematis, and these are the toughest and most typical of their groups. All are bare in winter unless they have 'E' for Evergreen, and are climbers without 'shrub' under their names.

Wall Shrubs and Climbers

	FLOWERING SEASON
Actinidia chinensis Cream flowers, eatable fruit, gooseberry flavour, large leaves*	August
Akebia quinata Brown-purple tassel flowers (S)*	May
Aristolochia sipho Large leaves hide the Yellow-green saxophone-shaped flowers*	June
Campsis radicans (S) Vivid Vermilion tube flowers, self-clinging, a 'must' for mild gardens*	Aug.–Sept.
,, *tangiabuana* 'Mme Galen' Orange-red	Aug.–Sept.

FLOWERING SEASON

Ceanothus (Shrub) *burkwoodii* Deep blue	July–Oct.
„ 'Delight' Deep blue	May
„ *dentatus Russellianus* Mid-blue	May–June
„ 'Gloire de Versailles' Pale blue	June–Oct.
„ 'Topaz' Deep blue	June–Oct.
Chaenomeles speciosa 'Boule de Feu', Vermilion (Best for fruit).	March–May
„ *speciosa* 'Cameo' Double Peach-pink	May–May
„ 'Falconet Charlot' Double Salmon pink	May–April
„ 'Moerloosei' Pale pink (fruits)	May–April
„ *speciosa nivalis* White	May–April
Clematis alpina hybrids All colours	April–May
„ *armandii* White	May–April
„ *florida* hybrids All colours	May–June
„ *Jackmanii* hybrids All colours	June–Oct.
„ *lanuginosa* hybrids All colours	June–July
„ *Montana* hybrids All colours	June–Oct.
„ *Patens* hybrids All colours	May–June
„ *Viticella* hybrids All colours	July–Sept.
Cotoneaster buxifolia vellaea Bright red berries (E)	June–July
„ *franchetii* White, red berries (E)	July
„ *horizontalis* White, red berries	May
Escallonia Ingramii Rose-red	June–July
„ *edinensis* Pink	June–July
„ 'Donard Brilliance' Crimson (E)	June–July
Forsythia suspensa atrocaulis* Sulphur yellow	May–April
„ „ *Fortuni* Bright yellow (N)	May–April
Hydrangea petiolaris White, self-clinging, Lemon-yellow autumn leaves (N)	June
Jasminum nudiflorum Yellow*	Nov.–Feb.
„ *officinale* White, scented	July–Aug.
„ *stephanense* Pale pink, scented	July–Aug.
Lonicera americana Rose-purple, scented (N)	May–June
„ *Henryi* Small Purple flowers (E)	May–June
„ *japonica Halliana* Creamy (E)	June–Oct.
„ *periclymenum serotina* Red-purple outside, yellow inside, scented (N)	July–Sept.
„ *Tellmanniana* Bright yellow (N)	July–Sept.
Passiflora caerulea* (S) Blue and cream	July–Sept.
Polygonum baldschuanicum White (N) (Magnificent but wages war)	July–Oct.
Pyracantha coccinea lalandii White flowers, red berries	May–June
Vitis inconstans veitchii 'Beverly Brook', self clinging. Autumn tints	May–June
„ *quinquefolia*† Virginia Creeper, self clinging Autumn tints	

FLOWERING SEASON

Wisteria chinensis Mauve (S)	May–June
„ *floribunda alba* White, lovely against red brick (S)	May–June
„ *macrobotrys* Lavender, the longest of all tassels (S)	May–June

It should be said that unfamiliar names in all these lists do not necessarily mean rare and difficult species—some will be treasures for every garden when they are better known.

Those who do know them all, and more, will be indignant that special treasures of their own have been ignored, while others have been left in. This has been unavoidable, for it is impossible today to write a complete gardening book that will give full and detailed accounts of everything. There are too many plants, especially flowering shrubs, so the selection has had to be in favour of the easiest species for beginners and the best flowering value for space in small gardens.

Garden Recipes

Though many ornamental trees and shrubs have edible fruit, this is often wasted because no one is quite certain how to treat it. The following recipes have been gathered through the years from helpful readers of the *Observer* and others.

The berries of *Mahonia aquifolium* can be stewed and will make tarts, but are not really nice; the 2-in.-long fruits of the climber *Actinidia chinensis* can be stewed and eaten for their gooseberry flavour. No jam recipes are available because it has not been long enough in cultivation to have acquired any. A number of the flowering crabs make ordinary crab-apple jelly to standard recipes, but the really attractive fruits for jam making are the small peaches on 'Aurora' and 'Clara Meyer'. They fit the recipes used by commercial peach growers in Canada for wasp-bitten or otherwise damaged fruit.

Peach Jam

Peel, slice and remove stones from 4 lb. of not too ripe peaches. Simmer gently with $\frac{1}{2}$ pint of water, with about two dozen of the kernels in a muslin bag hanging in the preserving pan, until the fruit is well cooked. Add 3 lb. of sugar and when this has melted boil the jam fast till it is at setting stage. Remove the muslin bag with the stones in, and pour the jam into the jars for normal covering.

Peach Jelly

Take equal quantities of cooking apples and peaches, wipe them clean and halve them without coring or stoning. Cover with water in a preserving pan, bring to the boil and then simmer till the fruit is soft. Strain through a jelly bag. Measure the strained juice and add 1 lb. of sugar to each pint. Boil this fast till it sets when tested.

Japonica Wine

The fruits of any japonica will make wine, provided you wait until they turn yellow and are just a little soft, like a ripe pear, for they are something between a pear and a quince.

Cut 4 lb. of fruit in eighths as for jam, and pour a gallon of boiling water on them. Add two sliced lemons and crush; an old-fashioned 'copperstick' can be used but anything clean that will smash them up will do. The best container is something of china, big enough to hold a gallon as well as the fruit. Cover with muslin to keep out wasps and flies and stand in a warm room for five days.

Strain the juice; an old pyjama sleeve tied at the end and spread with tapes on a clothes-horse is good, as with the jelly. Add 3 lb. of sugar to each gallon of juice, stir till dissolved, then mix $\frac{1}{4}$ lb. of yeast with $\frac{1}{2}$ pint of juice until it is creamy. Stir this into the juice.

Pour it into a bread crock, bean jar, or salt jar that is earthenware, and has a lid or can be covered with muslin. Stand in a warm room (65–75° F., ordinary room temperature, not a cold shed) for five weeks. By then fermentation will have finished, for it is going to bubble. The lid must be capable of being lifted, for the carbon-dioxide the yeast produces as it turns sugars to alcohol must escape.

Then strain it clear, using the pyjama sleeve trick, or blotting-paper inside a funnel; in this ball-pointed age it is easier to buy filter paper from a chemist, and this is best. Then pour it into clean bottles but do not cork them until the wine stops bubbling, otherwise the corks may fly out in the night and wine come frothing out. When all is quiet, cork, label with the vintage year, and it will be drinkable in nine months. It is rather like a dry sherry, but the alcohol content depends on luck. It will have a powerful kick and a flavour that would baffle a wine expert.

Japonica Cream

The following recipe for Quince Cream is from *English House-wifery* by Elizabeth Maxon, 1769:

'Take quinces when they are full ripe, cut them in quarters, scald them till they be soft, pare them and mash the clear part of them and the pulp and put it through a sieve. Take an equal weight of the quince and double refined sugar beaten and sifted and the white of eggs, beat it until it is as white as snow then put it into dishes.'

'Double refined sugar' is replaced today with castor sugar which needs no sifting; an egg beater would be easier for adding the egg white. This is a dish for eating at once, and adding castor sugar and egg white to the first stage of 'Japonica Jelly' would be a good trial recipe for only a few fruit.

Japonica Seed

All recipes mean cutting the fruit up and the seeds can be taken out like apple pips. Dry these in the sun and store until February, then sow in pots or boxes in a greenhouse, or in the open in April. The greenhouse-raised are away quicker and should be planted out when they are about 4 in. high. They take about three years to reach fruiting size.

Chaenomeles are very much easier than quinces, and all old quince recipes apply to them. If more was known of how to use them they would be a good garden fruit. The species *C. cathayensis*, which has short and spiny shoots, has the largest fruits, up to 6 in. long. Raising the named varieties, like 'Knap Hill Scarlet', will mean colour and fruit variation, for named varieties and hybrids do not come true from seed. There might be an extra good fruiting one in seed from a specimen that always fruits well.

Chaenomeles Cheese (see page 85)

Quarter and core the fruits but do not peel them. The skins add both to the flavour and firmness of the preserve. Put the prepared fruits into a vegetable steamer over a pan of water and cover them. Steam until they are quite soft. Sieve the fruit coarsely (through the coarse sieve of a mouli-legumes for example), then weigh the resulting pulp and for each pound allow a pound of castor sugar. Put the sugar and pulp into a large preserving pan and bring to the boil. Then stir continually, for it burns easily, until the mixture is stiff and starts to come away from the side of the pan. Turn into jars and seal as for jam.

A firm Chaenomeles paste to be cut into slices for dessert is made in the same way, but when cooked turn into shallow tins or dishes and dry in a cool oven for several hours until quite firm to the touch. Turn out like a cake, wrap in foil, and store in tins in a dry, cool larder or cupboard.

Suppliers of Plants and Seeds

The majority of the annuals, biennials, perennials, bulbs, trees and shrubs can be obtained from any good nurseryman, but this is little help to the beginner who knows only his local chain store or garden centre. Fewer and fewer firms remain who keep a full range of species, just as good grocers grow rarer and rarer in an age of supermarkets. The firms that follow are those that the writer has dealt with for many years, most of them have been established for over a century, and there is a hope that they will stay 'unmodernized' as long as this book stays in print.

The seedsman with the most complete collection of everything that can be raised from seed including trees, shrubs, alpines, herbaceous plants and vegetables, is Thompson and Morgan Ltd., London Road, Ipswich, Suffolk. There are many firms more famous than this one, that began in 1855, and sells its seeds without pictures on the packets, by catalogue only. This in itself is a useful reference book, for if Thompson and Morgan do not stock a seed it is probably unobtainable.

Messrs. George Jackman and Sons, The Nurseries, Woking, Surrey, and Messrs. Hilliers, West Hill Nurseries, Winchester, Hants,. are the two best tree, shrub and herbaceous plant nurseries for range of stock. Both also have a good collection of roses and fruit trees, but on trees, shrubs and climbers they lead Britain. Their prices for good-quality produce, true to species or variety, and supplied by road or rail at the right planting time are very much lower than those charged in garden centres for trees and shrubs in containers to plant when in flower. If you insist on seeing your plant flowering and taking it away with you, you must expect to pay extra, just as butter beans tinned from a supermarket cost more than those weighed up in a bag from an old-fashioned grocer. Again their catalogues are good reference works, and they charge 15p each for them (but well worth it).

There are still more good rose nurseries, for it is far easier to keep a range of varieties in one line than in the many lines a large general nursery must have. Messrs. E. B. LeGrice Ltd., Yarmouth Road, North Walsham, Norfolk, are excellent, especially for the newest, and they have raised a great many of the modern varieties that are spreading into every garden today. Messrs. Hilliers are, however, better for rare old kinds and species, just as they stock old-fashioned apples for those who still wish to grow them.

The alpine firm that most nearly approaches the famous firms whose rock gardens filled the long bank at Chelsea Flower Show (and began again beyond the Embankment gate), is Robinson's Hardy Plants, Greencourt Nurseries, Crockenhill, Swanley, Kent, with Messrs. Ingwersens Nurseries, Birch Farm, Gravetye, Nr. East Grinstead, Sussex, also excellent. We are so small an island that there is no gain in buying plants locally, and if they must come by post, they may as well come from a specialist with the species you require, rather than a firm that will 'substitute' a common alpine you already have for one they have never heard of.

The sundries are easy and most garden shops should stock the very few chemicals mentioned. Ryania pesticide can be bought from Messrs. W. J. Craven Ltd., Port Street, Evesham, Worcs.; S.M. 133 from Chase Organics Ltd., Gibraltar House, Shepperton, Middx.; and there are many makers of derris and pyrethrum. The makers of Amcide are Messrs. Albright and Wilson Ltd., 3 Knightsbridge Green, London, S.W.1., but it should be obtainable through the Farm and Garden Department of Battle Hayward and Bower, Carholm Road, Lincoln. Alginure Compost Heap Activator is made by Oxford Horticultural Laboratories, Drayton St. Leonard, Oxford, but again this is an emergency address or one to give your local shop so they can buy in bulk wholesale rather than send you one tube with heavy postage. Marinure, the powder dried seaweed activator and high potash organic fertilizer, is made by Messrs. Wilfred Smith (Horticulture) Ltd., Gemini House, High Street, Edgware, Middlesex. Almost anything in the sundries line from vine eyes and gypsum to tubular heaters and cold frames can be bought from Messrs. E. J. Woodman and Son Ltd., High Street, Pinner, Middlesex.

There are many more excellent firms, and the place to see their products is growing on the nursery or at one of the flower shows from the R.H.S. Hall and Chelsea to Southport, and the flower tents of the agricultural shows all over Britain.

Index

Note: botanical names used throughout book and assembled in comprehensive lists are not here indexed unless omission would mean omission of a theme. The lists are on pp. 256 seqq.

294